P9-CFI-613

DISCARD

268.432
MCN

McNeel, Bekah

Bringing up kids when
church lets you down
11/2022

Bringing Up Kids
When Church Lets You Down

# Bringing Up Kids
# When Church Lets You Down

*A Guide for Parents Questioning Their Faith*

Bekah McNeel

WILLIAM B. EERDMANS PUBLISHING COMPANY
GRAND RAPIDS, MICHIGAN

Wm. B. Eerdmans Publishing Co.
4035 Park East Court SE, Grand Rapids, Michigan 49546
www.eerdmans.com

© 2022 Bekah McNeel
All rights reserved
Published 2022
Printed in the United States of America

28  27  26  25  24  23  22      1  2  3  4  5  6  7

ISBN 978-0-8028-8209-7

**Library of Congress Cataloging-in-Publication Data**

A catalog record for this book is available from the Library
of Congress.

*For the Healers,*
*especially Moira and Asa*

# Contents

# Baptism and Burritos

You can go your own way.

—Fleetwood Mac, "Go Your Own Way"

"At least you're not pregnant."

That's what my mom said when I called from college to tell her I was considering getting re-baptized.

While most parents worry about their kids getting hooked on hard drugs in college, mine were worried about a shift in my theology. My conservative evangelical college in California and my conservative evangelical home church in Texas differed on just a handful of doctrinal issues, and my parents worried about every one of them.

Theology was central to their parenting. So when I challenged one, I challenged the other. When I doubted one, I doubted the other.

As a baby, I had received paedobaptism — "infant baptism" to those who don't like to sound pretentious. It was supposed to signify that I belonged to God's family. As an infant, I had been completely unaware of what was going on. This invalidated the baptism, according to my new professors and friends.

The college taught that baptism was for people who were very much aware of what was happening to them. It was for those

1

who could articulate belief in a handful of key Christian doctrines. Baptism was for individuals who identified as "believers." That's why it's called a "believer's baptism"—or credobaptism to those who do like to sound pretentious.

My new professors and friends convinced me that only a believer's baptism really counted. Counted for what? I have no idea. I just didn't want to be wrong in their eyes.

As far as my parents were concerned, my 1984 baptism, though inarticulate, had fully inducted me into God's family It counted. Wanting a believer's baptism was like bringing my own fast food to a family meal. By getting rebaptized, I was rejecting the brisket of the covenant, which was served family style, and insisting I wanted my salvific cheeseburger individually wrapped. It wasn't hurting anyone, but it was rude.

Had I made this phone call five hundred years earlier, I might have been killed.

In the sixteenth and seventeenth centuries the paedobaptists were burning the other team, the Anabaptists, who were credobaptists, at the stake. Or drowning them and calling it, sardonically, "third baptism." Even during the Protestant Reformation, when Martin Luther created an *entirely new church* to separate from the Roman Catholics, apparently believer's baptism was a step too far for many.

If you hang out around a lot of conservative seminaries, this all sounds about right. If you don't, let me assure you that the debate is alive and well.

My mom wasn't going to tie a rock to my feet and throw me in a river, but we both catastrophized our family's first theological schism in our own way—lots of hyperbole on her end, lots of milking for sympathy on my end.

I never went through with my believer's baptism, but I had seen the merits of informed consent and was no longer certain about visiting such sacraments upon unwitting infants.

Three years later, I was twenty-three and still unsettled on the issue, along with many others. I'd just come home from graduate school in London (a far more secular and eye-opening experience, detailed later in this book), and I wanted to devote my time and energy to exploring a Christianity independent of nationalism and colonialism.

I started my career in ministry at an infant-baptizing church that did not ordain women, not because the church's theology aligned with my new passion in life but because it was the only church I'd ever known. Without ordination there was almost no path to an actual career in full-time ministry in this denomination, but I was idealistic and certain there was a glass ceiling that could be graciously and submissively shattered.

My dad, despite raising me in this same conservative branch of Presbyterianism that did not ordain women, believed that I was going to be the CEO of a Fortune 500 company, or the president of the United States. I had just gotten back from the London School of Economics, and he was ready to watch me take over the world. Instead I was wasting my twenties on what he knew was a dead-end road. "Incredulous" is a mild way to describe his initial reaction, though he did the supportive dad thing in the end.

My grandmother, who is nobody's feminist, took me to dinner one night to tell me she felt like the church's leaders were taking advantage of me. They were exploiting my willingness to work for peanuts, raise my own salary, and run myself ragged, she said.

I ignored their excellent advice, interpreting it as some kind of persecution. Such was my insufferable self-righteousness.

My first boss, the pastor of a college ministry, played it cool at first when I expressed progressive political views on immigration and taxes—or doubts about specific doctrines. Tim Keller was on the rise in New York, convincing pastors in our denomination

3

and others it was counterproductive to be angsty about things like science and art, and that the way to college-educated, urban America's heart was through some level of shared appreciation, not political harangues. If the nineties were about creating an alternative Christian world, the 2000s were about finding value in the previously scary secular world. After decades of Jesus being the mascot of the Religious Right, it was cool to say that the good Lord was neither Democrat nor Republican. Rigidity, in theory, was passé.

As long as we agreed on the very evangelical majors—homosexual marriage was a no-go, atonement was necessary, abortion was murder, the Holy Trinity was a mysterious yet inarguable fact, and so on—my boss assured me we could work through the minors, and I could keep my job befriending college students and mentoring them through disordered eating, exams, and other campus crises.

I was close to finding a restful place of ambiguity on infant versus believer's baptism when my boss summoned me to his office.

"Remember how I said I would tell you if there was ever a doctrine that you had to come to agreement on?" (The "or else you'll be fired" was implied.)

I nodded.

He held up a pamphlet. On the cover: a baby and a bowl of water.

"This is one."

For me to work with college students, I had to affirm that infants should be sacramentally baptized. Because if there's one thing weighing on the minds of college students, it's paedobaptism.

The list of "minor" theological issues we could agree to disagree on turned out to be very, very short. The only thing on it, in fact, was "Why is masturbation wrong?" It was definitely wrong; that was not negotiable, but we could debate about why, exactly.

For example: Is it wrong because Jesus said not to lust and it's really difficult to masturbate without lusting? Or is it because sex is intended for the pleasure of your spouse, as an act of giving? Unsurprisingly, that second one mostly gets used on women. (If you're squirming already, I feel like you should know some form of the word "masturbation" appears eleven more times in this book. It is something I feel strongly about. We will revisit this exact argument, in fact.)

Everything else stayed on the agree-to-disagree list for about ten minutes, and then my boss or my boss's boss would need to know I was "on board."

"Take your time and read this," he said, handing me the pamphlet. "But you're going to need to come around."

Rigidity, in practice, was still on trend in the Presbyterian Church in America.

I didn't lose my job over baptism. I decided it was none of their business, told them what they wanted to hear, and went on talking to zero college students about infant baptism.

At twenty-six, I married an inherently skeptical, devastatingly handsome architect who could see the flaw in any plan from miles away. Lewis is a gentle, egalitarian kind of Christian, and when he started attending church with me, he quickly cried foul on the whole thing. He thought it was ridiculous for a church not to ordain women. He didn't like the white, bright, polite social scene and church's rigid hierarchy. With his love and admiration emboldening me, I started to push back—to question the elitist and patriarchal elements of the church, to rock the boat.

It did not go well.

So by twenty-eight, I was leaving my new position as the director of children's ministries at the same church where I had worked with college students, leaving the denomination into which I had been baptized as an infant, and trying to leave Christianity altogether.

I was trying to leave because the pimple of white evangelicals' racism and greed had become a purulent, oozing head. Barack Obama was running for reelection and I was disturbed by the way Christians talked about him—questioning his birth certificate and overemphasizing his middle name.

I was trying to leave because I felt like the church had embraced a "might makes right" version of social Darwinism, which I reject. Social Darwinism insists that if someone is on top, they belong there, and those with wealth and power are the right ones to follow. At the same time, I *had* started believing in scientific Darwinian evolution, which large swaths of the church reject. We were running out of Darwins to agree on.

I was trying to leave because the church where I worked felt like a spiritual East Berlin, riddled with spies and informants willing to sell you out to save their own skin. At the center of it, a man with the pastoral instincts of a startled moose was regularly explaining how combative and uncooperative I was.

Once we agreed that I would leave my job at the end of the semester, two months away, he required biweekly check-ins to make sure I was sticking to the script. I was to tell my closest friends, the community I had served for years in various capacities: "I'm pursuing other opportunities." That, and no more.

"They'll want to know more," I insisted.

He gave me a patronizing, pitiful smile. "No, they won't."

And for the most part, they didn't.

I was trying to leave Christianity because the crippling voices of condemnation and shame in my head were so loud I had to rage to hear myself. I *was* combative and uncooperative because I was angry and hurt. Nobody likes to feel like that, but everywhere I turned for help, I was met by somebody with good manners, a Labrador, and a house in the right zip code advising me to come back when I could see past my "woundedness."

6

I was failing to leave Christianity because, as it turns out, even with all my doubts, I still believed that Jesus had been telling the truth, even if my particular church was full of shit.

In my imagination, Jesus met me at the bus station as I was buying my one-way ticket out of Christianity. He was unfamiliar and familiar as he offered me a fried pie from the imaginary vending machine, took me to an imaginary park nearby, and talked with me through some very nonimaginary pain.

He listened to my story. He didn't tell me that it was all my fault or that I was too wounded for my thoughts to be valid.

As he flicked the crumbs from his sturdy work shirt, his dark-skinned fingers scarred with two thousand years of carpenter's nicks and cuts, he said, "To hell with all that. It's death. Come with me, and let's start living."

He had the words of life. Where else could I go?

First off, I could not just go nowhere.

Even at my most devastated, I was savvy enough to know that a twenty-eight-year-old who left the church where her friends and family attend—thus ending her career—probably needs some consistency in her life.

It wasn't that I was alone. There was a small exodus from the church shortly after I left. My parents and many of my closest friends all left for their own similar-but-different reasons. There was solidarity, but not stability.

My poor, sweet husband is just one man, and this was a bomb-squad-level mental health situation. The social and financial instability was not helping the anxiety I did not yet know how to manage. I drank half a bottle of tequila every night.

I needed some spiritual structure.

We settled on the back pew at a different church that offered communion every Sunday and had a pastor who wasn't offended if I skedaddled during the sermon. Every prayer, every cheesy story in the sermon, every benediction chafed like scratchy wool on a sunburn; but there I was, in the back row, waiting for communion. It was the one time in the week I felt connected to God. What few pastoral words I heard I shot down in my head like bottles on a fence.

Meanwhile I began exploring my political, civic, and social world without a pastor or parent to tell me what they thought Jesus thought of Barack Obama, gentrification, marriage equality, or Medicaid. I had been donating to the Sierra Club and reading Gloria Anzaldúa since graduate school, but now I could do these things with impunity. I took a job in journalism—exploring, questioning, demanding proof from people in power instead of the other way around.

I avoided conversations that would require me to articulate my beliefs and morals. At work I dodged conversations on abortion. At church I nodded along while people talked about the power of prayer, looking agreeable so that they wouldn't try to convince me—or worse, pray for me.

Surprisingly, the indecision did not weigh on me at first.

By nature, I hate having things up in the air. Especially moral things. But after walking away from a world of dogma, to simply shrug felt impishly emancipatory. Each shrug reminded me that I had pulled the plug on the church's control of my thoughts and behaviors. Its authority pixelated and faded to black. For a while I didn't know how much of my theology or moral conviction had gone with it. I didn't love the void; I just loved that it was nobody else's business.

For two years I lived in this unplugged zone. Going to church out of habit, taking the Eucharist like it was a prescription drug, and argufying the sermon.

Then I had a baby, and everything changed. We were back to goddamned infant baptism.

This time I was sitting in a Chipotle, holding the infant daughter to whom the potential baptism in question applied. At the table with us sat Brian, a kind and helpful pastor at the church where we sat in the back row and didn't listen.

The harsh light of parenthood shone into my ambiguous haze of faith. Brian didn't want to debate or split hairs. He couldn't fire me or burn me at the stake. He was ready to answer any questions we had for him, but his only question for us was: Do we need to get a commemorative building block with her name embossed on it or not?

The question I was asking myself was: Is the Christianity I grew up with something I want to give my children?

Others are asking that question too.

This book is largely about that dynamic—between the children we were and the parents we are. It's about the choices we make when we decide to depart in large ways or small ways from the faith we once held. It's about the way faith and family mix to create extra confusion, and the wisdom we need to raise families while we struggle with faith.

Parts of this book are about how I, Bekah, am raising comedic, justice-loving Moira and snuggly, detail-oriented Asa with their creative, gentle father, Lewis. Other parts are about how other parents are doing things. You aren't here because I have answers. You're here because we all have questions.

Nefertiti Austin describes her minor crisis over the question of christening. As an adult raised with a cultural attachment to the Black church, but with a deep skepticism of the colonized version of Christianity, she made her own peace with a "hybrid of Judeo-Christianity, Eastern philosophy, and positive affirmations."[1]

But as an adoptive mother, she writes, "All of this was fine for me, but as August grew from toddler to snaggle-toothed kindergartener, I began feeling conflicted about how to shape his understanding of a power greater than himself. The pressure to instill a sense of wonder of the physical earth and mankind's generosity and shortcomings through spirituality was intense."[2]

She had baptized her child as a way to celebrate his adoption into her family, affirm the value of a single Black mother, her adopted Black son, and their family as a unit.

Before I tell you, dear reader, how I answered the baptism question and the thousands of questions implied therein, I want to sit in that moment. In fact I want to write a book in that uncertain moment.

This book is about the various places and ways that uncertainty shows up for parents who, having left or altered the faith they once knew, now must decide what to give their kids. It's about church attendance, Bible memorization, school choices, and sex talks. It's about forging new paths in racial justice and creation care while the intractable voices in your head call you a pagan Marxist for doing so.

I've sought the studied wisdom of researchers, theologians, and counselors as well as the lived wisdom of people who have to make these decisions every day in real time: parents who are struggling with faith. Rather than a neat, clean certainty, I hope that we find ourselves thriving in uncertainty. As joyful, peaceful people we can challenge the power-lust at the center of certainty. As biblical scholar Peter Enns writes: "Doubt is only the enemy of the faith when we equate faith with certainty in our thinking."[3]

Before we get into those explorations, however, I want to lay the groundwork. In the next three chapters, we'll dive into (1) the reasons people struggle with faith, (2) the need to reject certainty's overachieving sister, perfectionism, and (3) the history of how our faith and parenting both became so tangled up in the need for certainty in the first place.

In those chapters, you'll start to see more of where I'm coming from, where these stories are coming from. There are fancier names for various theological framings, but I'm going to call this one the "theology of aperfectionism." It places a high value on uncertainty.

Christians, as a group, are not fans of uncertainty. Comedian Pete Holmes calls the church experience he grew up with "certainty worship."[4]

An authoritarian tone marks conservative Christians wherever they go, in no small part because so many of those in leadership are white men. In politics, in marriage, in money management. Popular evangelical author Tim LaHaye takes a definitive stance on gender roles within marriage *and* on how the world is going to end. We have pastors like John MacArthur and finance gurus like Dave Ramsey and politicians like Mike Huckabee.

Many cultures and religious traditions didn't need evangelical culture warriors to convince them marriage was between a man and a woman for life and that children were to obey their parents. Authoritarianism isn't unique to any religious group. Certain aspects of "I come from a conservative family" resonate across race, ethnicity, and religion.

But the white evangelical guys got the book deals, policy wins, and pulpits. Dominant culture foists its opinions on everyone.

This isn't new, and it's not local. Christianity got where it is today by controlling all the levers of power. The church worked with European governments to spread not just the One True God, but the One True Culture, and the One True Economic System. The United States, through ongoing wars, political activity, and media exports, has kept the close tie between white Christian dominance and economic and political power throughout the world. In domestic affairs, Christians infuse moral absolutism into every realm, silencing dissent by citing God's authority.[5]

Onward, Christian soldiers! Marching into certainty.

Into this world of aggressive certainty we introduce our reasonable desire not to accidentally cause the death of our children.

Who doesn't crave certainty about parenting? It's offered to us in many ways: breast is best, "back" to sleep, say no to drugs— but most parents know that raising kids also undermines everything you thought you knew. About morality, about society, about the variety of fluids that can come out of one body.

INTRODUCTION

We parents simultaneously place our faith in various experts and doubt that they know what they are talking about. Or we think maybe something is malfunctioning with the kid. Or maybe we're just doing it wrong. Raising children is such a crapshoot, even for the most metaphysically grounded parents. For those of us in a crisis of faith, vacillating somewhere between murky and ineffable, it's eff-ing terrifying.

I spent two hours discussing infant baptism at a burrito bar, while other struggling parents spent months dropping kids at religious youth groups without going into church themselves. Some of those likely wished they knew how to help their kids find friends without sending them to a youth group where those friends might make them sign a purity pledge. Speaking of purity pledges, some of us don't want our kids anywhere near the shame and pathos in the way our religion addresses sex, but we also don't want our kids having sex at thirteen. We have no idea how to get one without the other.

Other parents spend years praying for their kids but feel no one is listening. Some long to pray for their children but are grossed out by prayer jargon. Some parents are searching for ways to comfort or correct their children with something other than the Bible verses used to control and manipulate them when they were kids.

To be sure, in many ways I am still in the Chipotle. Theological doubt is only a small part of my struggle now. I've always drifted in and out of doubt about God's existence and the specifics of what God is up to. I'm comfortable with it, except when I'm terrified by it. My struggle now, as for many others, is more a mix of doubt, disgust, and hurt that all add up to daily uncertainty.

Rather than seeking to replace that lost certainty, I want to collect the wisdom of those who are living in uncertainty. I share the approach of scholars like Enns or Rachel Held Evans, who describes the Bible like this: "When you stop trying to force the

Bible to be something it's not—static, perspicacious, certain, absolute—then you're free to revel in what it is: living, breathing confounding, surprising, and yes, perhaps even magic."[6]

This is a book about certain uncertain people—the faltering, the free, the resigned, the living—and how they parent. Part 2 is about the different breaking points that snap the tether people had to the faith of their parents, be they legal or spiritual parents. These are the issues that first engender sinking uneasiness and one day become irreconcilable for many—issues that these parents are certainly not willing to pass to their children. Part 3 is devoted to the secondary issues, those that, once we are untethered, are suddenly a lot less black and white than we had thought. Once someone declares, "I don't believe in hell," they still have to figure out what to do about taking their kids to church.

I can't tell you whether to use words like "sin" or how to teach the story of Jonah, and neither can the parents in these chapters. But I'm interested in how people talk to their kids about things they haven't fully resolved. We can be encouraged and enlightened by other doubting, disgusted, and hurt parents who are addressing matters of faith with their children, whether they have found their footing again or not.

Most are, like me, struggling with Christianity—evangelical and conservative Catholic mostly—but I hope our stories encourage anyone who has struggled with a faith or culture that claimed to have all the answers. Because that's what it's really about—seeking wisdom instead of answers.

Not every faith claims certainty as its end goal. We can all learn from that. Not every expression of Christianity is abetting the white power structure. We can learn from that. Some of these voices have come to conclusions, and others are proceeding with caution. Some have strong convictions; others have brave explorations. Some are in turmoil; others are at peace with the storm.

Sitting here, in our Chipotles and parking lots, I want to invite you into a conversation with other doubters and with those to whom we've looked for wisdom. We're not going to tell you how to raise your kids. We may not have the missing piece to your faith puzzle. At most, you'll gain helpful, usable wisdom, and at least you'll feel less alone.

*Part 1*

# THE ICY ROAD

The next three chapters are the "why" of this book. We walk through the cost of certainty-based, perfectionistic faith and parenting and set ourselves up to comb through the numerous twists and turns of "what" and "how" we might do things differently.

Chapter 1

# How to Lose the Faith and Keep It Off

I lost everything I had inside a couple years
Lost my faith, I lost my mind, I lost a lot of tears
I spoke up about these problems that I saw outside
People turned they back on me, you woulda swore I died.

—Lecrae, "Restore Me"

The man at the front of the room wore a floppy blond wig and a tie-dyed shirt. He spoke with a distinctive lilt meant to imply that he was gay. But he wasn't.

He was one of the founders of a Christian apologetics camp where I was a counselor, and he regularly donned these alter egos, each costumed caricatures of the enemies of the faith he was training young minds to combat. Real Christians, at this point in time, wore cargo shorts. The atheist professor wore a black turtleneck. The gay man wore tie-dye.

This role-playing was engineered to mimic the kind of encounters the campers might have in a college environment. The apologetics camp marketed itself by assuring terrified parents that it could equip their kids to keep the faith in the hostile wilds of the modern university. The weeklong sessions mixed all the traditional elements of Christian camp—emotional worship, silly games, and crushes on cute counselors—with seminars on how to "defend their faith."

The teens debated the gay character about whether the Bible allows homosexuality. They wielded their logical arguments and Bible verses like sabers, as they had been trained to do. They raised their hands, he called on them, and they volleyed a bit before he moved on.

And then the founder lost control of his audience.

The students—about two hundred homeschooled teens attending a midyear session of the camp—devolved into mockery and jeering. They taunted and booed and mimicked the caricature. As a counselor at the camp, watching things devolve, a quake rumbled deep inside me. Something about the jeering seemed inevitable. It was a chemical explosion from basic parody mixed with acidic certainty.

Eventually, the founder broke character. He gave the campers a stern talking-to about balancing truth and grace, about being loving at all times. He reminded them that his character represented very real people who could potentially be brought into the family of God.

I don't know how many of those queer real people were in the crowd that night. I know of one for sure. Her week at an apologetics camp designed to help kids defend their faith in college had showcased all the stumbling blocks Christians trip over: an insistence on absolutism in all areas along with arrogance and unkindness that cause personal pain and rejection.

People struggle with faith for so many reasons, but the breaks are rarely so clean that they can simply walk away or get over it. Many exist on a continuum between broken and whole, embracing and rejecting, wounded and healing.

Before we consider the various ways the struggle manifests in parenting—the church attendance, the sex talks, and so on—it might be helpful to understand a little more about why people struggle with faith in the first place.

## Doubt

For some, theological doubt is the largest part of the struggle. In fact, evangelicals, progressive Christians, mainline Protestants, Catholics, and all kinds of devout believers struggle with theological doubt. They don't see how a good and powerful God could allow suffering—theirs or that of others. They don't buy the idea of hell. It's all just too far-fetched, too inconsistent, too mystical, too exclusionary. Some religions make more room for doubt than others. Mine made none.

Wheaton College professor Michael Hakmin Lee studies deconversion—the process of losing one's faith—and says that every faith has "stress points."[1] Every faith has features that trip up the faithful. In evangelicalism, he says, biblical authority is a big stress point.

While doubt can lead to deconversion, Lee says, it is also a common and even healthy part of faith. What comes after the doubt determines the outcome of the struggle. The voices one hears, Lee says, are critical. This may be true in other religions as well. Speaking from experience, I can tell you the moment an evangelical begins to doubt, it can feel like they've wandered into the kitchen looking for a drink of water, and instead find their parents fighting about some long-held grudge. Before the interloper can utter a word of explanation, the parents quickly turn and try to win her to their side.

Parent 1: "See, Bekah likes our cozy house. She doesn't want a bigger house, do you, Bek?"

Me: "Ummm."

Parent 2: "No, Bekah wants her own room. She's tired of sharing with her little brother. Aren't you, Bek?"

Me: "I'm here for a glass of water."

One "parent" is the ardent believer, the other is an atheist wholly opposed to organized religion of any sort. They have been at each other's throats for most of the last century.

Anchoring the pro-religion team you have the likes of Josh McDowell and Tim Keller reasoning with you, or writers like Lee Strobel digging up historical evidence to support the historical accuracy of the Gospels. For those who are deeply connected to a religious community, you also have ordinary loved ones who, at the first sign of apostasy, as Rachel Held Evans writes, "treated me like a wildfire in need of containment."[2]

Matching them blow for blow, you have folks like Christopher Hitchens and Richard Dawkins, whose 2006 book *The God Delusion* offers no quarter to those even loosely connected to religion. That book, while incredibly rigid in its anti-religion stance, does offer some insight into why doubt is inevitable and why, for some, it ends in unbelief. Dawkins writes, "I can decide to go to church and I can decide to recite the Nicene Creed, and I can decide to swear on a stack of bibles that I believe every word inside them. But none of that can make me actually believe it if I don't."[3]

Whether the doubter continues to deconstruct or circles back to assurance, the whole thing is made more anxious by the volume of this discussion. The middle of a brawl is not a great place to have a crisis.

More recently, a wave of gentler discussion— unsurprisingly including more women, queer people, and people of color—has explored doubt with less pressure to pick a side. Doubt in the absolutist, white, colonial Christianity we have inherited has been faithfully nurtured by leaders like Randy S. Woodley, Barbara Taylor Brown, Lisa Sharon Harper, and Layton Williams, who invite us to reform and interrogate our faith more than accept or reject it.

Ultimately, Lee says, the biggest determiner in whether someone's faith "migrates" to a new expression or is ultimately rejected is whether or not the person stays engaged with a faith community. That's easier than it sounds, because faith communities can be a struggle all on their own.

## Disgust

When I started this book, I needed to take some time off from my education journalism gig. I told my editor, a Jewish woman from Brooklyn with a long career in hard-hitting news, that I was writing about parenting while struggling with faith.

"What kind of faith?" she asked.

"Well, any faith, but it will focus a lot on evangelicals."

"Ooooh. That's a great idea," she said. "Everybody is wondering what the hell is up with those people."

By "those people" she meant white evangelicals. Throughout the book you'll notice I sometimes use just "evangelicals" and sometimes add "white." I'm trying to differentiate as much as possible to be fair to the Latino, Black, Native American, and other evangelicals who—while they may wrestle with the theological and moral conservatism of their religion—have a different relationship to power and white supremacy.

But "evangelical" itself is a slippery term. Most efforts to define and study it use four doctrines: biblical inerrancy, being "born again," evangelism, and the atoning work of Christ (the most conservative version of Bebbington's quadrilateral, theology people). But, I don't actually believe those doctrines define an evangelical. Daniel Silliman's research into the origins of evangelicalism, particularly its flagship publication *Christianity Today*, confirms something I've always felt about evangelicalism: it's not a set of well-defined beliefs. Silliman concludes evangelicalism as we know it now is an association, and claiming other evangelicals is sort of the main criterion. In launching *Christianity Today*, the midcentury founders envisioned it as the standard-bearer of yet-undefined evangelicalism, and "they dealt with doctrinal issues as they came up in conversations about specific people. The question, in each case, was concrete: do we want this person in or out?"[4]

This book partially exists because of how challenging it has become to associate with evangelicals who are acting on their whiteness more than their theology—"those people," as my editor said.

Three weeks before our conversation, a bunch of God-fearing white evangelicals had stormed the US Capitol sporting Confederate flags and face paint. What the hell is up with these people? In addition to theological doubt, disgust with the behavior of Christians pushes a lot of folks, myself included, away from Christianity, or at least from the institutional church. In the foreword for the essay collection *Empty the Pews*, the famously "exvangelical" Frank Schaeffer writes, "Christianity is improbable. When its cultural presence fades, be that through the Roman Catholic sex-abuse meltdown or because of the Trumping of white evangelicalism, all that's left is disillusionment. . . . The grim 'witness' of how Christians have behaved and voted is too heavy a blow for faith in magical thinking to survive."[5] Don't underestimate disillusionment. It's subtle, but powerful, like betrayal. It feels like getting punched in the gut when you were expecting a hug.

The title of Dan Merchant's 2008 documentary *Lord Save Us from Your Followers* says it well.[6] On January 6, 2021, the politicians and congressional aides barricaded in their offices were probably praying that exact prayer. The Trump years took a toll on what was already a dwindling population of American evangelicals. From 2009 to 2019 self-identifying evangelicals went from 25 to 23 percent of the population,[7] and fewer than half of American millennials now identify as Christian of any sort. Pew doesn't ask the survey respondents why they left. But references to the growing toxicity of white evangelicalism in particular comes up in many anecdotal accounts, like those in *Empty the Pews* and numerous podcasts.

It's not just Donald Trump and the Christian nationalists who stormed the Capitol on his behalf. It's not just purity culture,

Westboro Baptist Church, or the Moral Majority. The Bible has been contorted to justify the dominance of the Western empire for centuries. Boston University scholar Christopher Rhodes examines these close ties as they show up in day-to-day news. In an October 2019 post entitled "Why 1492 Was Even More Important Than You Learned in History Class" he wrote this:

> Columbus, for his part, saw himself as not only an explorer but also a Crusader, who sought to spread Christian influence to the Indies and use the wealth he expected to acquire to fund a new round of Crusades to retake the Holy Land. The Church blessed these efforts . . . to now assert the influence of Christendom on the world. This process would lead to conquest of the Americas and set off a larger colonial project that, over the next several centuries, led to European powers cooperating and competing to conquer much of the rest of the world and create circumstances and institutions that reverberate today.[8]

Those institutions include slavery, exploitative economies, and destabilized governments, and most rely on the social construction of race to justify all of this exploitation. Race and racism have led to boundless suffering, often at the hands of the very same church. In just the last one hundred years racism has not merely infected but actually *shaped* our public sphere. Our schools are shaped by segregation and redlining, banks by predatory and exclusionary lending, courts by mandatory minimums and underfunded public defenders. Ridding ourselves of racism isn't as simple as anti-bias training. It requires reshaping in the most practical of ways.

Rather than speaking against all this injustice, the biggest pulpits in white America consistently undermine the cause of social justice. From the op-ed that elicited Martin Luther King Jr.'s "Letter from a Birmingham Jail," to John MacArthur's Statement on Social Justice, white Christians have publicly and consistently sided against racial progress, and in doing so they have held down the white women, children, and poor people who stand to benefit from it as well.

I sympathize with that desire to disavow the embarrassing members of the family. In fact I do it regularly. I have published national op-eds criticizing John MacArthur and Nebraska Sen. Ben Sasse for their thinly veiled white supremacy and misogyny. I don't want to believe in the same God the crusaders did. Or the segregationists. Or the Trump army. Whatever plague made them that way, I don't want to catch it.

Some people are more tenderhearted. They are grieving, because a faith that nurtured them so well has been so ugly to others. My six-year-old often tells me, "I'm acting mad, but underneath I'm sad." Maybe that's me too. Maybe I'm sad and scared, afraid my faith is fundamentally toxic. Thankfully, the true spiritual father of my generation, Mister Rogers, told us to look for the helpers. Christians have done awful, terrible things in the name of Jesus for millennia. But they've also done wonderful things. Hospitals. Food pantries. Preachers who supported abolition. Martin Luther King Jr. The YMCA. The YWCA. Mother Teresa. Dorothy Day. Sojourners.

Clearly, being a Christian doesn't make you a good person, but it also doesn't make you a bad person. There are other forces at work: politics, compassion, greed, racism, justice, fear, ambition, tradition, love, disposition, and pride. The Bible might speak to these, but they also speak back, influencing how we interperet, understand, and live faith.

In his famous 1927 "Why I Am Not a Christian" address to the South London Branch of the National Secular Society, British logician Bertrand Russell argued that fear was the thing speaking back: "It is partly terror of the unknown, and partly, as I have said, the wish to feel that you have kind of an elder brother who will stand by you in all your troubles and disputes. Fear is the basis of the whole thing—fear of the mysterious, fear of defeat, fear of death. Fear is the parent of cruelty, and therefore it is no wonder that cruelty and religion have gone hand in hand."[9] I think he oversimplifies, but in practice, he's not entirely wrong. Sometimes that cruelty is as big as genocide. Sometimes it stays in the family.

## Hurt

Spiritual hurt can be the acute pain of specific rejection and bullying. It can also be the chronic ache of poor mental health that comes from being rejected and bullied for most of your life.

My friend Jonathan talks to a lot of wounded people. He's a counselor, pastor, and author of several books, including *The Company We Keep*, about biblical friendship.[10] He also happens to have been one of my closest friends when together we attended a Christian college, a site of much wounding for many people. We spoke in January 2021, just before our shared birthday. In his roles at Parkside Church and Fieldstone Counseling in Ohio, Jonathan talks to a lot of people who have been hurt by Christianity in general, a church in particular, or a pastor.

What most of those people need is time, he said, maybe even time to step away from the church for a while. Time, however, is usually what church leadership is most loath to give them. "There's such a rush to preserve the church and its reputation," Jonathan told me as we chatted on the phone.[11] It comes from seminaries and training that focus more on preaching with doctrinal purity than with actually caring for real human people. When he was looking into seminary, he recalled, only three of the ninety-six units required for a master of divinity focused on biblical counseling. He got an MA instead.

In their rush to protect the church, Jonathan said, pastors too often place a millstone around the sufferer's neck by excusing, rationalizing, or minimizing the hurt. It's this hurt-after-the-hurt that so many survivors of abuse—inside and outside the church—say creates the lasting rupture in the relationship. The pain of not being believed, being blamed, or being hushed for the sake of someone else's reputation is, as writer Lilly Hope Lucario puts it, "having the knife twisted."[12] The pastors attracted to the pulpit as "contenders for the truth" often don't have the flexible disposition required to patiently minister to hurt and angry people, Jonathan explained. They are trained as fighters, apologists, and debaters, he said, "so any kind of conversation with hurt people ends up being adversarial."[13]

In the one hundred years of doctrinal fighting over modernism and fundamentalism that shaped the church of the twentieth century, many of the young pastors celebrated for their bold stance on the inerrancy of Scripture have matriculated into leadership positions. Their shared belief that the primary challenge to Christianity is weak and wishy-washy doctrine has informed seminaries, denominational training, and the leadership qualities preferred within the church. It's a hypermasculine world of ego and supremacy, Jonathan said. This perplexes him, which doesn't surprise me. Jonathan was and is a gentle guy. He's married to his brilliant college sweetheart, and he and his four daughters cook elaborate meals, which he shares on Instagram Stories.

It is safe to tell Jonathan you are mad, sad, excited, or hurt. Emotions are allowed. Too often, he acknowledged, emotions are suspect in the church. If someone acknowledges pain and anger accompanying their doubts and criticism, it's common for church leadership to dismiss the doubts and criticism. Emotion clouds judgment, they say. Feelings and facts must be kept separate in biblical interpretation and in conflict resolution.

When deconstructing Christians go into counseling (the good kind—not the kind that is basically a hunt through your inner temple of doom in search of *your idol*) it takes a while to buy into the process. Or at least it did for me. The counselor wanted to talk about my feelings, and I had no idea how, or what the point of that was, or whether it was safe to do so.

It's a good thing I did though. Because as much as rigid dogma and emotional suppression had done to drive me out of the faith, it was emotions that kept me there. Not fear, as Bertrand Russell would say, but longing. I will never stop longing for redemption, for all to be whole—and that has been more powerful than any dogma.

Doubt, disgust, and hurt. Those three broad categories of struggle are by no means the only ones, and the particulars look different for everyone. Now combine that with parenting.

## Chapter 2

# White-Knuckle Parenting

And it's hard to dance with the devil on your back, so
shake him off.

— Florence and the Machine, "Shake It Out"

From ages twenty-eight to thirty I lived without answers. After leaving my church and ministry career, I went to counseling and started a new job. I also explored the world and different faith traditions I'd been curious about for years. In sharp contrast to my previous life, no one pressed me for decisions. I was breaking up the monolith of my faith. As it broke down into grains of sand, I was sifting it through my fingers while I watched the waves roll in. Then came the babies.

In the blurry, sleep-deprived fog of cluster feeding (or setting a feeding schedule), sleep training (or co-sleeping), and the all-around bad trip that is parenting during the first year of a child's life, I defaulted to my natural state, one familiar to many new mothers: anxious perfectionism. I stopped being cool with the gray areas, leaning into the sandy shores of faith; I started trying, again, to get it right.

I was collecting Good Mommy badges from my own parents, the mommy alumnae Facebook group from my fundamentalist college, the church ladies whose opinions I ignored on almost every other matter, the child development experts I regularly interviewed as a journalist, my new liberal friends, my childless friends, the mom friends I had stayed connected to from my old church, the authors whose books were recommended to me, the people who recommended those books, random NPR interviewees, angry bloggers, smug bloggers, self-righteous bloggers, and the teenage girl who babysat for us.

This continued until I had a second child and my brain broke.

You can kind of pull off perfectionism with one easygoing firstborn. You cannot do it with a toddler and a newborn who demands to be held at all times in the feverish mouth of Texas summer. I started stuttering, pulling out my hair, and rocking and humming to self-soothe. I would clutch the baby not in love but in panic, pacing and keening while my husband watched helplessly and the toddler, ever the advocate, screamed, "Stop it, Mommy!"

My husband insisted I get help. I resisted, because resisting help is part of what's wrong with me. (I know this now.) I don't know how I even got well enough to get help, but by the time the baby was two years old, I finally did. Postpartum anxiety seemed like the most natural explanation. I went with that for a while, but there was something else going on. My husband concurred. "It was like a lot of things I'd seen from you before, but all at once, and way more intense," he said one day. Therapy was helping, but I suspected that a girl whose spirituality had been as heavily policed as mine might have had some other things going on. I visited an intercessory prayer ministry to see what we could unlock.

Intercessory prayer is a lot of sitting and asking God questions, waiting for images to come to mind, interpreting images, letting the prayer guides put their hands on your shoulders. As a former Presbyterian and current WASPy person, I am wildly uncomfortable with this sort of thing, but again, I was finally well enough to admit that I was really, really unwell, so I was in "try anything" mode. As we prayed, one of the women said, "Ask the Holy Spirit to show you how you move through the world." The picture that came to my mind was a woman, me, driving up a steep and narrow mountain road in the sleet, with luggage piled high on her car and screaming children in the back. Her knuckles were white as she clenched the steering wheel. If I didn't get it just right, we were going to fall off the cliff.

Perfectionism was making my life about as fun and safe as that car journey.

## Perfectionism, Defined

Perfectionism is the relentless drive to conform to standards, and to accept nothing less. Psychologically, some of us are just bent this way. But what I'm going to talk about in this chapter is cultural perfectionism—the culture of never good enough.

Cultural perfectionism has dramatically shaped conservative Christianity, allowing churches to withhold spiritual validation from anyone whose lives and beliefs do not mirror that of the men entrusted with interpreting God's word. Ever felt like your pastor or parent would always find some sin you could be working on? Or that your Christian friends always wanted to talk about "the condition of your heart" even after you'd apologized for something? Like God's blessing was the carrot dangling out there to keep you trying harder?

That's perfectionism. Not yours. Theirs. Ours. It's a group thing. Cultural perfectionism shows up in the church when critics, doubters, and wounded people are told to keep quiet until they have resolved their own issues. It shows up in workplaces where mistakes are overemphasized and the sky's the limit on every performance metric. Children in perfectionist families are endlessly criticized, and the list of rules is a mile long—including everything from "elbows off the table" to "no heroin in the house" enforced with equal intensity and "room to improve."

Here's the kicker: It's killing you because it is supposed to. Cultural perfectionism is supposed to keep you locked in the car, on the narrow mountain pass, too scared to do anything but keep your eyes on the icy road.

What's coming may raise hackles for my white readers. Hang in there with me. It's going to feel like I'm wandering into lefty field. It's going to feel like I'm just talking about race and white supremacy because it's currently en vogue to do so. I'm not. I'm talking about it because if perfectionism is the icy road, then white, capitalist culture is the mountain, and we'll never find freedom unless we acknowledge it. You don't have to even be that invested in social justice or racial reconciliation to care about the toxic effects of white supremacy on our daily lives. I'm not going to try to convince you that you need to march or put a sign in your yard. The whole project of ending white supremacy would actually be better served if you just rejected perfectionism.

Perfectionism is, as Kenneth Jones and Tema Okun explain, a characteristic of white supremacist culture.[1] They don't just mean KKK white supremacy, but the everyday institutions, beliefs, and behaviors that keep whiteness on top. Not just the belief that physical white skin is better, but the belief that white cultural ways are the right cultural ways—or even believing that without knowing you do.

When I was first opening myself to the many things affected by white supremacy, I joked that the thing I said most often was, "Oh, shit. This too?"

This too.

Race-, class-, and gender-based perfectionism has a lot to do with American religion and parenting, where they come together, and how it all falls apart.

## What's Race Got to Do, Got to Do With It?

White, patriarchal culture keeps itself in the boss's chair by setting white, patriarchal standards for workplaces, family structures, political power, church leadership, and countless other things. It can then withhold power from anyone who does not measure up to its "perfect" standards—you don't get promoted if you don't act white and male enough; you don't get the tax benefits if your family structure isn't right.

The white church has long controlled who can and cannot lead it based on a self-serving interpretation of the Bible by those inside the cultural power apparatus. Black pastors could not be ordained in many churches until the second half of the twentieth century. Women still cannot be ordained in many. The prosperity gospel equated worthiness and wealth. Traditions and institutions like the National Prayer Breakfast have led many churches to value the spiritual health of business leaders and politicians over the spiritual health of ordinary folks.

Nefertiti Austin points out that white culture (including white feminism) often dictates who gets to be seen as a good or worthy parent, who can "get away with an *oops* pregnancy" (she mentions Bristol Palin), and whose struggles are a result of systemic injustice versus personal failure.[2]

While KKK-style white supremacy rigidly targets nonwhite people as less than, cultural white supremacy offers a car to anyone who wants to drive the icy mountain road. It promises that "you too can have power and approval and blessing" if you just measure up to the standards of white culture, and thus reinforce them. Whatever color your skin is, perfectionism says, if you can white-knuckle it to the top, you'll love the view.[3]

You cannot, of course, reach the top. The standards keep going up, to keep you working harder, spending more, performing more to win a spot in the hierarchy. White people, by virtue of their caste,[4] get to enter closer to the top with infinitely more benefits, but perfectionism isn't the top of the mountain. It's the icy road.

We're all on the icy mountain road. We don't all have the same view.

It always struck me how convenient it was that a man called into ministry could one day be taking home six figures and leading an international organization, while a woman called into ministry would be considered "blessed" by her role as a perpetual volunteer in his church. I went to college with women who believed that they were called into ministry and therefore needed to marry a pastor.

Or consider how quick wealthy white folks are to hold up a token Latino or Black manager in their company as a testament to the beneficence of capitalism, a testimony to hard work. But they are never going to make it to the top of the mountain. No one is. We're all just in a long line of cars, driven by people on the same dangerous road. The white, straight males may be higher up the mountain, but they aren't chilling at a chalet on the top. They're white-knuckling it too, with a millionaire in front of them. Or a billionaire. Or a politician. Or a head pastor. Or a head pastor with a bigger church. That's what we signed up for when we let white culture tell us to measure our worth in dollars and influence. Inequality and striving all at once, all the time. No justice, no peace.

### Perfectionism under Threat

So perfectionism has you working really hard to earn your blessings, constantly moving the goalpost just a little beyond what you can reach. That's the carrot. Here comes the stick—the threat of what will happen if you stop or resist. The more their position is challenged, the more the folks near the top feel anxious and spread that anxiety to those who are beneath them on the mountain. They start doomsday forecasting about how if this power structure is toppled, we will all lose. The economy will crash. The Bible will be outlawed. The kids will do drugs. Don't believe me? Flip on Fox News.

That anxiety seeps into our daily lives in the form of compulsive perfectionism. We must be good enough to prevent the demise of society. We keep our eyes on the road and grip our steering wheels. Compulsive perfectionism, however, isn't about being biblical enough, Republican enough, or wealthy enough. You can be none of those things and still struggle with perfectionism, because it has become the *only way you know how to interact with the world — refusing to accept anything less than perfection.* You can be a perfectionist liberal, or a perfectionist atheist.

Austin writes that perfectionism is one of the things Black people have turned to trying to dull the pain of oppression.[5] That is some insidious shit.

I had been compulsively perfectionistic long before I was pulling out my own hair and moaning. I was driving that icy mountain pass to nowhere, believing I could find respect in the male hierarchy of ministry, approval from my parents, admiration from my peers, adoration from my husband. When I became the parent of two brilliant, beautiful, and very strong-willed children, I simply cracked. There were too many standards to meet and too much reality keeping me from meeting them.

Even when I was most crippled by it, however, I had an inner rage against perfectionism. I wrote satirical blog posts about how stupid all parenting advice was. I desperately wanted to be free, but I was no match for a culture of perfectionism that had been more than a century in the making. As long as I stayed on that winding, snowy road, I was going to be a tense, white-knuckled mess. Rather than just "learning to relax" while I drove, I needed to get off the perfectionism road altogether.

## For the Bible Tells Me *Soooooooo Much*

When both faith and parenting are wrapped up in perfectionism, getting off the icy road can throw everything into confusion. Getting off the road requires a process known as deconstruction—questioning faith, capitalism, the trustworthiness of the people around you. The whole enterprise of driving up the mountain pass becomes mired in doubt and questions.

So you're left wondering what you're going to tell your kids. Not just "What do I tell them about God and how do I explain faith?" But, "How do I explain anything? How do I make the million decisions I need to make today?" Should we sleep train, give a pacifier, or, in my case, baptize them into the family of God? What do we tell them when they ask us what happens when we die? And what do we tell them when they wonder why we won't buy a plastic unicorn that poops glitter slime into a toilet?

From day one, children require endless decision making—with the threat of lifelong dysfunction or apostasy if you're wrong, or so certain experts tell you. As we make those huge and ridiculous decisions, we hope that our kids are learning how to make decisions too. The great hope of parenting is that they will honor their own bodies, choose loving friends, tell the truth, and one day pursue a vocation that makes the world more beautiful. But that seemingly simple goal feels miles away, on the other side of a lake filled not with water, but with doubt and decisions. And it has been scaring parents for generations.

As scary as it can be to doubt, deconstruct, or step back from parental certainty, it's also the beginning of the "decolonization" process and the healing that brings. Decolonizing, literally, is the process of kicking out conquering invaders, and restoring autonomy to the people who were in a place first. In this context, we are kicking out colonizing forces from our heads, hearts, and homes so that we can govern ourselves according to the Spirit that dwells in all of us. We are refusing to play our part in the current power structures. Whether colonization tells us we should be conquerors or we should be conquered, we cannot be One until we get rid of the hierarchy. Colonization uses perfectionism, shame, and oppression to uphold itself. When we follow those voices to their source, that's usually the place where we have been grafted into the colonial project, our entrance ramp to the icy mountain road.

We have been colonized by capitalism, leading to constant competition, which drives us to overcommit our kids in endless sports leagues and extracurriculars so that they will have the winning resume. We have been colonized by white supremacy, which leads us to fear losing our position in society, and then isolates us in racially and economically homogeneous social networks. We have been colonized by American Christianity, with its unattainable standards, leading us to feel unworthy of love, constantly trying to fix ourselves and everyone around us.

Decolonization is essential to the well-being of those outside the dominant culture. It is survival for Black families, indigenous peoples, communities of color, queer folks, single parents, American Muslims (or people of any faith that might be mistaken for Islam by ignorant Americans), people living with disabilities, and countless identities formed at the intersections of those. To whatever degree we benefit from the dominant culture (and most of us do to some degree), we must wean ourselves off the poisoned promises of a mountaintop view so that we can help stop the cycle of hurt and brokenness. Hurt people hurt people, but healed people heal people.

Even if you are the one who stands to lose the most from decolonization, you too stand to gain. It is fundamental to *imago Dei* to be able to recognize itself. To refuse to honor the image of God in others is to reject the image of God in ourselves. Absolute dominance, oppression of others, and power hoarding corrupt us. They enslave our souls and corrode the image of God in us.

In Matthew 16:26 (NKJV), Jesus says this: "For what profit is it to a man if he gains the whole world, and loses his own soul?" Decolonization gets the dominant, power-hungry voice out of your head so the Spirit can speak through other voices. That's freedom. The freedom to discern, to decide what you take and leave. The more we listen to these voices once relegated to the fringe, read their books, put them in the pulpits, the more the world begins to decolonize.

I'm not saying Christians have to scrap the Bible. I'm saying we open ourselves to the possibility that John MacArthur versus John Piper does not represent the breadth of possible interpretation of the Bible. Or think of any other two white, male Protestants with the same first name who have built their entire ministries on certainty.

In her writing on decolonizing Christian discipleship, public theologian Ekemini Uwan suggests we ask the following questions to determine whether our theology has been colonized:

- Does this theology call me to a deep love for God that causes me to pursue holiness and radical love for my neighbor?
- Does this theology benefit the privileged at the expense of the marginalized?
- Is this theology good news for everyone, regardless of their racial and socioeconomic status?
- Does this theology cause me to look in the mirror and marvel at God's handiwork instead of despising my reflection?
- When I close my eyes and picture Jesus, do I see a white man or a brown-skinned Palestinian man?[6]

## Joining the Resistance

Just as we don't need to scrap the Bible, we don't need to scrap all parenting advice. But we really should question whether the generations of Americans raised by "experts" are really the healthiest and most whole version of humanity. I had a hard time watching the events of January 6, 2021, and thinking, "Yep, we're definitely getting this right."

Resistance to profitable, politically expedient perfectionism has long been found in the private homes of Black families, working class single moms, and same-sex parents, but it is only recently that their stories have even begun to be mainstreamed as anything but tales of woe or deviance.

I want to be careful here that I don't equate the struggles of Black and white, queer and straight, marginalized and centralized parenting. It is infinitely easier to parent when you know your children are safe, when basic needs are met, when bigotry isn't working against you. Nor do I want to steal their wisdom for my own gain. Ending oppressive perfectionism as a tool of white supremacy and patriarchy is first and foremost a matter of oppressed peoples' self-liberation. They are not "saving" me, and I am not "saving" them. But as the beneficiary of white supremacy's promises, I have a role to play in calling bullshit on the whole enterprise, and the only way to do that is to go a different way, to follow someone new.

As people at the margins put their work and words out into the world, people at the center of power—white, straight, middle class folks—would do well to trade in the exclusionary, competitive worldview we've been promoting, and instead affirm what the people on the margins are saying. In doing so, in following their lead, those at the center will become co-conspirators in ending oppressive systems that are killing marginalized bodies and consuming souls at the center.

I think of how grateful I am to be raising children when we have voices like Nefertiti Austin, who, in explaining the concept of Black adoption, celebrates Black communities' resistance to defeat, while acknowledging the obvious pain of violence toward Black familial relationships. It is common, she explains, for Black children to grow up with extended family and close neighbors without the formality of guardianship or any biological imperative: "Calling back to the multi-generational family unit of pre-colonial Africa, we did not need social workers or dependency court, just the blessing of the elders to raise a child within our community."[7] That's resistance, and it's also grace. Grace to any parent who needs serious support.

The value of "chosen family," commonly celebrated in the queer community, is another deep well of wisdom from which all anxious parents can drink. Andrew Solomon recounts his own anxieties in becoming a gay, biological parent in a world that assigned lesser value to norm-breaking lives. "I do not accept competitive models of love, only additive ones," Solomon writes. "Every increase of love strengthens all other love in the world, that much as loving one's family can be a means of loving God, so the love that exists within any family can fortify the love of all families."[8]

A recent spate of mom bloggers—Glennon Doyle, Denene Millner, and Kristen Howerton—have emerged to push back on perfectionism and embrace a resistance approach to faith, culture, and parenting. They are wildly popular, because there's a lot of folks who need a voice to listen to that's not urging them back onto the icy road. In liberating themselves, these parents all chart paths to freedom—exit ramps from the road of perfectionism.

**New Ways to Parent**

Some who have struggled have found their way out, either into a place of cohesive, confident faith, or away from it entirely. It's not that they no longer struggle, but that they have emerged from "the dark night of the soul."[9] Some have even rebuilt a community. Cindy Wang Brandt's parenting conference, Parenting Forward, is a "hallelujah" for progressive Christians who are ready to get to it with parenting for justice, mercy, and kindness.[10]

Those who have left Christianity behind entirely will raise their children according to other values—maybe from other religions, all religions, or none at all. They will point their kids to moral and ethical leaders and find community while pursuing the common good. Even though these folks have found an inner peace from which to parent, those who were raised in a faith different from the one they now have will still, I suspect, find themselves second-guessing a decision or two, maybe even white-knuckling a bit. We who have been formed by perfection ism have had our decision-making apparatus tinkered with. We never learned to trust ourselves or hear the voice of God for ourselves.

Eventually, God spoke to me through Brené Brown, whose work on parenting imperfectly really is freeing, Nikole Hannah-Jones, who helped me pick a school, and Pixar's *Inside Out*, which gave me some tools to talk about emotions with my kids when mine were still creased and wrinkled from years of suppression. But when it comes to faith, explicitly, I'm still sorting through the rubble, wondering what to keep.

In a guest appearance on the *Dirty Rotten Church Kids* podcast, Brandt acknowledged the uniquely difficult position of our generation of parents. While former generations typically passed faith wholesale to those that followed them, she said, cultural shifts have led many to deconstruct their American Christian faith, asking of each doctrine: Do I believe this? Parents who are deconstructing their faith have much to "grapple with as they're raising kids who are having to form their faith for the first time," Brandt said.[11] I'm not alone in asking myself: Is Christianity something I want to give to my children? What kind? What else? Learning to decide, to trust our own spirit, or the Spirit of God in us, is part of becoming fully human.

After I saw myself white-knuckling it up the mountain, the women guiding my prayer told me to ask God how God wanted me to interact with the world. I saw a vision of myself running

on my own two legs down a wooded mountainside, not on a narrow road but bounding between trees, letting gravity draw me
further along through a world teeming with messy, exploding,
unruly life. That's how I want to parent, but often the voices in
my head are so loud. Telling me I'm messing up the kids. Telling
me I'm disappointing. Telling me I'm going to regret whatever I
just did or did not do. When I feel the loud perfectionism coming for me, I go back to the prayer cycle that led me to that free,
adventurous vision of parenting.

The cycle begins: Spirit, quiet every voice but yours.

## Chapter 3

## Sleep Training for Jesus

There's a battle outside and it is ragin'
It'll soon shake your windows and rattle your walls.

—Bob Dylan, "The Times They Are a-Changin'"

There was a fire burning in the backyard. It was small and controlled, and from the center came the anguished screams of twenty tiny, blue demons as they were banished to the pits of hell whence they came.

My father was burning my Smurfs in a hole in the backyard. It was the eighties, he was a new evangelical, and this is how the church was teaching people to deal with the devil's sneaky stranglehold on popular culture. After the Smurfs it was My Little Pony. End times theology was big in those days—I think AIDS had something to do with it. So after some sermons on "the horned beast" in Revelation, my parents were told to get rid of sneaky devil culture by ridding the house of unicorns.

This is how my blue My Little Pony unicorn came to have a giant hole in its forehead, where the horn had been sawn off. Even if they used scissors, the dehorning was probably, in the language of the church, a more biblical act, like a sawing. Or cleaving. After that it was probably cast into the garbage. Not tossed. Cast. I accounted for My Little Pony's gaping head wound by pretending she had been the victim of a tragic gangland-style execution.

My mom likes to describe their conversion from free love and recreational drug use of the seventies to the Moral Majority of the eighties as some sort of plot twist. It was not. Their generation followed a steady pattern of choosing the most extreme option available, as evidenced by the havoc wreaked on my toys. My parents—as new Christians whose pre-Jesus lives had been, according to my mom, singularly debauched—were convinced they needed not just to climb the monolith of biblical morality, but to free solo it. No slips allowed. If they fell off the sheer marble face of their new faith, they feared, they were going all the way down.

It turns out my parents were not alone. As new parents of the 1980s, they had inherited generations of angst and anxiety about getting both Christianity and parenting right. No, not right. Perfect. They, like so many other parents of their time, were influenced by a variety of external expectations that came to define the family culture in which many of us were raised, and out of which many of us would try to raise our own.

To better understand how we arrived at my charred Smurf collection, let's take a look at a few of the intersecting factors at play in both parenthood and the church during the era in which millennials like me were born.

### A Century in the Making

Ann Hulbert traces two main schools of parenting advice—"hard" and "soft"—through one hundred years of radical social, scientific, and technological change in America.

"Hard" approaches, Hulbert explains, emphasize discipline, independence, and toughening up. "Soft" approaches emphasize nurture, bonding, and careful attention to the emotional needs of children.[1] Every generation in the twentieth century produced its own set of child rearing experts from each of these schools of thought.

Hulbert identifies the fundamental question: "As children—and just as important, their mothers—prepare to meet the pressures and allures of an increasingly materialistic and meritocratic society, is it more discipline or more bonding that they need at home?"[2]

My parents were definitely in the "hard" camp, with notable exceptions. We were spanked, but we were also rocked to sleep. They did not regularly help us with our homework, but toilet training was pretty low key. When I got suspended for smoking cigarettes in tenth grade, my parents left the issue between me and the school, saying I'd been punished enough. I think most parents pull from each camp as they try to survive; and this works, because despite their different tactics, parenting advice generally shares the same goal: raising up the next generation to preserve the soul of America amid social change.

The advice, Hulbert notes, is largely dispensed by white men and aimed at white middle-class women, in a sense professionalizing motherhood, laying the fate of the nation in mothers' hands.

Politicians, preachers, and experts never hesitate to tell parents that they have a role to play in creating a perfect society, as defined by a white, patriarchal vision of America. It is designed to keep us spending money, looking pretty, and acting nice. In a capitalist society like ours, "perfection" is "winning" so everything is a competition. You're spending *more*, looking *prettier*, and acting *nicer*. These standards were set hundreds of years ago by people who wanted to make a lot of money in the "New World," and they have been entangled with our private and spiritual lives ever since.

We're about to go on a little historical romp here, so hang on tight. It's not going to perfectly tie everything together, or cover every intersection of parenting and power, but I hope it gives a general idea of how (mostly, but not exclusively, white) parents have been drawn into the advancement of various agendas.

*The Way Things Were Built, 1492–1919*

America was a literal collection of colonies, built by literal colonists who retained the values of literal colonialism even after they decided they didn't want to be taxed for it anymore. They wanted to grow in land and profits, believing they had the divine right to do so because the "savage" indigenous people didn't measure up, nor did Black people or most later immigrants.

Removal and genocide of original land inhabitants. Country quotas for immigrant visas. Preservation of racial hierarchy through slavery, eugenics, whitecapping, and Jim Crow. Those are all part of our colonial DNA.

Women, indigenous peoples, and Black people continued asserting their rights, demanding that the legal structures created by white Protestant men reflect the *imago Dei* they claimed to believe in. The founding fathers didn't intend to include people different from themselves in the civic life of the nation, but later generations were forced to accept change as marginalized people used the words of the Constitution to pass laws that would have James Madison spinning in his grave.

Enslaved people were freed. Immigrants welcomed. Women enfranchised. Indigenous nations had some itty-bitty bits of sovereignty restored. As halting, incomplete, and precarious as this hard-won progress has been, it felt like a magnitude 9.1 earthquake to the guys on top. Guys equal white men, and top equals supreme position—ergo, white supremacy.

The men at the top got nervous, and the ladies right under them were like, "Hang on, babe, I got this."

*White Ladies Keep It Going, 1920–present*

Elizabeth Gilbert McRae has profiled the ways in which twentieth-century women enlisted to be the "constant gardeners"[3] of white supremacy by virtue of their role in the home.

While laws were changing in the public sphere, women could preserve the racial hierarchy in the private, domestic sphere, and in effect circumvent the law. "Employing a politicized formulation of motherhood, white segregationists across the ideological spectrum practiced a politics that emphasized performing whiteness as synonymous with 'good' womanhood, cultivating a politics that minimized their racial identity and privileged their identity as parents and mothers," McRae writes.[4] For instance, it was women who organized to keep schools segregated. The education of children was the mom's lane, they claimed, and they wanted the state to get out of it. So it was women who took to the streets in places like Boston to put a domestic, maternal face to segregation—to make it seem like segregation was a matter of safety, not oppression.[5] Women also used their "natural place" on school committees to ensure that the narrative around the Confederacy could be properly laundered by textbooks. That's why I grew up reading about "states' rights" instead of slavery as the primary cause of the Civil War.

These tasks gave the work of white motherhood a sense of importance, tying it to the anxiety of their husbands: losing power. Believing in a zero-sum narrative of winning and losing, even those who want to see a more racially just society are not willing to risk their children's future prosperity. The thought of truly rejecting systems built by white supremacy and the privilege those systems convey freezes white parents in their well-intentioned tracks. Fights over school boundaries, affirmative action, LGBTQIA rights, and where to place government housing all call on the "concerned" and organized parents to speak out in protection of their children. Wherever equity is advancing, you'll find white, middle-class moms having a viral meltdown at the town hall meeting.[6] The thrust of their argument is this: Don't mess with my efforts to raise perfect, high achieving Americans.

*My efforts.* Did you catch that? What could have been a collective commitment to provide equitable public education and opportunities for all children has remained inherently private, and thus competitive and exhausting. White supremacy shaped the system, and now we are all so tired.

*The Invention of the Mommy Wars, 1970–present*

While they were helping their husbands maintain power over nonwhite people, many women were simultaneously growing discontented with their own second-class status. The feminist stance of the 1960s was simple enough: Women should be able to control their bodies and to work outside the home if they wanted to. Some things would need to change in order for that to happen. Enter the Equal Rights Amendment, *Eisenstadt v. Baird* (which legalized birth control for all Americans), Ruth Bader Ginsburg's entire career, and the infamous *Roe v. Wade*.

As controversial and potent as it became later, abortion was not an early rallying issue for conservatives. The battle over the ERA, however, was pivotal. With an argument resembling that of the segregationists, conservative Phyllis Schlafly claimed that the ERA was attacking the home, stepping on women's turf and minimizing the work of motherhood. In 1972 she mobilized conservative religious housewives into political allies in the fight against the Equal Rights Amendment, cementing motherhood as a theater for the culture wars.[7]

Ironically, those same conservatives would continue to pursue economic policy that made it impossible for many families to survive on one income. This irony still regularly shows up, even though women have more presence in the workplace than they did in 1972. Forty years later, in 2012, political commentator Hilary Rosen said that Ann Romney—whose husband, Mitt, was running for president—could not relate to middle-class women because she had "never worked a day in her life." The political right responded by dredging up the ol' Schlafly playbook, making the economic argument into a domestic one and claiming that Rosen was minimizing the role of motherhood. It was never about motherhood, blogger Denene Millner has pointed out: "[Politicians are] masters at turning nonissues into politically expedient grenades—the kind that expertly explode any unified stance that women, mothers, and the middle class might take."[8]

## Meanwhile, in the Pews

While parents were duking it out in schools and statehouses, Christianity was experiencing its own tumultuous era. Christianity's broader struggle between fundamentalism and modernism raged during the twentieth century, as the fundamentalists argued for biblical certainty against the modernists, who wanted to subject the Bible to literary criticism. Now, this is an older struggle, but here are the relevant highlights. Get ready for historical romp number two, same rules apply.

### What Does the Bible Say about Slavery? 1800s

The Presbyterian church had already split twice in the nineteenth century, once over revivalism and once over slavery. Actually, most mainline denominations split over slavery in the lead-up to the Civil War. However, they wouldn't necessarily have put it that way.

Jemar Tisby traces a core sleight of hand—using the Bible to justify racial oppression—through several centuries. One of the oldest battles over whether the Bible should be literally or critically interpreted was the argument over the slave trade. Slavers pointed to passages of Scripture that seemed to condone slavery. Abolitionists and Black theologians claimed that more correct interpretation emphasized liberation and the dignity of man. The Bible literally says "slaves obey your masters." But a critical, contextual reading made American chattel slavery untenable. The debate over enslavement, Tisby explains, laid the groundwork for any talk of social gospel or social justice to be conflated with liberalism, a low view of biblical authority—or even written off as communist or Marxist by politically conservative Christians.[9] This was a popular criticism of the Civil Rights movement, and it remains a popular rebuttal to social justice movements today.

*What Does the Bible Really Say about Everything Else? 1900s*

In the twentieth century, Presbyterians in particular would find themselves at the heart of an ongoing battle between fundamentalism and modernism—with white supremacy culturally aligned with the former. Their most famous school, the renowned Princeton Theological Seminary, would become a battleground for fundamentalism versus modernism. It was a loss for the fundamentalists that led to the establishment of a new seminary, Westminster.

While the academic portion of the debate originates within Presbyterianism, American Christianity as a whole was splintering like a wooden man with a stick of dynamite up his ass. The dynamite was biblical authority. The spark that lit it was social change. The twentieth century brought all kinds of new fodder for the debate over how to interpret Scripture. The Scopes Monkey Trial brought up the literal versus literary interpretation of Genesis. Suffrage and feminism opened the debate about how to interpret the apostle Paul's statements on women. Leviticus had its own day in the spotlight—not regarding haircuts, shellfish, menstrual hygiene, and many of the other things it addresses, just homosexuality.

The fight over using a literal interpretation of the Bible to govern any and every sphere of life hit a particularly shrill note in the 1970s through the 1990s, as many of today's parents were being parented themselves. So my toy unicorn was literally a satanic object in the house. The Smurfs literally had to be cast into a small lake of fire. The dispute over liberalism roiled throughout mainline American denominations, and my parents found Jesus in one of the most conservative offshoots of them all, the Presbyterian Church in America. Biblical literalism was used to explain the movies we couldn't watch, the spankings we were getting, why we couldn't go trick-or-treating, why I couldn't snuggle on the couch with my boyfriends, and why my boyfriends needed to be boys.

## The Perfect Storm, 1970-2000

By the end of the 1970s, multiple conflicts had converged with parents at the center: the long debate over soft versus hard parenting, the fundamentalist-modernist schism, the fight to preserve white supremacy through segregation, and the cultural war over the definition of the American family. Enter Dr. James Dobson, the man who was ready to speak to all of it at once using Focus on the Family. The organization advised parents on practical matters, lobbied Washington, and published arguments against evolution, homosexuality, and abortion. It was a one-stop shop for all things culturally (white evangelical) Christian. They even had a video club. The Ezzos, Gary and Anne Marie, also weighed in, shifting the parenting conversation from an expert-led continuous improvement to an absolute pursuit of standards outlined in God's eternal and unchanging Word.

By this time, parents, the group we've already identified as chronically anxious in their pursuit of perfection, were in a war zone, told they are both the starting place and last bastion of traditional family values, literally *Growing Kids God's Way*. As Hulbert put it: "At stake was not merely the growth or social adjustment, or emotional health, but anxiously calculated moral worth—as much the parents' as the child's—the regimens suggested."[10]

The conservative parenting experts dispensed most of their advice in the service of what would be called "traditional family values," which University of Virginia sociologist James Davison Hunter calls "a certain idealized form of the nineteenth century middle-class family: a male-dominated nuclear family that both sentimentalized childhood and motherhood and, at the same time, celebrated domestic life as a utopian retreat from the harsh realities of the industrial age."[11] Meanwhile, this nuclear family ideal was made impossible for generations of Black families who had been disintegrated by slavery, racial violence, and economic exclusion. During the 1980s, while white families were being enlisted to defend "traditional family values"—marked by cisgender, heterosexual legal unions and stay-at-home mothers—the Reagan administration opted to solve the anguish and pain of the crack epidemic by throwing a lot of Black parents in prison. The United States also destabilized Central American governments they feared would turn to communism and ally with the Soviet Union. The interference created an ongoing immigration crisis that has separated families through migration, deportation—and more recently by border patrol agents removing children from their parents.

For those who have seen *Hamilton*: When I talk about the 1980s, I do the same voice distortion Lin-Manuel Miranda selected to introduce the Adams administration. The meltdown demon voice.

The terrified new parents of the 1980s—for me and for many readers, our parents—were given Dobson and the Ezzos and told not to stray lest we, their children, surely die. They spanked, they gendered, they prayed, they private-schooled, they boycotted, they voted, they sleep trained, they dehorned My Little Ponies—all to keep us from the pain of life without God.

## The Latest Version of Perfect Parenting, 2000-present

By the time my generation became parents, pop neurology had replaced moralism and everyone pretty much agreed that no strategy was going to produce perfectly obedient, perfectly self-controlled, or perfectly anything kids. Now it was about being the perfect parent—neither permissive nor authoritarian, but "authoritative."[12] There's a liberal version of this that does not impose labels or competitive demands on children, and a conservative version that emphasizes manners and overtly prepares kids for a competitive world. There's also a distinctly Christian version.

Take, for instance, the 2000 book *Parenting without Perfection*. It seems poised to take some pressure off—and to a certain degree it does sign on to the whole "the experts cannot give you a perfect child" thesis. Author David John Seel Jr. leads by calling out the lie that is the family Christmas card—the book is from pre-Instagram days—and how we need a faith that allows for struggle. But he tips his hand when he suggests that he's offering advice for those struggling to parent in the midst of "weakened families and toxic youth culture."[13] The imperfection, the book suggests, is the "world's." We can still do it right; we just can't expect the world to be right, or our kids to be undamaged by the imperfect world. We aren't called to produce perfect children, just to embody Christ in our household.

Oh, is that all?

Like many other evangelical authors Seel has some more certain advice on what embodying Christ looks like. Take it from me, even if the only thing you are perfectionistic about is your own Christlikeness, you're still on the icy road of perfectionism. Because Christlikeness, in our culture, is still a construct interpreted by straight, white men, and it still leads to all the other standards and measures that straight, white men have set for American life. The hard part for those of us who grew up with burnt Smurfs and mutilated unicorns is finding the confidence to take what we need from all of this expertise, all of these values, and parent in our own way.

## The Best They Could

I spent my twenties furious that my parents embraced the Dobson model so thoroughly—that they refused to push back and had therefore given in to the pressure of cultural and religious perfectionism. But my burnt Smurf baggage is mild compared to what many of my peers carry. I knew my parents loved me. I never worried they would abandon or injure me. I was just angry that the monolith I inherited was hard to climb. Then came graduate school, and then the failed ministry career. Once I began smashing the granite face into smaller and smaller bits, I felt I'd been lied to and manipulated. I was crying with each necessary blow, terrified that there would be nothing left.

In the end, I'll take a pile of rubble over a giant rock. One can be a sandy beach where we can all hang out, and the other is the sheer face of El Capitan where only the people as reckless as whatshisface from the documentary are hanging on.

But when I had kids, I realized how scary it was not to have a big, reassuring monolith to cling to. What if I picked up the wrong pebbles? What if the sand slipped through my fingers? Ruining children is as much a liberal anxiety as it is a conservative one, and now I was listening to both sides. I was rejecting white supremacist systems but couldn't completely ignore the doomsday prognostications of the personal price I would pay for doing so. Also, there was Amazon and the endless ideas of what to buy in order to perfect your children. I felt so lost.

The inheritors of perfectionist legacy do not like to hear, "You're doing the best you can." Similarly, I do not like "most improved" trophies. Both affirmations carry the stench of inadequacy. Like, "You're falling woefully short, but considering your overall mediocrity, we'll take it." When I was parenting a two-year-old and a newborn, I was, by perfectionist standards, woefully inadequate. I lived half my day in a fugue state and the other half clenching my jaw. The stress I added to the house was destructive. I started whispering frantically, "I'm doing the best I can I'm doing the best I can I'm doing the best I can" to some invisible taskmaster as the messes piled up. As we were late to birthday parties. As I forgot to put more diapers in the diaper bag. As months went by and I still couldn't fit into my pre-baby clothes.

I didn't know anyone could hear my whispered mantra, my desperate attempt to self-soothe, but one day my two-year-old climbed into my arms and looked up at my face.

"Where's my princess costume?" she asked.

Honestly, the task sounded insurmountable. I had no idea if I'd be able to search the house for longer than five minutes without crying. I told her I didn't know where the costume was but I'd try to help her find it. My daughter smiled up at me.

"Because you're my mommy, and you're doing the best you can."

It was a humbling moment. On the one hand, filled with the incredible grace of toddlerhood. She accepted the *effort* as an act of love, even if the outcome wasn't perfect. On the other, her repetition of my mantra cut to the marrow of my pride. I was not the all-knowing, all-powerful, all-serene mother I'd wanted to be. She knew it.

And then I remembered that my parents became Christians just before they had me. Someone offered them certainty in the scariest moments of life. Of course they took it! If someone had showed up with some new redemptive certainty I'd never tried before, I think I'd have taken it too. I've tried. I've looked for certainty in baby brain science, "Embrace the mess" mom blogs, pediatricians' offices, and education. Thankfully, I was never mentally healthy enough to pick one and perfect it.

It might be tempting to be angry at our parents for trying to free solo El Capitan in the middle of the perfect storm, but the reality is that they were just as uncertain and just as scared as we are now. They were beaten up by perfectionism, and patriarchy, and consumerism, and competition just as much as we are. Most of them were doing the best that they could, and they need us to look back at those efforts with compassion.

*Part 2*

# EXIT RAMPS

The next six chapters are the "what" of the book. As in "what happened?" What are the reasons people's faith begins to shift? Most people get off the road of certainty and perfectionism as a result of questioning, being hurt by, or becoming disillusioned with a certain view of authority—whether the authority of Scripture, the church, or people in positions of power. That makes a lot of sense as the general starting point for change and discovery, but the particulars of our journey will have an impact on how we raise our kids.

Chapter 4

# Sword Drills

'Cause though the truth may vary
This ship will carry our bodies safe to shore.

—Of Monsters and Men, "Little Talks"

While I've been wrestling with the dilemmas described in this book for years, the struggle didn't become a book until about ten months into the coronavirus pandemic. Yes, a super convenient time. With all the anxiety and fear swirling around, I found myself involuntarily calling up a lot of Scripture I had memorized as a child.

".... will never leave you nor forsake you . . ." (Deut. 31:6, NIV)

".... plans to give you a hope and a future . . ." (Jer. 29:11, NIV)

".... neither height nor depth, nor anything else in all creation, will be able to separate us from the love of God in Christ Jesus our Lord." (Rom. 8:39, NIV)

I found real comfort in those easily accessible meditations, whispered by my spirit, as we went through the chaos of school-

at-home and work-at-home and piecing together daily schedules
out of ever-fraying scraps of routine. They were there when I
needed them. My kids will one day face their own challenges,
and it seemed like a good gift to put a deep well of blessing in
their hearts and minds to prepare them. I wanted them to have
access to the generations and millennia of comfort sacred texts
provide. The question was, how? Flash cards? Reward charts?
Stitch them onto decorative pillows?

I learned most Scripture through Sunday school, which was
all about competitive Bible memory and "sword drills" to see who
could flip to a chapter and verse the fastest. I had neither the desire
nor, frankly, the energy to do that with my kids. Sword drills, a
longtime favorite game of Sunday school teachers and Bible club
leaders, have been around since at least 1894, when the Presbyterian periodical *The Church at Home and Abroad* made mention of
them.[1] The "sword" in sword drills comes from Ephesians 6:17, in
which an author who did not know his letter would one day be considered "the word of God" refers to the "word of God" as the "sword
of the Spirit." In some drills, the chapter and verse are called out at
random. The teacher calls out, "Ezekiel 13:10!" and the class races
to flip to the obscure passage buried somewhere among the major and minor prophets, kings of Judah, Levitical law, or shorter
epistles of the New Testament. The onion skin pages of the Bibles
inevitably tear. Another kind of sword drill has the leader choose
verses by topic—some apps will even provide lists of verses on topics from abortion to zeal—so the drillers will know how to use the
Bible in topical discussions or, more likely, debates.

This is my problem with sword drills and Bible memorization
games: They make a competition out of something that could
be contemplative, and they treat the Bible as a book of debate
fodder, a jangly bag of disjointed ammunition. Games like this
either explicitly or implicitly teach that the "sword" is something
to be wielded in battle against other people whose ideas don't
measure up, rather than something to be used to encourage and

heal others and ourselves. I wasn't trying to outfit my kids for a battle of wits against scientists, doctors, or socialists. I was trying to connect them to a wellspring of life they can draw from as they encounter cyberbullies, vicious public discourse, mental health challenges, and addictions.

It's certainly possible that those sword drillers and Sunday school Bible memory champs tapped into such a wellspring through rapid-fire Bible memorization. I just didn't think one more competition, incentive program, or reward chart was what my family needed. I wanted them to experience the *beauty* of Scripture, so I turned to music. Music is a great memorization tool, and it is why I can still recite the books of the Bible and certain parts of the Westminster Confession of Faith.

I found a folksy, acoustic album with Bible verse lyrics and put it on in the car one day. Within a minute, both of my children had hands over their ears and were screaming at me to turn the music off.

"Mom! This music is terrible!" shouted six-year-old Moira.

"Björk! Björk! Just turn on Björk!" shouted four-year-old Asa.

I glared at my forty-year-old husband, Lewis, the culprit behind their love of Björk, Mazzy Star, The Black Keys, Fleet Foxes, and Fiona Apple. As a classically trained singer, Lewis has always maintained that bad music with Jesusy lyrics is more offensive to God than great music with non-Jesusy lyrics. So now the budding *Pitchfork* critics in my backseat had zero tolerance for chirpy kids' voices and campy guitar. I sighed, switched to Björk, and looked for another natural way to give my kids some meditative Scripture.

One night, as I walked my nightly pandemic sanity walk around the neighborhood, I called my childhood best friend, now the mother of a four-year-old.

"Are you going to have your kids memorize Bible verses?" I asked.

"You know . . . I don't know," she answered, no doubt conjuring up her own days as a sword driller. She thought a moment longer before answering, "Not the way we did it."

We started talking about the many things in that category of "not the way we did it." Church. Sex. Politics. That conversation would eventually become this book. As we talked, it became clear that my dilemma about *how* to help my kids hide some Scripture in their hearts was actually a dilemma about *why* I wanted them to do so.

## The Final Word

The sword drills and Bible memory of my youth came from a very particular place—a belief that the Bible was the authoritative word of God and that knowing it verbatim inside out and upside down was the only way to truly know God. We were taught that every "jot and tittle" of the Bible was a direct revelation of the unchanging nature of God and offered explicit instruction for how to live in the world. Our pastors would belabor the particular Greek and Hebrew participles and conjunctions used in the text as though they were the Rosetta Stone of God's mysterious ways. They were particularly good at taking those single words—"submit," for instance—and turning them into policy.

Most of us raised with religious certainty probably had an authoritative Scripture as the foundation. Words like "inerrant" and "infallible" make the foundation solid and immovable. Everything from Sunday soccer tournaments to premarital sex was prohibited with a helpless shrug, a wordless reference to the popular slogan of the culture wars, often seen on bumper stickers: The Bible said it, I believe it, that settles it.

Only, in my house we struck the middle clause. We did not need to "believe it" for a matter to be settled. Truth was truth—we were expected to conform our minds and beliefs to something that was already settled. Something objective, not subject to interpretation or discussion. So our bumper sticker should have read: The Bible said it, that settles it, now fall in line.

But that's far from how the Hebrew, and ultimately Christian, Scriptures evolved, writes historian Karen Armstong. Holy texts have always been dynamic—timeless truths recorded in metaphor, myth, poetry, and stories. While modern theology has made God a finite character in the drama, someone we can analyze and understand, Scripture was never intended to be an owner's manual or biography. The actions and even the direct teachings of the characters in the Bible have been filtered through the spiritual wisdom and intentions of the people who wrote it down in their time. "The art of scripture did not mean a return to an imagined perfection in the past, because the sacred text was always a work in progress. The art of scriptural exegesis was, therefore, inventive, imaginative, and creative. So to read scriptures correctly and authentically, we must make them speak directly to our modern predicament," Armstrong writes.[2]

Highly contextual and originally communicated through rituals and oral traditions, Armstrong writes, holy Scriptures primarily worked to draw individual humans into ineffable union with God and one another—they were far from static texts, inerrant on history, science, and comprehensive knowledge of God. "The art of scripture was designed to effect radical change in those who studied it, not to give divine sanction to their own inescapably limited views."[3]

We Christians aren't alone in our, perhaps misplaced, efforts to live faithfully to an ancient, sacred text. Wherever there are holy Scriptures, there's usually some branch of fundamentalism taking them literally, some debate over what they really say, some group trying to out-orthodox the others. Armstrong points out the irony of this in her exploration of the *sola scriptura* doctrine of the Reformation—the teaching that Scripture alone is the authority on Christian belief and living. The Reformation was largely made possible because of the printing press, which allowed more people to access the written word. Once more people could read the Bible, each aspiring theologian believed their interpretation of it was the most loyal to the text. Which led to squabbles. "*Sola scriptura* had inspired a mass of irreconcilable opinions simply because the reformers had fallen in love with their own ideas, but found their proof texts proved nothing."[4] They created new catechisms and creeds to, as Armstrong puts it, "filter" the Bible into a systemized theology. I grew up swearing fealty to the Westminster Confession of Faith as sincerely as to the Bible.

The printing press froze the Bible in place. I remember a pastor telling us that we were supposed to bring our Bibles to church so that we could check to make sure that everything he was preaching was directly taken from Scripture. Like the Bereans did in Acts 17. The Bereans did not have *Thompson Chain-Reference Bibles*, friends. The Scriptures they were searching in Acts 17:11 could not have been found in the drawers of hotel rooms, and they didn't include the book of Acts! They didn't have Bibles to bring to church. They were holding Paul's teaching up to an evolving, ritualized tradition by which they knew God. So it's sort of funny—don't you think?—that we froze Scripture in time and try to live our modern lives according to its words.

## The Sword of Damocles

Holy Scripture, instead of being the ancient and mystical sword of the Spirit, is often, in the modern world, the sword of Damocles. In the myth, the ambitious courtier Damocles is allowed to sit on the king's throne for a day, enjoying all of the royal riches and opulence. But the king has arranged for a sword to hang by a thread over the throne as a reminder of how precarious a king's position is, how fraught with dangers. If the sword of Damocles is the ruin awaiting those who disobey God's word, the thread suspending it is interpretation.

After the printing press, Judaism and Islam had their own advocates for a printed, bound, never-changing version of God's word in the form of ancient text, but, unlike Christianity, their interpretive rituals, actions, and traditions still carried their own authority. Both ritual-based and *sola scriptura* faiths prove plenty malleable in the hands of scholars, preachers, priests, and clerics as they find rigid ways to apply ancient texts to modern life. Whether authority is based on a continuing revelation or a set canon of Scripture, it can be used to control the flock.

Deborah Feldman, who grew up Hasidic, has described some of the internal debates on what was and wasn't kosher in her community. She notes times the community received new policies on how to live faithfully.[5] Though she chafed under the rules and cultural restrictions of her orthodox community, she knew the heavy cost of leaving—communal rejection and, according to what she'd been taught, spiritual death. The only way to escape the sword of Damocles, for her, was to question its sharpness. Discovering the dissonance between the King David she'd been taught and the King David-the-rapist-and-murderer depicted in Scripture created the first "loss of innocence" in Feldman's faith. "There was a specific moment when I stopped believing in authority just for its own sake and started coming to my own conclusions about the world I lived in."[6]

The Talmudic scholars in her community and the Christian apologists in mine both twist themselves in knots trying to make Scripture consistent so that it will be useful as a guide to life. She describes scholars looking for loopholes in the Torah that would allow the use of prams on the Sabbath. My parents referred to Levitical law to explain why we could not get tattoos. But we cut, colored, and exposed our hair regularly. We did not keep kosher. Whenever my siblings and I pointed this out, there would be some long, winding discussion of how Jesus replaced some laws but not others, and that the reason for the law—that tattoos were pagan markings—still stood. One day the youth pastor revealed that he had an ichthus tattooed on his calf, and now my little sister is a successful tattoo artist with two full sleeves—some things really are a slippery slope.

The interpretive backflips and knots are meant to make sure dangerous questions do not go unanswered, that behaviors don't go unchecked. Ultimately, they are to preserve authority.

When I think about raising kids in this scary world full of diseases, violence, and fast cars, I really see the appeal of a sword of Damocles. It worked for me. It kept me a virgin until I was married. It kept me off drugs and out of trouble. But talk to adults who grew up under a sword dangling by a horse's hair and you will not find peaceful, joyful folks. You will find people like me, who, if they could afford it, have spent thousands of dollars on therapy trying to rid themselves of the fear of a sword falling through their skull.

## Floods and Fish

So I don't want to raise my kids under threat of death.

I don't want the Bible to be debate fodder.

I don't want them memorizing Bible verses out of context just to earn gold stars or Bible Bucks.

Then come the other wrinkles: Jonah. Noah. The serpent. The Red Sea. The Bible stories we first introduce to our children are way more fantastical than most fairy tales and cultural myths of Santas and tooth fairies. Kids are drawn to those stories, and many adults continue to draw great comfort from them.

Who are the giants in your life?

Is Jesus asking you to step out onto the water, trusting he won't let you sink?

Where are you surrounded by lions? Do you trust God to keep them from eating you?

I wonder if these are our introductory stories *because* they are so fantastical. Like we are saying, "See kids, you have to believe in God, because God does all this crazy stuff!" So we've given them the

66

sword of Damocles to keep them in line and a bunch of far-fetched folklore to convince them to stay seated under the sword.

A rigid, literal interpretation of the rules of the Bible also requires a literal, rigid interpretation of the events of the Bible. Any honest person trying to reconcile science and history is going to have some questions. For Christian fundamentalists, doubts about the inerrancy of the Bible are often a starting point for a crisis of faith. Suddenly the miracles, creation account, Levitical law, or some other ironfisted dogma of the church becomes untenable. If you've said it's all or nothing, some folks are going to pick "nothing."

I remember the day in graduate school when I thought to myself, "I think I'm going to need a faith that's not so vulnerable." My understanding of God just could not hang on whether or not dinosaurs coexisted with humans. Or whether a big fish swallowed and vomited a man. Or whether a flood covered the entire planet. In the end, the inconsistencies in the Bible did more to help me love it than leave it. I was reaching the point of tossing the whole untenable thing when I stumbled upon a girl from Alabama who was taking the sword of Damocles and beating it into a plowshare — showing us how life-giving Scripture could be.

**Thank God for Rachel Held Evans**

I'm not sure anyone has done more for people on their way out of fundamentalism than the late Rachel Held Evans, who somehow balanced criticism and love in a way that is both rare and achingly needed. Before her tragic death in 2019, Evans convened a growing group of disillusioned Christians who could no longer draw from the Bible a literal interpretation of science, politics, human sexuality, and gender expression. Through her blogging, books, and teaching, Evans became a patron saint of burnouts and "exvangelicals."

I'll admit I'm not always at ease with exvangelicals, even though I guess I technically am one. Fundamentalism's centuries of heavy-handedness really brought out the schadenfreude in people itching to see it taken down a notch by science and basic logic. It can be painful watching people mock the universal flood or the seven-day creation—things I once sincerely believed. People I love still believe those things. I also think that the ex-vangelical movement has become a cottage industry or even a secondary economy to evangelical megachurches and celebrities. They are like the street vendors waiting to sell T-shirts to the folks on their way out, but they aren't offering them any kind of hope or healing. Just the catharsis of snark.

The snark is merited, but for those of us who also found comfort and assurance in a loving God, an indwelling Spirit, and death-conquering Christ, there's a bitter edge to the memes and tweets. It's a reminder of all that we've lost, with no hope for a better future. That's why my ears perked up when I heard Rachel Held Evans echoing both my concerns and my longing. Evans was never sardonic about her issues with evangelicalism—the fundamentalist, politically homogeneous kind she grew up in—but was earnest in her observations, critiques, and questions. In all her books—particularly *A Year of Biblical Womanhood* and *Inspired: Slaying Giants, Walking on Water, and Learning to Love the Bible Again*—she doesn't ridicule and poke holes in the Bible. She takes it seriously. By looking at it for what it is, not what we've made it to be, Evans, Armstrong, and scholars like Angela N. Parker and Peter Enns unlocked a lot of power in the Scriptures. When we consider the Bible as it was written, as the lived experience of the divine in specific times and places, it empowers us to say, think, and do in accordance with the Spirit of God in our specific time and places.

Evans died before she was able to publicly explore parenting according to her hard-won worldview. Her children were very young, and I think we were all looking forward to her thoughts on the journey of raising them. We can get a glimpse of what might have been in her children's book *What Is God Like?* In it, Evans draws from the various metaphors of Scripture to describe not the absolute nature of God, but the lived experience of God. The absolute nature of God, she says from the beginning, is unknowable. The experience of God, by contrast, is forever accessible. "Whenever you aren't sure what God is like, think about what makes you feel safe, what makes you feel brave, and what makes you feel loved. That's what God is like."[7]

## The Scalpel of the Spirit

Rather than sweat over making sure my kids memorize Bible verses, we've decided to introduce them to God and help them become adept at listening, whether God is speaking through their conscience or through the Bible, through nature, or through a friend.

When I think of the sword of the Spirit, the word of God, and the holy Scriptures I know best, I think of another passage— Hebrews 4:12 (ESV): "For the word of God is living and active, sharper than any two-edged sword, piercing to the division of soul and of spirit, of joints and of marrow, and discerning the thoughts and intentions of the heart." The author didn't know they were writing what would one day be considered holy Scripture, and their idea of the "word" of God was not a leather-bound family Bible, but something more experiential, more incarnational.

In *The Message* Bible, Eugene Peterson translates the sword in Hebrews 4:12 as a "surgeon's scalpel."[8] A tool of healing, not of destruction. The word of God is not used against you, but to cut out cancers and blockages. It's a tool suited for our most intense spiritual struggles, the kind that leave our souls so entangled that we need the finest blade to cut us free while leaving us whole. Anyone who has found spiritual hope amid depression, anxiety, and addiction knows that dicey place.

A sacred text cannot fully communicate or encapsulate God or God's actions, but revelation and intimate spiritual knowledge are part of living in God's world. Sacred texts of every faith are part of that conversation and experience captured through-out time, and as such they are a wealth of help, comfort—and, yes, are useful "for teaching, for reproof, for correction, and for training in righteousness" (2 Tim. 3:16, ESV). But they are not like a magic book from a story by C. S. Lewis or J. K. Rowling. They do not flop open and unleash a god, only to have it contained again as the book is snapped shut. Scripture is not something we control or use to control others. When we discuss the sacred texts with our children, my husband and I want them to come away more free, more loved, more aware of God.

In our house we want our children to be more unified with the Christ, more tapped into the wellspring of the Spirit. There are Bible verses that draw us into union with Christ, and we will speak them often. There are stories, both biblical and not, that strengthen our hearts, and we will tell them. We will stop to consider God in nature and in service. We will allow our hearts and minds to be changed by our experiences of God and God's creative, unfolding word.

Where there are tough passages, stories that unsettle us, or teachings that seem to run counter to the God we know, we keep asking for wisdom. When suffering continues, causing us to question God's goodness, or when the world continues to un-ravel at the hands of the unjust, we keep doing what we know is right, loving like we know we should, and waiting for un-derstanding. We are OK saying, "Right now, I don't understand how that squares with the God we know, but one day maybe we will. That doesn't stop us from loving God and loving others."

Rather than finding in the Bible a sword of Damocles, a sword to slay debating foes, or a definitive answer on the size of the fish that swallowed Jonah, we will give our children access to Scripture, and it will speak to their souls in a way beyond anyone's control.

## Chapter 5

# Theater for the Damned

Don't count me out just yet
I'm not your little lost lamb
God might still get my world
Get it undamned.

—Over the Rhine, "Undamned"

Hell-for-nonbelievers may be the teaching responsible for more ex-Christians than any other doctrine. It is definitely responsible for a lot of anti-Christian sentiment. Hell is the big judgment that encapsulates all the little judgments people associate with condescending, mean-spirited, colonizing Christians.

And I grew up being totally fine with it!

When I was four years old, my dad's aged secretary died. It made sense to me that older people were supposed to die, and I remember feeling not sad, necessarily, but concerned. I was logical but still tenderhearted. I asked my mom if the secretary was in heaven, and she, ever earnest, replied, "I don't know. I don't know whether or not she knew Jesus." She then deftly seized her evangelistic moment and asked me if I knew whether I would go to heaven when I died. The alternative, I knew, was hell. Hence my concern for the secretary.

I could stop here and talk about how I was forever trauma-tized by the fear of hell, the threat of hell, or the possibility of hell. But I wasn't.

Death, my own and others', was inevitable. Something had to come next. Hell existed—best to avoid. Heaven existed—very nice option. I pictured it like Willy Wonka's chocolate room, but with more gold. So I knelt by my wrought iron bed at age four, my little nightgown tucked under my knees, eyes about level with the box spring, and I asked Jesus to live in my heart. That night settled a lot for me. My friends and siblings worried about hell and the end times and demons throughout childhood. I was just certain Jesus wasn't going to let me down. He couldn't. I'd said the magic words, and I passed into adolescence with very few worries.

This confidence didn't hang on the character of Christ or on Jesus's love for me. My worldview was entirely transactional. Like the ancient Hebrews in Egypt, I had blood on my door-posts. The angel of death had to pass over (Exod. 12:13). De-spite occasional emotional moments of closeness with Jesus, I wasn't hanging my eternal safety on his love. Emotions were not sturdy, not even God's emotions. I would bet my future on more certain things: reason, logic, transaction, and obligation. Certainty worship and perfectionism were born early in me.

As I learned more about theology in middle and high school, hell remained a functional, if harsh, reality. My inherent com-fort with harsh realities placed me somewhere between an in-sufferable prig and a total asshole. Not a day goes by that I don't thank God for holding social media at bay until I was well past the worst of it. I could have populated a Twitter feed that would haunt me forever.

My pride in cold, unflinching logic had a lot to do with the sexism I internalized as well. To justify the exclusion of women from leadership, many of us grew up hearing that women were too emotional. Being overly sensitive to cruelty and injustice was seen as a weak, feminine trait, and as someone who was constantly trying to earn the right to speak and be taken seriously in theological conversations, I had to show my strong stomach.

Condemning good people to hell on a technicality is a great way to prove you have balls of steel, especially when you have no balls. By the time I was in high school, I sneered at people who "just couldn't imagine a loving God would send people to hell." On the outside, I would shrug and say, "It makes me sad, but I trust God's goodness." My internal response was, Don't be such a whiny baby. There are a lot of things I don't like that are still true. Those people were weak-minded, I decided. God could be a rumbling volcano occasionally erupting sharks and monsters, and to me, if that's what was real then that's what was real. Best to accept it and adjust.

This worldview would remain with me until it was undone over the course of my twenties and thirties. First, I started actually forming relationships with the damned—people whose very tenderheartedness and love of humanity led them to reject my worldview. I learned more about how vast and diverse the world is, and the idea that I had, through accident of birth, stumbled onto the one capital-T Truth was less and less tenable. Could it be that the lake of fire was really going to be chockablock full of people who had no idea how they'd ended up there? And about that "lake of fire." That's not even the consistent description used throughout the Bible. The Bible is less clear on the exact details of hell than I'd been led to believe, giving me far less certainty with which to combat my growing unease about sending three quarters of humanity there. Suddenly the people who loudly defended the existence of hell sounded, like middle school me, somewhere between obnoxious and silly.

"What happens when we die" entered my realm of spiritual unknowns.

### What's the Hell?

It's not that my kids haven't asked about what happens when we die. Grandparents, dogs, and movie characters all died, and we had to answer some basics. Fortunately, death has been around from the beginning, and I have lots of material to pull from. Pretty much every civilization has had to come up with an answer for what happens when we die. Most civilizations have had a "realm of the dead" scenario, at the very least. Usually with a scary guard. Sorting souls of the departed into the winners (heaven), not-quite-winners (purgatory, temporary destinations, reincarnation, and so on), and losers (hell) has had a lot of iterations.

Not every religion has hell. But most have judgment. Most have criteria of some sort to get into some version of paradise. Most have an answer for "What if my life on earth did not meet the entry requirements for paradise?" Karma. Jahannam. Naraka. Annihilation.

Christian theologians coalesce around the idea of "separation from God," but very few agree on the specific features of what that entails. They also don't agree, entirely, on how to avoid hell, which makes the whole enterprise ludicrously scary. Evangelicals usually believe that trust in the death and resurrection of Jesus is the only criterion for avoiding hell. Traditionally, many Catholics have believed they have additional sacramental boxes to check to lock down their salvation, like last rites, confession, and baptism. Mainline Protestants seem less comfortable with sending virtuous nonbelievers to hell, and they have been more willing to consider exceptions to the strict "confess and believe" criteria for getting into heaven.

The destiny of stillborn babies, Gandhi, and Hitler have left Christians in knots, trying to reconcile the love and justice of God. Those who believe we must have explicit faith in Jesus have to deal with the babies and Gandhi. Those who believe everyone gets in, the universalists, must answer those who don't want to spend eternity with Hitler.

Worldviews relying on a cosmic ledger of good and bad to determine eternal destiny must deal with people who are at risk, or "on the bubble" as they say in the television world. Like

Mindy St. Claire from *The Good Place*. She lives in "The Medium Place"—a realm of eternal mediocrity—because after a lifetime of debauchery she intended to start a nonprofit charity. She died before she could start it, but her sister went through with the plan in her honor and helped a lot of people. This made for problems in the afterlife accounting department.

Whether you are dealing emotionally or logically with human nature, we do not easily sort into goats and sheep. Emotionally, nobody likes to send babies to hell. Logically, the sum total consequences of our actions, as *The Good Place* points out, are not easily counted. Neither are our beliefs. Christian theologians regularly make the specifics of the gospel so narrow that different branches of Lutheranism or Presbyterianism might hesitate to call one another "saved." Chaos.

With all this squabbling about who goes to hell and how to avoid it, it's not surprising that so many of my friends were terrified that they'd missed some crucial detail. It makes my own lack of fear seem like pure naivety. As an adult, I'm not certain what will happen to my soul when my body dies. I'm way less sure about what happens when you die, or when people on the other side of the world die. I still have my childlike confidence that Jesus has me covered, but in a different way. I believe that God is love, that Jesus connected me to that love, and that love transcends death.

In the McNeel house, this esoteric discussion of hell is not nearly as important as "What are we going to tell the kids?" When you are parents struggling with faith, you spend your date nights trying to figure out how to talk to kids about hell. Lewis, my husband, is a thoughtful, deep man who absolutely hates systematic theology, philosophy, and all other fields associated with men sitting around a table smoking cigars, theorizing, and pontificating. So while I was spinning my wheels trying to figure out how to integrate medieval theories of Sheol and concepts of reincarnation into our nontraumatic "hell talk" with the kids, Lewis summed it up in the length of one drive to the movie theater.

There are three options, he said: (1) Tell the kids the version we grew up with—that hell is a real place where you go forever if you don't believe in Jesus—because if it's wrong, they've lost nothing but a little anxiety, and if it's right they won't go to hell; (2) tell the kids hell doesn't exist—because the depictions and language they will hear in contemporary America are largely wrong—and give them lots of positive reasons to love God and love others; or (3) don't bring it up, because we have no idea and their journey is their own. We still haven't picked an option, which means we have defaulted to option three for the time being.

When they ask about death, we go with heaven. Psychologically, it just seems safer. I may not have been scared by hell, but I know enough people who were. I also don't want to introduce the idea of judgment—either eternal or earthly—until we've laid the foundation of what to do with shame and justice, two things my own theology of hell did not prepare me to handle in my own life.

## Going through Hell

Hell may not have scared me as a kid, but as a budding perfectionist I did experience a lot of the shame. I lived in constant fear of rejection, which made sense in a worldview with insiders and outsiders, membership and excommunication—earthly previews of heaven and hell. It wasn't possible to make Jesus abandon me. His people, on the other hand, seemed more fickle. My soul was going to heaven, but acceptance—being treated like part of the community—on earth was tied to approval. It was tied to my behavior and my ability to please various adults whom "God had put in authority over me." The messages I received on this were, shall we say, mixed.

Here's a theatrical vignette I like to call "The Mindf**k":

*(Scene: BEKAH is in elementary, middle, high school, and college. A chorus of PARENTS, PASTORS, and CHRISTIAN SCHOOL LEADERS surrounds her.)*

**CHORUS:** If the authority is happy with you, God is happy with you.

**BEKAH:** I'm doing it! I am so tired! But I'm getting it right!

*(Fade to black)*

*(Lights up on 27-year-old BEKAH who sits alone in a room across from PASTOR-BOSS)*

**PASTOR-BOSS:** Your need for my approval is idolatry.

**BEKAH:** But approval is the only gauge I've ever had to tell whether or not God was happy with me!

**PASTOR-BOSS:** You need to rest in [long winded explanation of substitutionary atonement].

*(Fade to black)*

*(Lights up on same stage, one year later)*

**PASTOR-BOSS:** We're not happy with you. You're fired.

**BEKAH:** But I thought—

**PASTOR-BOSS:** You don't have my approval, you never will. You're fired, and you need to go be thankful for this opportunity to starve out your idols.

*(End scene.)*

Please send inquiries to my agent.

Authority figures told me that acceptance was secure because of atonement, what Jesus did on the cross. He had died to cover my sinfulness, which God could not accept. Thanks to his death on the cross, now when God looked at me, God saw Jesus. I would not go to hell. Yet watching the families and churches around me, I got the message loudly and clearly: If the authorities disapproved of me, I would be treated as an outsider.

The fear of becoming an outsider trumped eternal security and wired my brain for shame. I felt like I had to hide my imperfections, just in case they were the imperfections that made me unacceptable. I knew my parents would never literally abandon me. I knew they loved me in that love-is-an-act-of-the-will way, but I worried that if I screwed up badly enough, they would see me as a lost cause and only keep me around out of a sense of obligation. I hid my imperfections as best I could until I could master them.

I'm going to give my parents this huge piece of credit: Their four children all grew up to do things they disapproved of, and they never rejected us, not even emotionally. There have been hurts, yes. But if I had known how deeply they would long for relationships with us despite unplanned pregnancies, tattoos, Democratic voting habits, and all sorts of other violations of our childhood taboos, I would have relaxed a lot. In fact, if I could go back and tell ten-year-old Bekah two things, they would be: (1) You will marry someone who adores you (separate topic, big concern for my childhood self), and (2) your parents are going to want to have a relationship with you forever. Not everyone has that. Some parents do reject their kids—for being gay, for being addicted, for being atheist. I never ventured into mortal sin territory, so I never feared being thrown out or disowned, but I still felt the weight of every disapproval like an anvil. Disapproval and rejection were theologically synonymous for me, and my emotional response followed suit. It still does, even after the theology has changed.

After a lifetime of hiding-until-perfect I smell rejection everywhere, like a fox on alert for hounds. My mom compares me to a duck—serene on the surface with legs paddling madly beneath me. A deep throb of unworthiness still pulses in my gut.

Like many weary, shame-ridden "evangelikids," I turned to Brené Brown, the researcher whose TED Talk would spawn an empire of leadership theory based on courage and vulnerability.[1]

Shame, Brown says, holds us back from sharing our true selves because we believe that we are unworthy.[2] Something deep inside of us is unacceptable. Vulnerability, the willingness to be our true selves in spite of that nagging belief, is how we connect to others. Those connections based on vulnerability are how we experience peace. We know that the people who accept us are doing so with full knowledge of who we are. We don't have a shameful secret hanging over us, whispering in the night, "If they knew, they'd stop loving you."

As a parent now myself, shame gains new significance. Parents are a child's first God-like presence.[3] How we treat them is how they will assume God treats them. We also know that psychologically we are social, tribal animals and we are wired to need acceptance from each other.[4] Our children get from us a sense of spiritual security or insecurity. If we aren't able to draw a clear line between approval of behaviors and acceptance of persons, they are bound to feel insecure with God and each other. They are bound to fear their own unworthiness. As a parent, it's on us to reduce the threat of rejection. We have to disentangle approval and acceptance. We have to be vulnerable so that our kids can be vulnerable. We have to openly accept ourselves and others so that they will feel free to be their true selves.

Sometimes, of course, our kids' true selves are exactly what we're afraid to unleash. The threat of rejection or disapproval can be useful to keep them from destroying the house, talking back, hitting their friends, and maybe even trying drugs. Kids want acceptance and approval, and if we can convince them that those things they crave will be denied, they will often fall in line. Either that, or they become sneaky, compulsive, insecure perfectionists who are more vulnerable to risky behaviors and addiction as they try to earn the approval of others who aren't their parents. There are no sure bets in parenting.

It *may* keep the house and the urine tests clean, but shame destroys the soul. The healthiest adults drink from deep wells of acceptance that aren't tied to approval or agreement. Wiser people than I can tell you how to parent like this. I'm learning from Brown, Tina Payne Bryson, Cindy Wang Brandt, Jessica Lahey, and Lisa Miller, among others. I commend them to you.

But what about the things for which we *should* be ashamed? How do we instill a sense of right and wrong? What about justice? Pain and alienation from others is hell on earth, and it's not caused by demons or pitchforks. It's caused by us. It will be, on one level or another, caused by our children. We have to reckon not only with, as Mr. Rogers said, "What do you do with the mad that you feel?"[5] but also "What do you do with the pain that you cause?"

## Hell on Earth

As I write this in 2021, healing is having a moment. The younger Millennials and Gen Z are helping us all "name our traumas" and "cut out the toxic people" from our lives. I've done a bit of this selective pruning myself, and, yes, it feels marvelous. But we have yet to figure out what comes next. The healing process doesn't end with blocking someone on Twitter or announcing publicly that we struggle with anxiety. What comes next has huge implications for public justice. For families, friendships, and communities recovering from hurt. We have to move past the "hell" we're living in and start moving toward "on earth as it is in heaven."

In 2019 *New Yorker* theater critic Vinson Cunningham wrote an essay called "How the Idea of Hell Has Shaped the Way We Think."[6] Cunningham, in the kind of witty, lyrical prose one would expect from a theater critic, catalogs the various features, boundaries, and admissions requirements given to hell over the centuries. He concludes that our obsession with hell has made us a more punitive people, on the right and the left. It's easy to point to "law and order" politics and say the right is the more hell-bent side of the spectrum. But, Cunningham points out, the Occupy Wall Street movement didn't exactly have redemption in mind for the bankers it sought to dethrone. Or how about cancel culture, which hadn't fully crested when Cunningham was writing in 2019? Good guys, bad guys, and ultimate ends are part of our national mythology.

Cunningham muses on the potential for a more restoration-based future, namely in the form of prison abolition. But our future is limited by our imagination, he argues. "To redirect our creativity and train it toward Heaven—and, by extension, our notions of the good life on Earth—would require a kind of revolution in our thinking," Cunningham writes. That revolution, I believe along with him, is restorative justice.

Restorative justice is a movement across schools and the criminal justice system to focus less on punishing bad behavior, and instead more on asking harmed people what they need to be made whole. Offenders then take part in making restoration.

Punishment of the offender does not restore the lost property or dignity of the person they harmed, but restorative justice seeks, inasmuch as it is possible, actually to give the victim back what was lost, and in many cases to restore to them the lost relationship with the offender. The community is also made whole by restored victims who are no longer living with a hole in their lives and restored offenders who are contributing rather than rotting in jail.

It happens in little and big ways.

Restoration happens when a kid must give back a stolen toy.

Restoration happens when an addict gets treatment and is able to contribute to and invest in the family members who were hurt by their addiction.

The idea of amends and repair is so easy to teach children. The Daniel Tiger ditty sums it up nicely: "Saying I'm sorry is the first step, then 'how can I help?'"[7] Children can be raised to believe that harm is common and repair is possible. We don't have to defend our perfect records at all costs. We don't have to earn approval by never screwing up. We can die and rise.

Jesus showed us the way. He died (for things he didn't do) and rose so that we could be repaired. So that our relationships with God and one another could have shalom. Catholic theologian Richard Rohr maintains that shalom is so synonymous with the character of God in Jesus Christ that even the idea of his death on the cross *as a necessary punishment for sin* skews the narrative too far from God's redemptive heart: "Once a person recognizes that Jesus's mission (obvious in all four Gospels) was to heal people, not punish them, the dominant theories of retributive justice begin to lose their appeal and their authority."[8]

But most of us weren't raised like that. Not by our parents, churches, or society at large. We were raised in a litigious world where justice was handed down by external forces, not worked out between people. A punishment for the wrongdoer and a token for the victim. Our defensiveness about right and wrong has made some conversations—the big ones about who we are and what amends we owe as a society—nearly impossible to have.

As a white woman in the United States in 2021, I've become more acquainted with appropriate guilt and culpability. I understand my role in systems that have hurt indigenous people through genocide and dispossession, and people of color through various forms of oppression, exclusion, and violence. It's a long and ugly history, and I am the beneficiary who, unless a radical change is made, will continue the legacy for another generation.

Of course, there are those who don't want me to feel that guilt. During their 2021 legislative session, Texas lawmakers passed a bill that forbids teachers to teach that "an individual, by virtue of his or her race or sex, bears responsibility for actions committed in the past by other members of the same race or sex; any individual should feel discomfort, guilt, anguish, or any other form of psychological distress on account of his or her race or sex."[9] A parent in Tennessee protested that teaching about segregation, even historical segregation, was overplaying the differences between children, implying children were culpable for something beyond their control.[10]

Whenever I talk about systemic racism with other white folks, they quickly reply with "I shouldn't have to feel guilty for something I had nothing to do with." The real worry, I suspect, for lawmakers and the rest of us, is not whether these teachings are historically accurate. The question is: What would accepting this guilt require of me? Restoration requires us to descend into the place of death. It requires us to look around and acknowledge the little piece of hell we have brought to earth, to die to it, and to rise without it. What death is required in order to rise into wholeness as a nation reckoning with racism? Death of my all-white school? Death of my investments? Death of my private property? Death of my belief that I deserve everything I have? Death of my self-righteousness? The suffering of guilt ends when we die to harm and rise to repair. Repairing the breach. Bringing peace. This could refer to a spat between siblings, the betrayal of a spouse, or generations of oppression. Alcoholics Anonymous calls it "amends." Racial justice advocates call it "reparations."

We know when we break shalom. We gossip, we lash out, we ostracize, we abuse. We know when we are bringing death to the world. Death of relationships, death of trust, death of our bodies, death of others. I understand the knee jerk reaction that comes after hearing that we are broken or sinful or in any way "bad." I have that reaction every time. Just ask my therapist. We fear if we admit our fault, the cost of reconciliation will be too much to bear.

We've never known brokenness without shame. We've never known justice without damnation.

## "Go to Hell, Rob Bell"

As Cunningham's essay points out, Americans are quite married to the idea of punitive justice. We're probably not going to give up on hell, even if doing so would make us braver, more willing to make amends, and less fearful of what it would mean to accept guilt.

Hell has become such a linchpin for Christian doctrine that to reject it, for many, is to reject the entire religion. At the same time, simply rejecting hell does not immediately make us better people. We've got to struggle a bit, because how we envision heaven and hell are good indicators of what we believe about the nature of reality, the nature of God, and the nature of justice. It's about what matters and what lasts. It's about the consequences and purposes we are embodying here and now.

Cunningham references Lucas Hnath's 2014 play *The Christians*, about the experience of a preacher who declares he no longer believes in hell. Pastor Paul, after he makes the big statement in the first scene, must contend with his associate pastor who questions his orthodoxy, the elder who worries that without hell people won't keep coming to (and tithing to) the church, the layperson who doesn't want to share heaven with Hitler, and the wife who feels that staying married would be to sanction the heresy. Along the way, Pastor Paul's intentions, timing, and hubris are called into question. If *The Good Place* explored moral chaos in the afterlife, *The Christians* explores moral chaos in this life.

When I recommended the play to my own pastor, he asked whether "Pastor Paul" was actually "Pastor Rob." He was referencing Rob Bell, who first became famous as the pastor of Mars

Hill, a Michigan church (not to be confused with the Seattle megachurch of the same name) established in 1999 and reaching eleven thousand attendees in 2005. His book *Velvet Elvis: Repainting the Christian Faith* was widely popular during my short-lived ministry career, though we hardcore conservative folks thought he was dangerous. His book *Love Wins: A Book about Heaven, Hell, and the Fate of Every Person Who Ever Lived* moved him from "dangerous" to "heretic" in the eyes of many. But he left those folks (and his midwestern church) behind and went on to be a career Christian celebrity. He even moved to Los Angeles. He tours. He podcasts. Rob Bell is doing just fine.

Hnath insists in the preface to the 2016 edition of *The Christians* that no character was based on a specific person, but rather a lot of people. The play doesn't ultimately side with Pastor Paul or any of his detractors. A simple rejection of hell, the play demonstrates, leaves a gaping moral hole in the universe. "And while the plot of The Christians is far from ambiguous, the play is a series of contradictory arguments. No single argument 'wins.' There's no resolution," Hnath writes.[11]

Bell—whom the play is, again, not based upon—shares a similar sentiment in the introduction to *Love Wins*. "If this book, then, does nothing more than introduce you to the ancient, ongoing discussion surrounding the resurrected Jesus in all its vibrant, diverse, messy multivoiced complexity—well, I'd be thrilled."[12] Uncritical rejection of hell is a short cut, in many ways, a way to get the good feelings and avoid the struggle, the discussion, the "what about?" It works both ways though. The threat of hell can be a lazy shorthand to get behavioral results or moral formation without the struggle, the discussion, the "what about?"

We need to talk to our kids now about how to handle the moral chaos of wrongs done by and to them, of shame, and living with uncertainty about what happens when we die. We need to help them believe that a God who is love can be trusted with the outcome.

I don't have all the answers, but I do have one resource to share: the Marvel Cinematic Universe.

Around age four, my son Asa became obsessed with superheroes and villains. He ordered his universe by good and evil. He wanted good to win and bad to die. Not just lose. Die. To foster and direct his budding sense of justice, I turned to our shared love of all things Marvel, namely the character of Bucky Barnes. Asa is too young to see the movies, but he knows Barnes through the various books and snippets I've allowed.

While most superhero stories involve the demise of the villain, the *better* stories, I told him, are the ones where the villain can be rescued and "turned good." In fact, the blurrier the lines between villains and heroes, the more powerful the story becomes. Marvel, while incredibly imperfect in terms of violence and war as a means to peace, does have characters to strengthen a mythology of redemption.

Barnes, for those who are not Marvel fanatics, was an American soldier in World War II who was captured, brainwashed, given the same super soldier serum that created Captain America, and used as an assassin by HYDRA, which had its eye on world domination. Barnes, as the Winter Soldier, would face off against Captain America only to be spared, rescued, and rehabilitated.

"Isn't it better that Bucky survived so Captain America could have his friend back?" I asked.

"Yes," my son answered.

"And now the good guys have another teammate!"

"Yes!"

But Barnes still had amends to make, as we see in the series, *The Falcon and the Winter Soldier*. He did not simply get to say, "I'm a good guy now, forget all that other stuff."

Other Marvel characters, like Nebula, the Hulk, Hawkeye, Loki, Ant-Man, Black Widow, and Scarlet Witch carry a certain amount of villainy and destruction in their backstories as well.

They struggle to make consistent choices. They don't always agree with the "good guys," and sometimes they are right.

Redemption is always possible and is always a work in progress. You can be fully loved and accepted while you work on the rest of it. My son gets this. I try to ignore the cigar-puffing pontificator in my head who says, "But what if Barnes had died at the beginning of *Avengers: Infinity War*—after his rehabilitation in Wakanda but before he joined the epic effort to save the world?"

Again, I'm going to let a loving God sort the afterlife. My job is to weave that love into this life.

# Chapter 6

# Black Jesus and Confederate Pastors

Black girl magic, y'all can't stand it
Y'all can't ban it, made out like a bandit
They been tryin' hard just to make us all vanish
I suggest they put a flag on a whole another planet.

—Janelle Monáe, "Django Jane"

A s a kid, I didn't think it was weird that my pastor had Confederate flags and memorabilia in his office. The disposition of pastors tends to influence the kind of people attracted to their churches. His love of Robert E. Lee and Stonewall Jackson led to a church full of Confederate history buffs and battle reenactors. I didn't think this was weird, because my grandmother cried when she talked about "the way they treated our boys" during the Civil War. With my childlike internal timeline this always made me assume she'd lived through the Civil War. She was born in 1933.

I didn't think it was weird, because my mom, her siblings, and many of our family friends graduated from Robert E. Lee High School, which opened its doors four years after the *Brown v. Board of Education* decision that desegregated schools. Confederate flags were all over her dance team uniform, yearbooks, and other high school memorabilia. I didn't think it was weird, because the other side of the story, the historically accurate side, was entirely absent from my life, by design. Decades of curriculum writers and national storytellers had made sure that I could grow up feeling good about whom I came from and how we came to have all that we had.

Modern segregation—not the legally mandated kind, but the white flight and economic reinforcement kind—left few in my day-to-day life to question those narratives. There were few people of color in our church—at times there were none. Can't imagine why. Though I did have my suspicions about the way history was shaded, I liked feeling good, having an identity rooted in a noble and honorable legacy. I suspected we were glossing over some things, giving ourselves a pass on some bad behavior, but I didn't think of oppression as essential to white southern identity.

That's a key to hold on to: Parents of all races want their children to feel good about who they are, but when we root that desire in anything but belonging, acceptance, and love as the birthright of all children of God, they are not equipped to live in a racialized world. Fear of not being "the good guys" renders white folks too fragile to repent, and thus we continue to hurt our neighbors of color. Meanwhile generations of people of color have fought to counter the racialized narratives that undermine their worth. White supremacy has lied to all of us, and we cannot let it continue to tell us who we are.

Over the course of my childhood, I became adept at explaining away racism, something sociologists call "system justification."[1] In the months before I left for college in California I grew deeply sentimental about my southern roots. I bought a shirt with a Confederate flag on it, a neon beer sign, a bumper sticker with something about Girls Raised In The South (GRITS). I went full redneck in a way I never had before, largely as an expression of homesickness. It was shameful, really, and now embarrassing how uncritically I embraced the white supremacist iconography. I fully endorsed the narrative of southern chivalry and godliness, ignorantly glorifying a myth that was evil to its core. Historians call this myth the "Lost Cause," and living in the South, I have to be extra vigilant not to pass it on to my kids. This is especially challenging because many southerners have lost sight of where the Lost Cause lie ends and Christianity begins.

Jemar Tisby devastatingly summarizes the Lost Cause in the context of Christianity's embrace of the myth in this way:

> The Lost Cause mythologized the white, pre-Civil War South as a virtuous, patriotic group of tight-knit Christian communities. According to the Lost Cause narrative, the South wanted nothing more than to be left alone to preserve its idyllic civilization, but was attacked by the aggressive, godless North, who swooped in to disrupt a stable society, calling for emancipation and inviting the intrusion of the federal government into small-town, rural life.[2]

It's like he wrote this after visiting my church.

Segregation and economic inequality, problems that extend far beyond the American South, also had their own "Lost Cause" type narratives to blunt the tip of the spear. I was told the differences in our neighborhoods, schools, and wealth was about values, priorities, genetics—anything to stop the reality of oppression from piercing my heart.

It kills me that Christians were the ones telling me to back away. The church was giving me alternative explanations. So I was slightly less surprised than many of my peers were by the church's support of Donald Trump, whose racist rhetoric and coziness with explicit white supremacists shocked the nation. Black people were quick to point out that if we were shocked and surprised at all, it was because we hadn't been paying attention. The roots of this complicity run deep. In fact, white supremacy has so thoroughly shaped American Christianity, it's hard to imagine what the latter would be without the former.

The two have certainly become inseparable to Katie.

## Christianity the Way We Know It

Katie is the editor in chief of *ESJ*, a journal committed to socially and environmentally sustainable lifestyles. She's a Black woman and parent to six-year-old (at the time of our interview) Castle, who is biracial. She's letting him grow out his magnificent curly hair and posts gorgeous thoughts from their journey together on her Instagram. On Sundays, that journey does not involve getting dressed up and hauling themselves to church.

Growing up, Katie said, her family was deeply involved in a Black church in Dallas, Texas. Even though the Black church as a broader entity is known for its resistance to white supremacy, Katie said she could see the ways the racism and colonial mentalities of American Christianity had seeped into individual congregations. Katie began to notice that Christians were consistently on the side of the most powerful. Not only was faith rarely used to advocate for those on the margins of society, but sometimes it was actively pushing and keeping people there. "I find Christianity the way that we know it to be extremely oppressive," Katie said when we spoke on the phone in spring of 2021.

When she began searching for a new church home for her and her son, she grew uncomfortable with churches' emphasis on connecting to God exclusively through the physical, weekly worship service. It was like they were telling her that without these institutions—many of which do not understand how white their culture is—she cannot know God, she cannot be "saved." But Katie does know God, she said, even if she's stopped going to church. "I know they look at me and think that I'm doomed, but I've never been more happy or more whole in my life." Away from the pressure and the weight of their expectations, she's experiencing shalom, the peace and wholeness God came to bring.

Describing a Christianity free from white supremacy, Cherokee theologian Randy S. Woodley uses deliberate terminology to push back on a spiritual transaction, salvation, as the main work of Christ. A one-and-done "ticket to heaven," Woodley argues, legitimizes a "conquering Christ" theology. In order to be saved, the conquered and enslaved are required to give up their faith, culture, and customs to adopt a version of "Christianity" suspiciously profitable for the colonizers and slaveholders.[3] By contrast, Woodley writes, the work of Christ was bringing about healing, wholeness, and shalom, all of which cannot coexist with oppression. "Shalom is God's community of creation or counter-kingdom of inclusion to a power-based empire of exclusion," he writes.[4]

Woodley and co-author Bo C. Sanders suggest that much of the Christianity we know has so bastardized the teachings of Christ, a radical anti-imperial socialist from the Middle East, it may not merit the label "Christianity" at all. "Christianity has been embedded within an imperial theology—a theology of creating injustice for 'the other,' often resulting in colonization. Therefore, if Christianity is to be associated with the life of Jesus the colonial forms of Christianity shouldn't be considered Christian."[5] But what else is there? A lot, it turns out.

It was eye-opening to Katie when speaking with her West African therapist who told her that the concept of Jesus that she had growing up in the American church was not at all like what the therapist knew of West African Christianity.

"It's completely different from what we've been taught," she said.

Katie told me this in an interview, but we didn't dig into it very deeply. Of course, the second we hung up the phone, I was off to the library. I'm a theology nerd at heart, so bear with me while I geek out a little on theological alternatives to the colonial Jesus.

**Theology Break!**

*African Christologies*

Theologians from sub-Saharan African countries, especially West African countries like Ghana, have done extensive work repairing the harm done by anti-African missionaries, who sought to replace African theology with a picture of Jesus and salvation interpreted exclusively to the favor of European culture. Yet they have not thrown out Christ, the God-man. Looking at the work of scholars like John Pobee and Bénézet Bujo, it's possible to see Jesus as a universal Christ, not a white or colonial Christ. Unlike colonial missionaries, Jesus does not replace or erase Bantu, Akan, or Baganda spirituality, but rather—as he did in ancient Israel—completes it.

"Ngaga [a traditional healer] willed to save man, but did not succeed in doing so; Christ did so fully once and for all. Christ has accomplished the work of Ngaga," writes Congolese theologian Buana Kibongi.[6]

Researcher Diane Stinton cataloged the many ways that Jesus is understood by African people as the ultimate exemplar of African values: life-giver, healer, mediator, ancestor, family member, and liberator. In reading Stinton's pan-African survey, I was most struck by the regular reference to one of my favorite Bible verses, John 10:10: "I came that they may have life and have it abundantly" (ESV). In the African context, abundant life was both incredibly important and far more holistic than we have taken it to mean in the West. I have been taught to think of the abundant life being one where I don't feel guilty, don't struggle with anxiety, and I love everybody. Beyond the condition of my spirit, I was taught, the Bible makes no promises.

In my theological training the verse had not been overspiritualized, but rather it had been underrealized. Abundant life is thoroughly spiritual and, in the African context, thoroughly lived in the flesh and blood of life on earth. In African culture, abundant life—the life Christ brings—is physical, communal, social, economic, political, and relational as well. Spiritual harmony leads to all manner of flourishing. This only works for African Christians if Jesus is also the healer of Africa's colonial wounds and devastation, and the conqueror of its oppressors. Jesus cannot be for Africans if he is not about their abundant, liberated life.[7]

That reclaiming of the colonizers' conquering Christ is, in this white lady's opinion, pretty badass.

### Liberation Theology

It reminds me of the liberation theology tradition of Latin Americans. Gustavo Gutiérrez, C. René Padilla, and Leonardo Boff, among others, developed a way of reading the Bible with freedom for the oppressed as the overarching theme, and their work has echoed through many movements of spiritual resistance, both academic and activist.

For some, borrowing from the spirituality of other faiths is a way to round out the more anemic elements of Christianity, particularly around liberation. My friend Denise grew up in a Mexican-American Catholic church, where the teaching and imagery of femininity was docile and subservient. As the single mother of a son who is entitled to, but often denied, special education services, Denise needed a bold and fiercely liberating image to cling to as she went to battle day after day. "There aren't very many Women Saints who are Fighters and Warriors," she said.[8] She suspected there had been women like her all along, women who didn't settle for the answers given, the meager allowances handed down. She suspected they had been there but that they simply had not been canonized. Her own faith tradition had diminished the way women's spirituality could be expressed, but others had not. She found the Hindu goddess Kali, a fierce warrior who fights for her people. Kali validated the divine nature of Denise's fight for her son, for her neighborhood, for her own people.

Liberation isn't just a theological concept; it's an act we can participate in. It's an embodied connection to the work of Christ.

## Womanist Theology

American womanist theology shares this holistic understanding of Jesus's work, pushing feminist theologians to consider race and class, and Black theologians to consider gender and class when they write about the liberating work of Jesus. Until the "least of these" is fully free, writes Jacquelyn Grant, the work of the Christ is ongoing, lifting God's people out of oppression.[9] Jesus, who regularly challenged systems of power in favor of those who were excluded, identifies with the most oppressed, the most in need of liberation—which in the biblical world, as today, undoubtedly included women, and today includes Black people. Thus, Grant, building on the work of William L. Eichelberger, goes so far as to say that because Jesus took on the form of those he came to liberate, that in today's terminology, Jesus is a Black woman.[10]

Taking in this theology is like coming up for air after a lifetime of Martin Luther and John Calvin. But as appealing as decolonized, indigenous, or liberating expressions of Christianity might be, they are difficult to find in the United States, especially in Texas. Most of the churches accessible to Katie are not preaching liberation of any kind, let alone indigenous, African, or womanist versions. She doesn't want to take Castle to church where he might experience the same microaggressions she has faced, or to overhear belittling or patronizing comments directed at her. She hasn't told Castle about Jesus yet, because she's still laying the foundation of spirituality for him and she doesn't want that to be corrupted by the white, colonial Jesus readily available around them.

As a white mother of white children, for me to live in solidarity with my Black neighbors, I have to be just as vigilant to make sure my kids don't adopt that version of Jesus either. We cannot have "my shalom" and "your shalom." It's the universal shalom or nothing.

Katie feels confident raising her son in alignment with the God who lives within, she said. She is connecting him to his Black heritage as well as preparing him, as a light-skinned male, to live a life of compassion. She is consciously teaching him to pursue kindness and love. "I hope that he knows that God can be found in all of those things. God is in him," Katie said. "I want him to stand in that power always." She's building his spiritual identity outside the institutional church, but not outside the essence of who Jesus was. "Religion is a very difficult thing for me these days, but I don't think faith is the same," Katie said.

That said, it does chafe that white people ruined Christianity, she acknowledged. "It's not fair that white people get to claim something else, and I don't get to touch it without being tainted."

## OG Christianity

Katie's comment wasn't a surprise to me. White supremacy ruining things has been the theme of my work in journalism for the last decade. I write about schools, immigration, and religion—all things made vastly worse by white supremacy.

The corrosive effect of racism makes religious systems toxic for everyone, my friend Anashay observed during a grueling antiracism workshop. We hopped on a call to check in after the class, each having witnessed a critical moment of emotional angst in the other.

For me, a white woman, as the myths of childhood melted away, I was feeling lost, angry, and not wanting to own my people. My sense of alienation from my ancestors was, from Anashay's perspective, an indictment of Christian perfectionism and its inability to hold two truths—love and imperfection—at once. "This religion has hurt so many people, particularly non-minority people, people of European descent. When you get to the point when you can't see anything good in your ancestors—" Here Anashay trailed off. I could hear the implied "you're lost, sister" in the silence.

In other words, my desire to write off people who don't measure up to my idea of perfection *is* the problem, and it's not unrelated to the very real issues in my family tree. I was embodying the insecure belonging that makes racism so difficult to confront and end. To dissociate from one's ancestors would be literal sacrilege to Anashay, who sees the Creator and God of her ancestors as love manifested in others and as a daily guide through this crazy life. "Sometimes the Creator comes to me as my mom," she told me when we talked again over Zoom, months later. Her mom's spirit transcended this world when Anashay was in high school. She was only thirty-nine.

Feeling love for her ancestors in their "perfectly imperfect" selves has led Anashay to immerse her children in a community based on belonging. Rather than putting her kids in the most competitive "good schools" she could find, she chose schools full of kids and families who would show her children the breadth of God's love. "I needed my kids to hear the real, authentic brothers, sistas, shawties and slang from *my* 'hood; I needed them to fall in love with all the dimensions of who we are as a people." She's not letting perfectionism get in the way of connection and belonging.

To Anashay, Christ is radical, accepting love. Not a rules enforcer and policy maker. The Creator doesn't keep score. The Creator sees strength and value in all people, especially those who were disruptive disciples often seen as "sinners" by the world and who were ultimately betrayers. "The more I fell in love with who Christ the person was, the further I moved away from 'religion.' To me, Christ was a true example of a disruptive leader! He embodied the spirit of what John Lewis would call 'good trouble,'" Anashay said. "He led with radical, agape, disruption. And he honored the humanity of all he encountered."

After the murder of George Floyd, more white churches began soul-searching ventures, enlisting antiracist trainers and launching book studies. Because it was during the pandemic while many churches were not meeting in person, some white pastors had their congregants tune into livestreams or recorded sermons from Black pastors. Our church launched Be the Bridge groups, using the materials developed by Latasha Morrison. Part of the process, for many white churches, is lament. It's sorrow. But Anashay is not interested in dispensing the sackcloth and ashes for the white church's repentance process. The disquiet I had observed in her during the antiracism workshop was the desire to get on with things. To get to the part where Black people acknowledge their God-given power and stop asking what the white people think about it.

Anashay runs a social-impact consulting firm called Disruptive Partners in DeKalb County, Georgia. The fundamental premise of Disruptive Partners is that the genius and collective power of the Black community already exists. She'll be the first to tell you that she wastes no time dwelling on oppression. To illustrate, she wrote down this story for me:

> We had just watched the 2019 film *Harriet* and in true fashion, my daughter (six years old at the time) managed to hit me with two back-to-back comments/questions: "Can you teach me how to pray to our ancestors and grandma Brenda (my mom) the same way Harriet did?" As if that wasn't enough, she then followed up with, "Man oh man, I feel so bad for white people." I paused and then asked, "Why do you say that sweet girl?" My six-year-old simply said, "*Because they can't be Black.*"

There was so much power in that statement. Out of the mouths of babes. As a family, we spend very little time speaking about "anti" whiteness, racism, and so on because we spend most of our time leading with pro-Blackness and all the diverse dimensions of our humanity. We made the decision a long time ago to disrupt messages of inferiority by leading with the collective joy, peace, and power of our Black community. This intentional shift from narratives of "powerlessness" and inferiority to our collective power was life-changing. Getting the white, eurocentric superiority complex out of our systems disrupts the cancer and deadly ideology of saviorism in our schools, communities, hearts and souls. It is the "good disruption" we need. Not to mention, it benefits everyone—especially members of the dominant culture. Why? Well, because it allows you to embrace your authentic humanity, all the "perfectly imperfect" pieces of you. Obviously Black, Indigenous, and people of color have suffered the most real and severe harm, but white folks have paid a certain price in the form of soul starvation & deprivation, primarily spiritual and social, for the advantages we cling to so dearly. Advantages that don't truly care about anyone UNLESS they maintain the current state of de-humanizing affairs.

"Love is confronting the lies we have been told," Anashay also said. "That is what authentic disruptive love is to me. It's rebuking any negative narrative that negates the humanity of any person. You lead with the promise of people. That is love to me. You do not lead with the constant problem. Right now, we have so many church folks of all races that are so heavenly bound, they're no earthly good. What the world needs now, more than ever, are disruptive leaders."

That doesn't mean she's overlooking history. In fact, it's her awareness of history that has led her to step away from the institutional church for a while. The southern church's emphasis on authority and obedience has roots in racial subjugation, which is a nonstarter for her. "Look at Nat Turner's Rebellion," she said, referencing an uprising of enslaved people in 1831 during and after which preachers and plantation owners leaned heavily on the Bible's submission passages. "Y'all know they used the Word to steal, kill, manipulate, and destroy (to quash the rebellion)." Rather, she's interested in seeing if there's a new and better spiritual community out there for her—one that celebrates the perfectly imperfect community, its ancestors, and the disruptive love of God.

Later, as I reflected on what she'd said, I found myself thinking that this kind of spirituality may be the only hope for me to be able to live with the weight of my own history. Instead of trying to dissect and retrofit old religious systems, she'd rather see Black people embracing their own spirituality, one that empowers and ministers to them. If white people want to truly follow and support it, that's fine, she said, but Black people set their own agenda.

People of color looking for new expressions of Christianity—outside the historical congregations and denominations their parents and grandparents attended—will likely find themselves in a "multiethnic" church, and often multiethnic or multiracial churches don't see how white they really are. In a 2021 article for *Christianity Today*, Korie Little Edwards writes that most multiethnic churches really just invite people of color to assimilate whiteness, ignoring where and how their leadership, doctrine, and worship might have direct roots in oppressive ways of thinking. "Racial diversity without power equality is not good news for anyone, especially not for people of color," Edwards writes.[11]

While many religions must grapple with the way they may have conflated race, nation, or ethnicity and religion, Christianity's unique history with racism and white supremacy call for a particular attention to the way forward. The path to shalom for Black, indigenous, Latino, Asian, Pacific Islander and Middle Eastern Christians will, I suspect, be paved by their own, whether that path is outside or inside an institution. The Black church in the United States has not been totally immune to patriarchal influence, but it is a clear source of power and liberation for Black communities. Some argue that other traditions, those not historically led by people of color, can also chart a liberating future by putting marginal voices at the center. Anglican theologian Esau McCaulley argues this way forward can be both "orthodox" and relevant to Black people. "I want to contend that the best instincts of the Black church tradition—its public advocacy for justice, its affirmation of the worth of Black bodies and souls, its vision of a multiethnic community of faith—can be embodied by those who stand at the center of the tradition."[12]

As an immigration reporter I kept close tabs on the work of Sister Norma Pimentel, a Mexican-American nun directing Catholic Charities at the Texas-Mexico border. She exemplifies what McCaulley describes. In her I found a lived devotion to both the Catholic faith and service in places where racism was tearing families apart, subjecting God's children to sickness and suffering. Similarly, when I asked her about reproductive healthcare for a November 2021 news story, she emphasized the possibilities within Catholic orthodoxy. Abortion is not an option, but neither is leaving immigrant women to manage a pregnancy alone. She advocates for radical involvement and support, not despite her Catholic pro-life stance, but because of the Catholic idea of what it means to be expansively pro-life.

One of my favorite quotations from retired Anglican priest and psychologist Martin Brokenleg, a member of the Rosebud Sioux branch of the Lakota people, spoke to both a rejection of a whitewashed Christianity and a hope of a universal Christ:

> The task of First Nations who want to place their story in a
> Christian context has been to set the teachings of Jesus on the

foundation of their First Nations way of thinking and under-standing. This is what I found in my own spiritual journey, as I explored the Eastern Orthodox Church. But what I found was Christianity in Greek clothing; I wanted Christianity in feath-ers, buckskin, and button blankets. . . . Eventually, if Chris-tianity is going to nourish Aboriginal people, it will have to look, sound, taste, and smell like a First Nations Ceremony.[13]

## Leaning on the Spear

Those who have been oppressed in the name of Jesus say the way forward for their communities is self-determination, freedom to be in relation to God, not in relation to whiteness. For those whose heritage oppresses others in the name of Jesus—my peo-ple—every day is repentance and pursuit of shalom. This means turning from ignorance to awareness. From the scarcity of com-petition to the abundance of solidarity. From color blindness to Black Lives Mattering. From justifying systems to, as Anashay would say, disrupting them.

I vowed to raise my children in that repentance. In our home, we prioritize the peace of truth over the pleasantness of lies be-cause things are wrong in the world. Looking away, rationaliz-ing, or reframing might make us feel better, but none of it heals. Rather than try to maintain or manufacture innocence for our kids, we teach them to pursue righteousness in an unjust world. We are walking with them to the tip of the spear, taking their hands and leaning hard into it. Together.

When Moira was four years old we made a pilgrimage to Montgomery to lean on the spear offered to the world by Bryan Stevenson and the Equal Justice Initiative. While we were there, we leaned on the spear of the Freedom Riders who left no excuse not to ride along. The next year, we leaned on the spears of Ruby Bridges and Sylvia Mendez and put our kids in an integrated school, where 96 percent of the students are not white. Their teachers teach history, not white history. Whenever we can we lean on the spears of Rosa Parks, Emma Tenayuca, Martin Luther King Jr., Dolores Huerta, Breonna Taylor, George Floyd, and thousands of asylum seekers by marching and making signs for protests.

We constantly lean on the spears offered to the world by Jemar Tisby, Austin Channing Brown, and Latasha Morrison by finding a church committed to anti-racism, because I'll be damned if my children will ever be anything but clear on what God thinks of white supremacy.

Chapter 7

# Holy Unions

If loving you is wrong, I don't wanna be right.

—Luther Ingram, "If Loving You Is Wrong"

I was sitting in the newsroom at my first journalism job, looking around at my young, enterprising colleagues—most of us were in our twenties or very early thirties—considering the difference in our lifestyles. Some dated both men and women. There were various long-term and short-term cohabitants. The unattached young'uns were assumed to be having attachment-free sex, almost as an obligation to youth and freedom. And nobody fired them! This wasn't a surprise to me, rationally. I knew I was the cultural outlier—ol' married me with one sex partner. Ever.

Emotionally, though . . . emotionally it hit me like a bracing wind—cool, crisp, and strong enough to make me catch my balance. I sat still, anchoring my soul as I explored the awareness of being unmonitored. Of having autonomy over my sex life and being surrounded by people with autonomy over theirs. I had been working since I was sixteen years old, and at twenty-eight I finally got a job from which I couldn't be fired for having pre-marital sex. Fired! All that unmonitored autonomy was wasted on me now because I was already married. But it made my head spin nonetheless.

I'd had a similar vertigo moment in graduate school when I realized that my classmates were all hooking up and no one cared. No one in authority told them to stop, called them in for a disciplinary meeting, or demanded repentance. In high school and college—the virginity-losing years for most of my generation—I would have been expelled for being sexually active. Expelled! I wandered through grad school too wide-eyed and terrified to do anything about it until I was safely back home, working in ministry, with the threat of termination to keep my pants on.

They would have done it too. I saw teachers at Christian schools lose jobs, college students expelled, and pastors defrocked. If they repented, there was usually a small measure of grace, but it was clear grace depended on a commitment to chastity within the evangelical sexual ethic.

Nonerotic errata can be tolerated in small doses, but not sex and romance. Everyone who has had a brush with conservative branches of religion knows that erotic sin has special rules. Christianity, Judaism, Mormonism, Islam, and Hinduism all have some form of sex ethic establishing pure and impure sex for laity. Buddhism and Catholicism require clergy to remain celibate. Sex is about purity. Purity of the body. Purity of the family. Purity of the community.

The entire conversation about sexual contamination and purity also has a racial component. Just ask mixed-race couples or the families of the hundreds, maybe thousands, of men lynched because they were suspected of having sexual intentions toward white women. Today many talk about same-sex couples the way their grandparents talked about mixed-race couples, and mixed-race couples still raise eyebrows in some settings. In fact, many of my friends remember being told that while they could be friends with people of different races, the room got chilly if they brought up dating. I'm not going to get into the nuances of the racial purity conversation—it would be a whole other book—but I wanted to acknowledge it as part of the purity pathos.

Gather any group of adults whose teen years were spent in evangelical youth groups and summer camps, and you'll hear stories about how the intense regulation and monitoring of our sexuality led to some pernicious hang-ups that followed us well into marriage. We don't want that for our kids.

No one tries to raise kids burdened by shame. Not the kind of shame that leads to isolation, addiction, and loneliness. But that's what perfectionism and certainty-based spirituality does. Purity is another form of certainty. It is the certainty of the body—an all-or-nothing proposition by which bodies, relationships, and families are deemed in or out, orthodox or unorthodox, clean or dirty, worthy or unworthy to participate in and represent God's family. Whether it's a lot or a little, many of us carry shame of not being quite pure enough, and we don't want to pass it on.

Even with my handful of hang-ups, I'm one of the lucky Christians who has never been forced to choose between love and God, not really. I just had to take some cold showers. Sex or no sex, unrepentantly dating a woman or a non-Christian would have meant expulsion from my Christian education or the termination of my various ministry jobs. Others have had to make that choice.

If the path to redemption requires a life without sexual intimacy, or at least intimacy with the person you love, I can see why many would get off that path. If life in the church is life as a marked or second-class person, I can see why many would leave.

For those who have achieved "purity," whether purity of the body was worth the torment of the soul might be an ongoing question as they try to sort through the myriad sexual dysfunctions couples report after growing up in sex-obsessed churches. I've sat with a lot of ladies who can't enjoy sex because they still sort of believe orgasms are for sluts. Then there's me, who kept track of the number of times we had sex *for two and a half years*, partially to make sure I was meeting my husband's needs, and partially to make up for a lifetime of feeling lame and prudish. For those who could scrape by with their own purity, but with beloved LGBTQIA friends or family members, the inability to condemn their loved ones often leads to larger unraveling. It raises questions about the criteria for being "in" and "out" of the family of God.

Sex and marriage is such a big, tangly issue for religious folks, I'm going to divide the discussion of sex into two parts. In a later chapter we'll get to the nuts and bolts of how people who reject purity culture talk to their kids about sexual ethics. Just because you don't want your kid wearing a True Love Waits ring doesn't mean you want them to run a high school sex ring. But that's later. In this part I want to explore how we parent against perfectionism and for belonging by embracing the families religion has deemed impure—whether or not we're settled on what our personal faith tells us about sexuality and marriage. For some that means accepting a family member or friend. For others it means self-acceptance. For everyone it means evaluating how measurements of purity, both sexual and otherwise, are already shaping our families.

A quick word: This chapter mostly addresses LGBTQIA issues, but I can't make you queer-affirming. I can't even make you tolerant. If you are a queer person struggling with the implications of that for your faith, which religion you can or cannot embrace, I cannot end that struggle. I'm not even going to try to address the various arguments and prooftexts regarding homosexuality. Others are doing that, and doing it well. This book is about parenting through the struggle, not ending it.

In fact, I would recommend skipping this chapter if you are *not* struggling. If you are confidently queer or queer-affirming and have a faith community supporting you, this chapter may be more triggering than helpful, because it recounts pain endured by families who don't fit the traditional religiously sanctioned model. If you are comfortable with traditional, heteronormative sexual ethics, there is nothing in here that's going to change your mind. This chapter speaks to people who are—as I was for years—struggling to sort through things we were taught to believe about sexuality and family, and how to help our kids shape the more inclusive world we want. The struggle is vital, but it's not something you need to endure again if you have already. That's my disclaimer.

For those who want to read on, for those in the struggle, here's the thesis: We'll never know what we believe or what to tell our kids until we are able to truly love all families, commune with all families, and worship with all families. Love has to come first. That's not wishy-washy; it's theological. God is love. It's the origin and the interpretive key. The hermeneutic, my theology friends, is love, and it cannot be applied with our brains only. I didn't make this up; St. Augustine did. He wrote: "Whoever, then, thinks that he understands the Holy Scriptures, or any part of them, but puts such an interpretation upon them as does not tend to build up this twofold love of God and our neighbor, does not yet understand them as he ought."[1]

I believe the experience of living together, praying together, parenting next to, and worshiping with diverse families makes our questions about sexuality and marriage easier to answer, because we answer them from a place of real love—love that is practiced as for real, all the way acceptance. It's not "I love you, *but* the Bible says . . ." and not "I love you, *but* I'm going to reject you because it's best for your soul." It's not "I'll make you think I'm affirming by being nice, and then, when you ask me point blank, I'll let you know I think your marriage is a sin." No, I'm talking about leading with your feet. Loving first, and letting love tell you how to interpret everything else. This isn't about reconciling a handful of Bible verses, it's about radically reorienting how we conceive of God's family.

Driving away or marginalizing queer families, single parents, and mixed-faith families makes us a less hospitable, more anxious, and more judgmental people. As we legitimize our reasons for shutting them out, we have to police the whole community more stridently—including our own kids. We begin to identify ourselves by our purity instead of our love, and eventually none of us are pure enough.

## The Family Table

Sicily was expecting to find love and community when she walked into a Bible study in her new neighborhood in 2016. Visibly pregnant and accompanied by her wife, Cheyenne, they settled at the dining room table and the friendly hostess began chatting with them. The woman assumed Sicily and Cheyenne were friends who had ventured out together to a new Bible study, as girlfriends often do.

The fact that Sicily was pregnant probably signaled heteronormativity to the hostess. The tie between the blessing of children and the straight, monogamous, two-parent nuclear family is automatic for many people. But Sicily was carrying a baby made with reciprocal in vitro fertilization from Cheyenne's egg and a sperm donor who shared Sicily's own Caribbean ancestry. As they chatted with the hostess, the family's construction became clear, thankfully before anyone else arrived. The hostess said to them, as Sicily remembers it: "I only want to do Bible study with doers of the word." She then got up and walked to another room.

Sicily was dumbfounded, unable to hold back tears.

The hostess's husband came to see what was going on, and Cheyenne took over, trying to extract her family while keeping things as peaceful as possible with the hosts, who lived in their neighborhood and would likely cross their path again. Cheyenne is a first responder. Keeping people safe is her job. She was in emergency mode. She explained the misunderstanding, told the husband what his wife had said, and declined his apologetic offer to sit and study the Bible with them. She told the man they didn't want to make anyone uncomfortable in their own home.

Cheyenne and Sicily were not there to stir up controversy or make a statement. They weren't making a stand for their rights. They just wanted to build a spiritual community. They made their exit without further incident, but inside, Sicily said, "My whole spirit was just shook."

Cheyenne was less surprised, having encountered more homophobia in her past. Sicily had, for the most part, enjoyed love and acceptance from people of faith. Her upbringing was unstructured, she said, but faith gave her a sense of rootedness. She knew, intellectually, that religion was sometimes hostile to the LGBTQIA community, but that hadn't interrupted her sense of community thus far. The Muslim family of her high school best friend, the nondenominational bilingual church she attended in high school, her own mother whom she calls a spiritual "chameleon"—all had accepted her.

Never the type to limit herself to the LGBTQIA community, Sicily put her energy into creating a stable, rooted, spiritually nourishing family. She married Cheyenne and sought a family-focused church where they could raise kids in Sunday school and vacation Bible school, and among all the loving presences available to children who grow up in the church. They found their way to Community Bible Church in San Antonio. When Sicily mentioned this in our interview, I winced. I know Community Bible Church. It's a megachurch incredibly popular for its family ministries. The preaching is engaging and winsome. There seems to be a ministry for every member of the traditional family—and even for single moms and people going through divorce.

In high school, most of my friends who were committed, active Christians went to youth group at Community Bible Church, and it was one of the few youth groups where non-Christians would willingly go along, because it was genuinely fun and welcoming. I totally see the appeal of Community Bible Church for someone like Sicily who was looking to put down roots in a small town big city like San Antonio, where newcomers don't always have the easiest time. But I also knew what was coming when Sicily said that in 2020 she and her wife inquired about having their family dedicated. In an email, one of the church's pastors at the time told Sicily that the family was welcome to worship at Community Bible Church but that the children of same-sex couples could not be dedicated publicly.

"We frame the ceremony not only as a dedication of the child, but of the family's public decision to demonstrate commitment to God's word, and we believe the Bible to define marriage as a lifelong commitment between a man and a woman," he wrote. "For this reason, our public Family Dedication is for families who have chosen to have a family within this definition of family as we believe the Bible to give us." Instead they were offered a private prayer session, where someone would pray over the children. Then the pastor wrote something that I've seen written, and heard said, many times in similar situations: "I hope that you can receive this as being said in love for your family, because it genuinely is."

It was not received that way. It never is. Statements like that are based on the sincerely held belief that cruelty, rejection, and shame are justifiable, even loving, means to an end, if that end is "holiness."

"It was heartbreaking," Sicily said. She was starting to get the message that "all the other families are good enough to sit at God's table, but not ours." When we talked, these rejections were in the past, but they were not gone. The coronavirus pandemic still had us all screen-bound, and the young family had welcomed another baby in the middle of it. They still had not found the right church, and now they were having to try everything virtually. Sicily was facing the decision many LGBTQIA families face: choose a queer-affirming church where activism was central to the mission, or a nonaffirming church with lots of families and a great children's ministry.

## The Myth of the Perfect Family

Rooting our family in acceptance and belonging is more than just being OK with gay. It's more than the slightly-nervous-hip-conservative hanging out with "tax collectors" like Jesus did. If we try to slather a veneer of acceptance on top of our judgment, it only delays the pain. It makes it all the more jarring and confusing when someone is treated, like Sicily was, as impure or second class. In our households and our churches, acceptance and belonging require that we let go of our own perfectionism, our own insistence that there is an ideal family or a hierarchy of families like Sicily described.

Every church I've been a part of has had "that family"—the fit mom, the successful dad, the beautiful kids. She cooks, he's an elder or deacon, the kids play sports and earn As. We assume they are good because they are so pretty. At one church I attended, a pantheon of young moms had different domestic realms over which they presided: The Goddess of the Crockpot. The Goddess of the Remodeled Master Bedroom. The Goddess of Stimulating Kids Activities. The Goddess of Skin Care.

"Have you seen her house? It's amazing."

"I got her braised cabbage recipe!"

"I bought the same moisturizer she uses."

The domestic goddesses became minor celebrities helping mere mortal church ladies plan menus, pick dresses, redecorate rooms, and find the perfect play groups. Going to them for advice was like praying at the temple of Athena or Venus. It was a little bit worship, a little bit envy.

Kids can tell who you wish you were, and who you wish they were. In fact, aspirational identity formation is a pretty big part of coming of age. I think we all remember those collages of celebrities and fashion icons on the inside of our lockers, the original vision boards. "The perfect family" is, in every sense, a myth. In one sense, it is mythological because it is not based on reality. Underneath shiny veneers are still broken hearts, resentments, and strained relationships. But even if it doesn't exist in reality, perfect family myths serve cultural purposes. They are stories from which we derive meaning and identity. In that sense, attainability doesn't matter. Myths are not our end goals; they are our origin stories. They tell us who we are and help us make sense of the world. By internalizing the mythology of the perfect family, you can have a lot of things. If what you want is high performers, clean faces, and multigenerational vacations—you can have them. You can have a family full of doctors and lawyers and trim, well-kept wives. You can have an army of little churchgoers (at least until they are about eighteen). You can have the admiration of everyone around you and see yourself reflected in insurance commercials and real estate ads.

As Duke theological ethicist Amy Laura Hall points out, you can have all that with increasing precision, thanks to advances in genetic manipulation. While many Christians might balk at this Huxleyan version of "the perfect family," Hall points out, most of us feel the pressure to create it out of the raw material that we have, however far from genetically perfect it is. "Women have explained (at times in excruciatingly painful detail) the pressure they feel under to conceive of parenthood in ways that involve meticulous timing and intense quality control," Hall writes.[2] So we have parents paying for more expensive tutors, driving farther for club sports teams, and vying to get into competitive kindergartens. My generation had elementary schoolers on diets and unambitious jocks pushed into MBA programs and law schools.

We're all beckoned to that icy road of perfectionism, making that perfect family, keeping it clean. We bring our kids onto the road with us and pack their luggage full of shame. That very shame we're trying to avoid by not making them sign a True Love Waits pledge, by affirming their sexuality, we can heap on them in a million other ways in our pursuit of becoming the perfect family. Sex has special rules in religion, yes, and that increases the anxiety, but purity is about so much more than sex. If we want to set our kids up for belonging, we should start practicing before it's time to discuss sex and choosing a life partner.

One of my worst moments as a parent happened when my daughter started at a new school for kindergarten. Each day of the first week, at pickup, the teacher gave me a glowing report on my eager, outgoing daughter, who was shaping up to be, like her more introverted and people-pleasing mother, "a delight to have in class." A real go-getter. Likely to succeed. On the second Monday of the school year I walked up to her class's table in the pickup area, grinning as I anticipated more positive feedback. Instead, the teacher told me how disruptive and fidgety she had been, how she hadn't listened. The teacher used a color spectrum chart ranging from red (worst) to purple (best) with a clothespin for each child moving up and down the rainbow to track their behavior. Moira's clothespin was on . . . red! (I was thirty-five years old at the time, and I am now mortified at how serious that sentence felt to me then.)

Moira, all curls and smiles, bounced toward me, and I, feeling as though her behavior was reflecting poorly on my parenting, immediately began chastising her. Her face fell. I'm embarrassed to admit I yelled at her in the car on the way home. She cried.

Day after day the bad reports kept coming. Her spirit was sinking, our rides home were emotionally chilly. I considered asking the school to move my daughter to another class. I became "that mom." I sent the school research on the clothespin system and its ill effects. The color chart system was so stupid, I ranted to anyone who would listen. She needed time to adjust to being in kindergarten! She needed compassion! This stupid color system was going to ruin how she saw herself. She's an exuberant kid! She needs to be able to express that!

And then one day I heard myself: The system *was* stupid. But it was only going to change the way she saw herself if it changed the way I saw her, the way I treated her. She hadn't been devastated by that first day "on red." She only started feeling shame when I started heaping it on. I decided to stop. We started talking about the behavior chart only when she brought it up, and when she did, I would tell her that no matter where her clothespin ended up, I was proud to be her mom.

"Guess what, mom!" she said one day, "I spent most of the day on red, but at the end of the day, I got it up to orange!"

High-fives.

"Guess what, mom! I stayed on green all day. And it was really hard because Oscar told a fart joke and I really wanted to laugh at it, but that would have disrupted class."

High-fives. Not because she stayed on green, but because she was proud of herself.

Sometimes, she would confide that it was worth being on red if everyone laughed at her class-disrupting joke. Rock on, kiddo. Put out a tip jar.

My fear had been that a stupid system would stigmatize me and my daughter, but I realized I could provide a potent alternative of belonging and acceptance. Just because not everyone approves of her exuberance, doesn't mean I can't affirm it. I freaking love it. Framing exuberance as part of her personhood, not her behavior, allowed Moira to cultivate it, and it became more and more life-giving to the people around her.

Her pizzazz came back. Her clothespin migrated up and down throughout the year, but she and her teacher became close chums, and Moira was able to take the feedback on her behavior—the manifestations of her exuberance—in stride, as helpful instruction from someone she trusted. She was learning to set and explore boundaries.

The next year, as the coronavirus pandemic had our school on Zoom part time and behind a mask the rest of the time, her first-grade teacher apologized for what an imperfect year it was shaping up to be. "You know though," the teacher said, "Moira is so joyful and adaptable. She's so understanding when we can't do everything perfectly. Sometimes when we teachers are complaining, one of us will say, 'Hey guys. Be like Moira.'" I felt happier about that than I ever could have felt of hearing my daughter was "a delight to have in class." Because she wasn't just like me. She was more free. Free of shame, freeing others.

Perfect family mythology does the opposite. It colonizes.

While I've been writing this chapter I've been listening to the chilling podcast series produced by *Christianity Today*, called *The Rise and Fall of Mars Hill*, about the toxic leadership of Mark Driscoll at a megachurch in Seattle.

Almost everyone I know had some kind of visceral reaction to the reawakening of religious trauma as they listened to Driscoll berate, manipulate, and bully his congregation. So many things were familiar and disturbing to me, but one thing stood out: Through all of his theological phases (he has fallen in and out with several theological movements during his career), he never gave up his belief in near-hyperbolic gender roles and the belief that the gospel would go forward by virtue of strong marriages, gender roles, hard workers, godly families, and homeownership. He never gave up on the American settler narrative that tells us we have to overwhelm the natives with our sheer numbers, our enterprising spirit, and our wholesome living. Only instead of the original colonized people of the Seattle area, the Duwamish, Driscoll wanted to outsettle postmodern academics and queers, and he wanted a wagon train of perfect families to do it. Despite subscribing to a faith that was built on single men, polygamists, working women, and eunuchs, we seem to think that the survival of churches depends on how many his and hers closets and two-car garages we can build.

You will never affirm diverse families if you believe, even deep down, there's only one perfect, pure way to be a family, or that the continuation of any faith depends on people getting married and raising lots of religious babies. Most faiths grew as a way to create in-groups. Jesus scandalized people by saying, "We're all in the in-group." That's why he and his disciples, and later Paul, were always breaking Jewish rules. That's what the whole preaching to the Gentiles thing was about. That's what the tax-collectors and parables and women at wells were about. Getting rid of our "in-group-out-group" criteria. But he didn't finish the in-group expansion; he just started it. He told us what the kingdom of God is about, and we apply that in our communities.

## Thicker than Blood

I was not surprised when Denise, the mother mentioned earlier, opened up her house to a queer young man fleeing abuse. It looked pretty much on brand for the woman who regularly collected signatures, crunched data, served on commissions, and dropped everything to come to the aid of her community. Sometimes it was other single moms. Sometimes it was other parents of students fighting for special education services. Sometimes it was her little corner of San Antonio, just outside the hot real estate of downtown, where politicians regularly seemed to have a blind spot.

Still, opening her home to the young man was a singularly profound experience for Denise and her son, Cristóbal. It had "that feeling like the ultimate church," Denise told me as I sat among a verdant jungle of house plants on her front porch, sipping tea from a mug that read "Te Amo." She ended up sending me home with the mug.

Now, having talked to Lalo, her statement makes sense. When teenage Denise needed somewhere to ride out a storm in her biological family, Lalo and Bernie, the married couple who served as youth ministers at St. Cecilia Catholic Church, opened their house. They treated her as family, because in their hearts she is.

Lalo told me that he is as dedicated to the family he's formed, which includes Denise, as he is to the family he was born into. He and Bernie never left the Catholic faith of their parents, he said, at least not in substance. They simply extended it. "We really opened our lives to the community," Lalo said. Despite being fairly conservative doctrinally, Lalo wasn't willing to shut his door to people whom the church saw as sinful. "We didn't lose our faith; I think we probably took it a step further, became more inclusive."

That's why no matter how many ups and downs Denise has had with the Catholic church, she still considers Lalo and Bernie spiritual parents, her beloved family. She too is forming a family beyond the walls of her home. As a single mom raising a son, Denise has given a lot of thought to the family she's forming, and how she's forming it. The blood ties she inherited, like the Catholicism she grew up in, were heavily gendered. Men were the bosses. Spiritual, emotional abuse—her own and others'—at the hands of men was routinely overlooked by those in the hierarchy who expected women to submit and comply.

Her own pain soon echoed back to her in many voices. When the sexual abuse scandal broke in the Catholic church, she was working at a nonprofit where survivors came for counseling. "It hit me really hard when I was in a space of wanting to be close to the Catholic church as a single, unwed mother," Denise recounted. She was drawn to the beauty but repelled by the treatment of children and young women like herself.[3] She began to form her own spirituality, just as she was forming her own family.

In some ways, Lalo explained to me, extending the family beyond biology is common in Mexican-American culture. *Compadres* and *comadres* enter your life at your christening; best men and maids of honor surround your marriage. They are not box-checking roles. They are active, involved, even authoritative roles. "It wasn't just *cariño*, an emotion," he told me. "It was people caring about how I turned out." Lalo recalls growing up surrounded by people who would even spank him if his parents weren't around, so active was the participation. Whatever you might think about spanking, Lalo looks back on it as evidence that they cared about how he turned out.

"Chosen family" is also a common concept in the LGBTQIA community, as so many have faced the rejection of their families and communities. Chosen family is based on acceptance and love. Denise knows how it feels to "not measure up" as an unwed mother. She also knows how rigid, narrow family roles can devour those inside them. She has become an active ally for the LGBTQIA community in San Antonio.

It was Denise who introduced me to Sicily and several other members of her chosen family who were interviewed for this book. They all knew what it was like to rebuild a spirituality and a family based on acceptance and belonging rather than perfectionism and purity.

### Close Enough to Touch

Religions have treated queer, mixed-faith, and unmarried couples—American Protestantism even treats aromantic, asexual, and celibate people this way—differently than straight, married couples who share a religion. At best, as second-class members of the community. At worst, as lepers.

These folks are not lepers, nor are they sick, nor is there something spiritually or mentally wrong with them. But faith communities often treat them in the same way the Jewish society of Jesus's day treated people with skin conditions—as threats to purity. In Matthew 8, Jesus heals a man with leprosy, which could have referred to any number of unsightly or painful skin conditions. In a world without microscopes and lab equipment, if it looked bad it was bad. More importantly, though, people with skin conditions were considered to be both physically and spiritually unclean, because disease was said to be caused by sin. If the rash cleared up, the formerly afflicted had to go through an elaborate ritual to rejoin the community. Yes, Jewish law regulated the original purity culture.

Hear me clearly on this one: Queer, mixed-faith, and single-parent families go through things that suck, just like the rest of us. They need practical healing just like everybody. But their identities are not the things that need to be cured. Too often when they come to church for encouragement and healing, those things are withheld because the church believes that the real issue is their sexual status.

The fact that Jesus physically healed the man speaks to his compassion, because skin diseases (unlike queerness) actually do suck, whether it was actual leprosy or psoriasis or crusted scabies.[4] Unlike many contemporary pastors, he didn't need a neato tagline about how the real cure was for "soul-riasis." The skin condition wasn't a metaphor for sin, just like it wasn't caused by sin. It was a sucky rash, and Jesus cleared it up.

So Jesus healed the man physically, but he didn't heal him spiritually. Jesus instead affirmed the man. Jesus touched the man *before he was physically healed.* He touched someone society said was unclean. He didn't need to. Jesus worked remotely all the time. I don't believe the touch healed the disease, physically. I believe the touch was intended to say, "The social and spiritual stigma attached to you is invalid."

He told the man to go ahead and go through at least part of the ritual he would need in order to be accepted back into Jewish society. He wasn't asking him to live as a contrarian, and he knew what society was and was not ready to receive. But between the two of them, the kingdom of God existed in that touch. In the kingdom of God, the man had always been clean. According to Jewish law, the touch would have made Jesus ceremonially unclean as well, but we don't see him going through any purification rites. I don't think he was trying to impress us with how brave and controversial he was. I think he was trying to tell us that these ideas of "unclean" were not of him. In him, all are clean.

Jesus's hermeneutic, the way he interpreted the law he came to fulfill, was love. It was acceptance. It was affirmation. Kids get this. Acceptance is life or death for them, so they understand its power.

When we were in high school, my best friend Lee and I worked at a Christian day camp. Day camp will wear you out, and on one particularly exhausted—maybe even a little grumpy or disheartened—day, Lee sat down for daily devotionals with her group of six-year-olds. The assigned devotional that day covered this story of Jesus and the man with leprosy. She explained that Jesus showed his love by touching the man, and that he showed his power by healing him. Touch, she explained, was a way of saying, "I love you. You are accepted. You're good enough for me." Lee closed her eyes to pray. As she spoke, she felt a little hand on her knee. And then another on her arm. And then on her shoulder. She opened her eyes to see her entire group touching her, telling her they loved her. Telling her she was accepted. Telling her she was good enough for them.

Kids get it.

Our kids can build their family ethic around where they see love and belonging. If we attend the weddings, the baptisms, the ordinations, the birthday parties, and the fundraisers, the marches, and the vigils, they will not wonder whether gay couples or transgender teens or single moms belong in the family of God. If we expose them only to a perfect family mythology, if important people disappear from their life once they become "impure," their family ethic will grow narrower and narrower, excluding more and more people. They may find themselves unsure of their own belonging. Do they measure up? Are they pure enough?

We are trying to give our kids a deep and diverse vision of family love, where belonging is secure no matter who they grow up to be, where they will always be safe inside, and where they will be a safe family for others. It took me a while to figure out how the explicit conversations would go with my kids. I went a long time without ever explaining why I was affirming, or how that squared with my faith. For a while my only "stance" was this: "I'm not sure how it all fits together, but the Spirit is leading me here." But the cool thing about the kids is that they never knew there had been anything to square. Their faith has never drawn lines around in and out.

I recently explained to my kids that our dear friend, Theodore, whom we had always known as a girl by another name, was, in Theodore's heart and mind, neither boy nor girl. That we loved them was not in question; Theodore had joined us on vacation. That we trusted Theodore was implicit; they often babysat. So when we explained transgender identity, religious rules didn't enter the conversation. I didn't have to have an exegesis of Leviticus or Romans all prepared, because that's not where my kids are starting from. They are starting from love for the people in their community.

Later, when they asked me if God was a boy or a girl, and I explained that God was neither, their theology had room for that. They were curious about how it worked—they don't think God is transgender or nonbinary—but the idea that a being could be personal while neither exclusively male nor female was not new. It was something they had already touched.

## Chapter 8

# Unholy Unions

Shame, shame, shame, shame on you
I bet you think you're a big man now
But I think you're a sick man now
And you don't know how to be a good man too.

—Lake Street Dive, "Shame, Shame, Shame"

The nine-year-old boy's face contorted with shame and offense as he ran toward us. Tears smeared through two days' worth of grime from camping, swimming, and hiking. The other two children—his older brother and my then-six-year-old daughter— were nowhere in sight, conspicuously absent as he sank into a camping chair between his parents and began to sulk.

"Moira is so mean," he said.

"Oh no!" I said, "What did she do?"

He would not elaborate. I imagined the worst.

His mom gave me a "Let's wait and see" cue, to stop me from thundering off in search of my daughter, demanding she make amends.

What had she done, we all wondered. Moira's a smart kid, but to be three years younger than this boy and still devastate him like that? What on earth had transpired?

Finally Moira and the older brother returned to the campsite. Moira looked sheepish, and the older brother was barely containing his laughter. Soon after, Moira quietly found the younger brother and slipped him a little apology note, made with some art supplies from our tent. Reconciliation achieved, Moira and the younger brother scampered off to play again, leaving the older brother sitting with the adults. When they were out of earshot, four adult heads whipped around to the older brother, who was still barely suppressing a smile.

"What happened?!" we asked.

Unlike his brother, he was more than happy to oblige us with the story. The trio had been playing a game that involved taking turns, and the younger brother had not been willing to give up his turn when it was over. The other kids had pleaded with him, but he would not stick to the rules. Finally, in a moment of hot-headed anger, Moira jumped up, and according to the older brother, delivered her annihilating insult.

The older brother choked with giggles as he told us what she had said: "She called him 'Donald Trump!'"

Of course, part of me—the larger part—was quite proud. Another small part was taking note at just how ruthless my daughter was willing to be when pushed. And the smallest part, just a little echo from the past, wondered if we should be more sad that our kids would never associate the president of the United States with de facto heroism.

For as long as I can remember, up until perhaps the Obama administration, respecting the president was a matter of patriotism. My parents hated the Clintons, but they were adamant that we speak respectfully of the president. Patriotism is a moral virtue to many Americans, and in my lifetime, that has largely meant backing the plays of the United States. It has meant supporting the various wars we waged, believing every other country would be better off to be more like us, and supporting our leadership as the leadership of the free world—whatever that means.

Calls for national unity carried President Joe Biden into office after Trump, but most of us know we've lost the Cold War unity around the myth of a United States that is great because she is good. While it might be bad for morale, it's good for morality. We should always be questioning our fealty to the most powerful country in the world.

I answered the little voice in my head, the killjoy trying to make me feel bad for laughing so hard: No, we should not feel sad. We should never have been so loyal to power and position. It took the Trump administration in all its unprecedented norm-busting to drive that home for some Christians.

Though they existed before, the cultural division lines, like cracks in the walls when the foundation of a house begins to shift, started showing up everywhere during the Trump administration, especially in white Christian churches. White Christians supported Trump more heavily than any other group, with just over half of white nonevangelical Protestants and Catholics, and a whopping 78 percent of white evangelicals lending their support to Trump over President Joe Biden in 2020.[1] Latino Christians were the next most favorable to Trump, but only evangelical Latinos gave him a favorable majority going into the 2020 election.[2] No other racial or religious group even came close to white evangelicals.

Meanwhile, white, evangelical non-Trump supporters were getting increasingly uneasy. Some became vocal. For some it was the white supremacist Unite the Right rally in Charlottesville, Virginia, in August 2017; for others it was family separation at the US-Mexico border. For some staying so closely aligned with Trump became untenable as early as the unearthing of the "grab 'em by the pussy" tapes shortly before the 2016 election; for others it was as late as the January 6, 2021, insurrection two weeks before he left office.

For the committed conservatives, leaving the church of Trump was as far as it went. They posted that they were "too

liberal for conservatives and too conservative for liberals" on social media or grew out their beards or voted for Joe Biden in the
Democratic primary. But they probably still went to the same
church and voted for downballot Republicans. They kept their
faith, but might avoid calling themselves evangelical. A few
made big public declarations about how evangelicalism needed
to be dissociated from Trump.[3]

For others, leaving the church of Trump led to a closer examination of how we got here. For example, how could the same
group that declared Bill Clinton unfit for office on the grounds of
his philandering now sing the praises of a notorious womanizer?
Once they started digging, they found a psychological and theological root system centuries deep. Turning back time to a more
"civil" or "united" time in both politics and the church was only
that—turning back time. Like mowed weeds, Trumpism would
be back. It might never really leave.

They found the roots of Trumpism were intertwined with
the roots of this conservative, white evangelicalism, two shoots
from the same seed. Both shared a view of authority manifested
in the home as much as in the pulpit and the voting booth. The
roots and their shoots, which along with authoritarianism included racial caste and patriarchy, could be more socially palat-
able than the fruit—rough speech, outright womanizing, and
cruelty—and thus were able to remain through centuries of
social progress, wrapping around our institutions and national
myths. But more and more people began calling it out. The bad
fruit of the Trump presidency wasn't a fluke. And many grew
impatient as religious leaders stayed silent on such "issues." Others grew frustrated when religious leaders waded into them.

It would be easy to make this a "both sides" discussion. To say
our opinion about which topics should or should not be taught
from the pulpit is entirely determined by whether we agree with
the pastor's stance on those topics. But it's more complex. Politics is not a "both sides" situation for anyone but the most privi-

leged among us. Spiritual people, religious people, caring people have to engage in politics, and we have to teach our children how, as the blindly loyal patriotism and nationalism many of us grew up with is no longer an option.

## Politics of Human Life

Politics is a determining factor in the flourishing or suffering of millions of human beings. Black human beings are incarcerated in grossly disproportionate numbers because of politically motivated laws. Transgender human beings have their careers curtailed and lives endangered by political pillorying. Female human beings have access to only as much reproductive health care as politics will allow. Politics holds heavy sway over the lives of fetal humans, immigrating humans, gay humans, indigenous humans, and the human victims of gun violence. People who have been embattled by history do not engage in politics for sport or pleasure. They are trying to survive.

God, I believe, is present in the relationships between people, their power dynamics, their struggles against injustice. God is not absent from the various mechanisms we use to help and hurt each other. Determining the proper relationship between faith and politics is not the same as managing the separation of "church and state." These are institutions, and keeping them separate is vital to a pluralistic democracy. Faith and politics, however, are inevitably going to overlap, because our faith and our politics both have a say in how we relate to other people.

Because of that, our faith *and* our politics show up in how we talk to our kids about core issues like generosity and justice. Even if we don't "talk politics" in the CNN watching, trivia memorizing, horse racing way, we have to talk about the help and the hurt done by various laws and policies. Whether they ultimately become voters, pacifists, public servants, or protesters, we want our kids to do so from a healthy spiritual grounding.

Whether dealing with national politics or interpersonal politics, spiritual grounding can give us insight and wisdom as we encounter what I'm calling the elements of power: authority, influence, and prosperity.[4] Authority is the right to exercise power. Influence is the ability to exercise power. Prosperity is the result of power used on your behalf. Of course, they don't stay so easily separated. These three elements feed one another to create a self-perpetuating cycle. That cycle shapes history.

## Take Me to Your Leader

In 2014 Kathryn moved to San Antonio with Venture for America, an economic development program that places entrepreneurial-minded college graduates into startups and small businesses around the country. She'd been matched with a tiny company inside San Antonio's tech incubator. The incubator has a hip, urban vibe, and many of the people in its orbit attend the same hip, urban church in downtown San Antonio. Kathryn's boss was one of them, and he created, in her words, "a really toxic work environment."[5] She raised concerns about line-crossing behavior, only to see members of the incubator community rally to defend her boss—most frequently, she said, it was incubator staff who were *also* involved in the hip, urban church. "I kind of found out on the back end how much they knew," she said. "It was like I was just wrapped up in this system where this powerful, quasi-charismatic guy with a lot of sway was being protected by these other guys."

While his conduct with her grew more and more abusive, those surrounding him continued to justify his behavior, implying she should forbear, forgive, and support her Christian boss. They deferred to him because he was a major player at the incubator and in the church.

When Christians started falling into line behind Trump two years later, it made a certain kind of sense to Kathryn. Brash. Irreverent to the liberal establishment. Guardian of conservative "in culture." He made people feel as though they had a pit bull at the door, snarling and snapping on their behalf. But inside, there was a little wink, a shared chuckle as they baited the snowflakes. "It's not just the satisfaction of finding someone who hates the same people or things that you do—it's the sense of acceptance that comes from knowing you are not alone, the high of feeling like you belong," wrote journalist Adam Serwer, making sense of Trump's brazen cruelty and the cheering it elicited from his followers.[6]

Now that Kathryn is in Nashville getting a master's degree in counseling, she says she sees that the parallels are even deeper. The messages embraced across the United States—including those about leadership in Washington and Wall Street—are the same in the church. "Exploring the American cultural messages . . . I could just pull out pages from my textbook and put them next to harmful messages that the evangelical church taught. They're very hard to distinguish," she told me.

No white evangelical church would ever say it was modeled on Washington, DC, or a state legislature. Some have proposed churches should operate like businesses, but that quickly gets the stink eye from people who know the church is supposed to be something holier. The church should look different. But it doesn't.

Powerful American institutions are usually led by people who fit the American ideal of a leader: ambitious, charismatic entrepreneurs with ample hubris and vision. Leaders who are not white, straight, wealthy men must know how to play well with white, straight, wealthy men. Playing well means not threatening their status. Not rocking the boat. Everybody has to be on board. Everybody has to submit to the mission, which so many times is synonymous with the man. The man—as Kathryn had discovered at the incubator—need not be kind, principled, or humble. He need not have the best interest of others at heart. He need only have a strong personal brand, enough charisma to sell it, and absolute assurance in his personal vision. Those contributing to their vision on any given day would be treated like family. Those in the way, even for a moment, are steamrolled.

Months before Donald Trump won the 2016 election and the press corps began its collective lament of "What could we have gotten so wrong about people's support for this guy?" *Vox* had identified one particularly salient feature of the primary voters who vaulted him to victory: Trump voters love authority.[7] They run strong authoritarian households, in which parents deserve to be obeyed solely because of their position as parents. They believe in institutional hierarchies wherein those on top are due respect because of their position. They defer to executives—the people whose role lends them the power to execute their will. Executive branch of the government. Executive pastor. Executive director. Chief executive officer. Those in charge have authority, the right to execute their will.

Kathryn, as it turned out, was working for a leader with authoritarian power and watching an authoritarian leader ascend to the presidency. While she still held out hope that she would find leadership based on integrity in the church—people who treated others with dignity because they prioritized the oneness of all, not their own set-apart status—she was at the beginning of a disappointing journey.

While looking for institutions with integrity, Kathryn got married and had a baby. Her home became the place where she could model mutually submissive, integrated, earned authority for her daughter, Ella. She wouldn't assert her authority based on her position or insist that Ella obey authority figures without question. She's teaching her daughter to trust her own spirit, knowing that one day Ella will speak truth to Kathryn's power as her mother. (If you're a parent, you know the sting of being called out by your child.) When Ella has a desire or opinion, Kathryn—while still making decisions based on what's healthiest and most appropriate—takes note so she can understand her daughter better as an individual, honoring the child's unique thoughts, personality, and spirit.

This is, of course, so much easier said than done. I swore I'd never say, "Because I said so" or "Because I'm the mom" to my kids. But sometimes I just need them to put on their damn shoes. It's a struggle, we can all agree; but for parents who see the myriad problems of authoritarianism writ large and small, it's worth finding the language and rhythm that allows us to organize our homes around mutual respect.

Kathryn wants Ella to know how to weigh authority and to be wise about the leaders to whom she submits. She also wants her to know how to hold leaders accountable with integrity. Psychologists say this sort of mutual respect has numerous benefits for children, but it's a whole-house commitment. If there are two parents in the home, both have to participate—especially, in our patriarchal world, male parents. Fortunately, Kathryn is married to Cameron.

**Spheres of Influence**

Cameron grew up wanting to be a certain kind of guy. He looks the part: nice hair, strong jaw, earnest blue eyes. He wishes he were taller, but he has a natural swagger that makes it so he's the only one who notices. By high school, he had figured out how to be the kind of upstanding young man who might be tapped as a future leader in his family's Christian circles. But once Cameron left his "insulated" life as the captain of the "God squad" in high school, he no longer felt like he was leadership material. "I went off the rails in college," Cameron said.[8] He joined a band. Did drugs. Slept around. All the while still imagining that he could figure out a way to get back onto the God squad, back on the leadership track. After college he tried to pick back up where he'd left off. Finally, with a darkness nagging at him, Cameron said, "I realized I was totally dis-integrated."

It was a heavy burden for a young man trying to fit into one of the most influential groups of Christians on the planet. Cameron grew up around The Fellowship Foundation, the folks behind the National Prayer Breakfast. The Fellowship provides informal mentorship and spiritual support to Christians in positions of "influence," under the working theory that this is how the gospel will spread. This happens primarily in Washington, DC, but also in small groups around the world. People in the Fellowship's orbit start small group Bible studies, often inviting local leaders in a given place or profession. Not only does the Fellowship network among those already in power, it also feeds the network from the inside by recruiting promising young men and women into these small groups. The select few work as "interns," living in a fraternity house situation in the DC area.

The Fellowship is looking for people who are influential or who will be influential. It seeks people who can, because of their innate giftedness and drive, carry the gospel more effectively than people like Cameron can—or so he believed. He longed to be one of the young men singled out as a rising star, someone worth discipling and drawing deeper into the network of powerful men in Washington, DC. "I grew up very much revering that group of men, and I'll be honest I still love many of them dearly and respect their mission," he said. "But as a child . . . I desperately wanted to be in with that crowd, and I never was. And I mostly felt like it was because I wasn't man enough. I didn't have the social aptitude. I wasn't hard-charging enough." He didn't fit the model for the kind of leader who exuded authority or influence. Cameron, with his guitar and his laid-back demeanor, said he felt like a "sideshow" to the main event: charismatic, dominant go-getters.

Because the Fellowship is so secretive, it's hard to know how many churches and Bible studies are led by those inside its orbit. But the model has become ubiquitous: Invest in the leaders, the ones with influence, because they will then set the world to rights. It's a sort of spiritual *noblesse oblige*. A trickle-down spirituality.[9] But what are we saying when the people with the most spiritual influence are the people with the most economic, social, and political influence? What do our children hear when we make connections between the grown-up version of being cool and popular, and spiritual value?

People like Cameron, who grew up questioning their place in a spiritual hierarchy, understand the radical nature of what Jesus came to do: to invest in the margins, to leave the ninety-nine for the one, to party at the wrong house, and to hang out with the wrong folks. Maybe those "wrong folks" weren't just—as the hip pastors tell us—the edgy sinners. Maybe they were the people without influence, who weren't going to make him look more credible. Jesus wasn't just being risky with his reputation, he was being, in terms of trickle-down spirituality, inefficient.

If you decide to base your spiritual investments on influence and judge value by financial and political prosperity, those two things will be tied together throughout the ministry. Trickle-down is the opposite of proximity and solidarity. It reinforces hierarchies—a downward direction is part of the model—instead of radically distributing spiritual resources according to people's inherent dignity.

I know Kathryn and Cameron well enough to know that they share this value with me: I never want my child to wonder where they fall in the hierarchy of God's love. I never want them to use a hierarchy of influence to determine who is worth their time, who is worthy of help, who should be in authority and who should be shoved aside. But if this attitude is not reflected in how we are investing or voting or explaining the gravely consequential political actions of our day, our kids will suss out our real beliefs. They will wonder about their place in the hierarchies when they see that all the politicians, pastors, and venture capitalists look and sound . . . the same.

Together, Cameron and Kathryn, now with their daughter Ella, are on the hunt for a spirituality that does not prize authority and influence in the same way, and it affects their politics, the way they view civic leadership as well. They are looking for integrity and compassion. They are looking for a spiritual practice and civic posture that stands with, feels with, struggles with those who are not destined for financial or political greatness. They are looking for leaders who are near to the brokenhearted, because they are the brokenhearted.

## What Does It Mean to Be Blessed?

The Bible makes it abundantly clear that Jesus cast his lot with people on the margins, the underdogs, the exiles. The God of the Old Testament places a high priority on care for the poor. The Spirit continually moves through people and places overlooked or disregarded by those in power. Yet white evangelicalism's embrace of authority and influence have revised that motif. Jesus is the model of a manly man. Yahweh exalts the faithful and exiles the wicked. The Spirit moves in the hearts of powerful people to advance a triumphal kingdom. Capitalism, when crossbred with spirituality, tells us that prosperity is a sign of virtue and poverty is a sign of vice. Those who are ahead have a good work ethic. Those who are behind must have slacked.

In childhood, prosperity looks like making the team, getting good grades, and being attracted to and attractive to the right people. We call those who are popular and achievers "good kids," the ones your parents want you to hang out with. Those who are not, the underachievers, must be into drugs or something.

It's a false equivalency of the highest order. Prosperity does not equal virtue. Not all prosperous people are virtuous. Not all virtuous people are prosperous. If instead we see prosperity as the result of power acting in your favor, we have clearer eyes about who prospers and why. We don't ask, "What did you do to deserve this?" but, "How much power is in your corner?" When you look at poverty as the result of someone being left defense-less, of someone having power used against them rather than for them, it changes the way you relate. You are faced with the questions: Will I share my prosperity? Will I take some of the power working for me and share it with you?

The goals we set for our American kids will either plant the seeds of what we now know as Trumpism, or they will plant the seeds of its opposition. If the goal is to gain power through authority, influence, and prosperity, they will grow up in the garden of Trumpism. If the goal is to share power through integrity, compassion, and generosity, they will grow up in the garden of opposition to Trumpism and all that it entails. They will often find themselves, as many of us ultimately did during the Trump administration, in a place of protest.

## Protest Is Prophetic

Throughout the Trump administration, and in many times before, Christians—of all denominations, not just evangelical—who are comfortable enough with the current hierarchies of authority, influence, and prosperity have issued calls for unity. They have urged us to come together, and to find a gradual, placid way forward. They want kids to grow up being proud to be Americans. However, Christians who are wholly uncomfortable with current hierarchies of authority, influence, and prosperity have faithfully declined to sit politely at a table set to discuss, but never change, the status quo.

The resistance-based actions and words of people like Dorothy Day, Martin Luther King Jr., Jim Wallis, Fred Shuttlesworth, Sarah Bessey, and Rosa Parks are part of a centuries-old tradition of religious protest. Incorporating our children into that protest is integral to their understanding of authority and how their spirit would have them relate to it. I wonder how many people my age have participated in a "life chain" event as kids and a Black Lives Matter rally as adults. I suspect many. At the life chain, we stood silently praying around the town square linking arms and holding posters with messages about the sanctity of life. At the Black Lives Matter event, we marched through those same streets chanting messages about the sanctity of life. Even Jesus and the Reformers participated in religious protest. In speaking out against the corruption of the religious establishment they were upsetting the authorities, influencers, and prosperous of their day. They were poking powerful bears.

Queer pastor, journalist, and theologian Layton Williams goes so far as to say that protest is, at one point or another, an unavoidable part of the life of someone committed to the way of the Christ. "To be a faithful Christian in a broken world is to live in protest of what does the breaking and what is broken, in the name of love, wholeness, and healing."[10] Protest is a form of love for the oppressed, a love that is wholly the business of the church. It is also an act of political contribution. In the summer of 2020, as Black Lives Matter protests swept the country in response to the murders of too many Black Americans, many referenced the work of journalist Nikole Hannah-Jones who, in her 1619 Project, pointed out that America has been blessed by the protest and continued struggle of Black people: "Yet despite being violently denied the freedom and justice promised to all, black Americans believed fervently in the American creed. Through centuries of black resistance and protest, we have helped the country live up to its founding ideals."[11]

The tendency among Christians, who benefit most from existing hierarchies, is to chastise protest and pushback as "stirring up division." But Williams points out that those divisions already exist. They exist between the authorities and the oppressed, the influencers and the brokenhearted, the prosperous and the impoverished in any hierarchy—church or civic. Naming them and seeking to bridge them will always feel unnecessarily combative to those being called to relinquish authority, influence, or prosperity. "As long as civility is defined by the existing system of power, arguing or dissenting in any way that destabilizes the system is deemed uncivil," Williams says.[12] In other words: If everyone approved of your protest, it wouldn't be a protest.

If we parents want our kids to be faithful protesters, we have to be OK with them getting into trouble. We have to worry less about their college applications, their networks, and their prospects, and more about their willingness to go where the Spirit is calling. We want our kids to engage in politics when it helps them live out their values, when it helps them help others, change unjust systems or bring peace in times of war. We want them to vote, run for office if they want to, and protest whenever they need to.

But I never want them to let the rules of politics govern their conscience. I don't want them to be more loyal to a political party than they are to their own spirits, or to put their hope in a candidate who promises to keep them safe, keep them on top, and to use power in their behalf. I don't want them to be silent for the sake of civility or cheap unity. Nor do I want the contemporary white evangelical idea of authority, influence, and prosperity to shape their vision of spiritual health and the way of Jesus. I want them to think like Jesus and those who knew his leadership model best.

So the last shall be first, and the first, last.
(Matthew 20:16 NASB)

Blessed are the meek, for they shall inherit the earth.
(Matthew 5:5 ESV)

God chose the weak things of the world to shame the strong.
(1 Corinthians 1:27 NIV)

## Chapter 9

# War Games

Roll away your stone, I'll roll away mine.
Together we can see what we will find.
Don't leave me alone at this time,
For I'm afraid of what I will discover inside.

—Mumford and Sons, "Roll Away Your Stone"

It was a hot summer day in Austin, Texas, and I got off a yellow school bus along with the rest of the campers from Worldview Academy. We walked in groups of three onto the University of Texas campus. My group of fourteen-year-olds stopped a college student on his way to one of the academic buildings and asked if he had a few minutes.

Then we asked him if he knew what would happen when he died.

If you've never done street evangelism, this sounds borderline psychotic. If you have done street evangelism, you know it also *feels* borderline psychotic. Leading with "What happens when you die?" is the most unnatural way to begin any conversation, let alone a conversation with a stranger. All four of us—the team of three and our spiritual quarry—felt it.

I don't remember how the rest of the conversation played out, but here is the first line of my journal entry from that day,

June 10, 1998: "Well, today was evangelism. We went to UT and witnessed. I witnessed to a guy that was just confused." I probably meant that he was confused about his eternal destiny, God, and religion—I go on to give him the pseudonym "Doubting Thomas" in my journal as I pledge to pray for him. Reading it now, knowing how we must have looked, three young teens roaming around on a university campus in search of someone to save, the college student's confusion is highly relatable.

What on earth were we doing there?

We were, as Worldview Academy had promised our parents, preparing to defend our faith in the scariest of all secular institutions: the college campus. I attended, and later went on to work for, Worldview Academy. I was drawn to it because it explicitly took on what it called a false dichotomy between faith and reason. As a bookish kid, I didn't like the idea that the two most important parts of my identity—Christianity and academic ambition—were at odds. As early as fifth grade I was eager to make faith compatible with certainty. It made me feel better existentially and fed my budding ego.

In the back of the very same journal that includes the June 10 entry about "witnessing," I wrote out a seven-page treatise on the impossibility of being a merely "four-point Calvinist" explaining how the five "points" of Calvinism were not separate points at all to be accepted or rejected, but were merely logical implications of a single theological truth. I was fourteen going on 1517.[1]

The faculty at Worldview Academy were and are all incredibly smart men from whom I learned a lot, including how to argue for a version of the Christian faith that was logically airtight. My hungry mind loved words like epistemology, cosmology, and ontology in the same way I loved systematic theology. I liked treating faith like something in which one could become an expert. A cold, logical, badass expert. At Worldview Academy, I found that hard edge I was looking for.

The founders of Worldview Academy were striking back at what they saw as a softness and silliness in contemporary Chris-

tian culture, a passivity they saw as leaving students intellectually defenseless when they went to college with no good argument for challenges to a seven-day creation and objective truth.
They wanted less emphasis on fun and fluff, and more emphasis
on sacrifice and intellectual rigor.[2] Students like me wanted that
muscle. We wanted to be respected. We wanted to rhetorically
devastate some atheists. The promise to parents was that students, many of whom had been homeschooled, would not be
led astray by the ideas they encountered in college. They would
not fall under the spell of professors and lecturers purporting to
have a more intellectually satisfying, more scientifically tenable
alternative to biblicism—the belief that the Bible, and everything
in it, is factually, literally true as written.

This was a big worry for parents. On the book table at my
church, University of Texas professor J. Budziszewski's book
*How to Stay Christian in College* was a hot commodity, less among
the students for whom it was intended, and more among their
parents. The book gets right to it. In the second sentence of the
second paragraph of the first chapter, Budziszewski warns that
"from the moment students set foot on the contemporary campus, their Christian convictions and discipline are assaulted."[3]

Dang, J.

Evangelicals, of course, aren't the only ones worried about
their children being led astray. Recent college graduate and author Aurora Griffin speaks to the fears of Catholic parents. Before she gives her forty tips for students—which include finding
Catholic fellowship and professors, making pilgrimages, living
the liturgical year, only dating Christians, drinking moderately
and legally, and not doing drugs (the advice is terrific if staying
Catholic is the goal)—she encourages parents to pray. She writes:
"This book is also for you, parents who worry (rightfully so)
about sending their children to secular colleges, fearing that they
will come home to that first Thanksgiving dinner as atheists.

This is a real threat, so you must be vigilant in praying for your students and encouraging their walk with Christ."[4]

That's why Worldview Academy took us to the University of Texas—to get all the intimidation out of our systems. They told us how faculty members had decimated evolutionists in debate and assured us we could be well-equipped to do the same. We would not be bringing a WWJD bracelet to an intellectual gun-fight. Christianity belonged in the academy, they insisted, where it had been for centuries. We couldn't abandon academia—we had to win it back, bring it back to the place where the Bible and Christian orthodoxy were the final authority. Of course anything deemed final, canonized, or settled is a precarious place from which to study the human genome or astrophysics. "*Niente merda,*" mutters Galileo from his grave. Inquiry and creativity run afoul of what we think we know all the time.

The war with academia was really a symbol for the war with the culture, of course. Wherever science, philosophy, and arts ran afoul of a fundamentalist interpretation or application of the Bible, that's where the war was. College was like culture wars concentrate.

My main goal for my children is not that they have a ready answer in a debate with their professors or with their conservative family members or with their political adversaries. As a person whose spirituality has been enriched by the freedom to explore and challenge, I absolutely want that freedom for my kids. I want them to ask "why" and dig into paradoxes and run all over God's big, beautiful world, running afoul of what we think we know. Unlike Griffin and Budziszewski, I'm not writing a book about how to keep your kid in a particular kind of faith. But I'm also not trying tee up your kid's atheism. I believe that it is possible to know God—just not all of God, or with certainty. So if not rigid orthodoxy applied to all areas of life, what *should* we be giving our kids to integrate their minds and spirits?

I had to understand the disintegration before I could answer that for myself.

## Winning in Heaven and on Earth

For so long, the mysteries of the universe were the domain of religion because they seemed to be the domain of God or gods or spirits—unseen movers and causes. Everything from stars to seizures carried an air of mysticism. Power rested in the hands of the one who could interpret the "will" of these unseen forces and suggest how people might keep themselves in good standing. We know, historically, this worked out great for some interpretations and poorly for others. Dominant faiths did not check their influence at the door of government, economy, or academy. In the West, Christianity's view of the world reigned supreme. In India, a form of Hinduism dictated society's structures. North Africa and the Middle East became the "Muslim World." Buddhism became synonymous with national identity in many Asian countries.

Those faiths that endured minority status were, to varying degrees, persecuted. Most infamously, the Jews. Francisco Sanches and Baruch Spinoza were two of the Jewish scholars forced to abandon the practice of their faith during the Inquisition, and rather than the intended full embrace of Christianity, these two (and one would presume more like them) turned to logic, math, and natural science to explain the world. "Don't ask me for many authorities or reverence for 'authors,'" historian Karen Armstrong quotes from Sanches's 1581 *Quod Nihil Scitur* ("That Nothing Is Known"), one of the foundational texts of philosophical skepticism, "since this is of a servile and unlearned spirit, rather than of one who is free and wants to know the truth. I shall follow only the reason of nature."[5] That hostile tone was a new development born of the cruelty and oppression of the Inquisition, Armstrong writes.[6] Spinoza would go on to say that Scripture could and should be judged rationally on its own merits, without pastors or rabbis doing the interpreting. It should be subject to reason, just like any claim. If it made false claims, no clergyman should be allowed to salvage its inerrancy by creative interpretation.

And soon began the age of the Enlightenment, when, despite millennia of more complex and interactive interpretation, scriptures throughout the world religions would be subject to new scrutiny, required to stand alone as any other historical or scientific text. When what would be called "fundamentalist" branches of world religions answered this scrutiny, they could have said, like Armstrong, that the scriptures "had never pretended to be amenable to scientific demonstration, so a 'scientific' approach to scripture could only produce a caricature of rational discourse that would bring religion into disrepute."[7] Instead, they accepted Spinoza's premise. For the sacred texts to be valid, they had to be true in the same way that a map of the stars or a human anatomy book was true.

Fundamentalist branches of several religions stuck with modernity, none with more gusto than fundamentalist Christianity, which now has an entire museum dedicated to a seven-day creation and books of charts one can purchase to foretell the date of the end of the world. OK, maybe not the date, but the rough timeline. Such intellectual gymnastics, rather than proving the intellectual respectability of religion, made it the constant punching bag of what nineteenth century theologian Charles Hodge called "a large class of scientific men."

The 1925 Scopes Trial, in which the teaching of evolution lost the legal battle but won the public relations war, entrenched the battle lines between faith and science as we know them. The trial continues to provide a useful typology for the entire cultural war that would follow: American Civil Liberties Union lawyer Clarence Darrow, the rational, well-spoken underdog up against a fuming, grandstanding, but ultimately fumbling William Jennings Bryan with the power of the conservative political landscape on his side.

With science embattling them on one side, Christian fundamentalists also had to deal with the social and theological ramifications of German schools of higher criticism. As in the Scopes trial, fundamentalism doubled down on biblical inerrancy. "The Protestant Reformation had insisted on *sola scriptura*. Scripture was, therefore, the life and soul of Protestant Christianity; it was all they had, and when it was attacked, fundamentalists felt that their very selves were violated," Armstrong writes.[8] As Bill Jack, one of the founders of Worldview Academy, would say, he defended a seven-day creation so vehemently because if God couldn't get it right in the first three chapters, how can we trust anything in the Bible?

And that is what we kids getting off the bus at the University of Texas were walking into. That was the battle, that was what was at risk. If we couldn't win the debate, our faith was doomed.

But wait. There's more.

Restoring the Bible's influence in academia, storming the ivory tower, was part of "capturing the culture for Christ," a phrase commonly used in the circles of my youth. Francis Schaeffer, one of white evangelical Christianity's favorite thinkers, taught that the academy is the birthplace of ideas that make their way into the arts, then the culture in general, and finally theology and the church.[9] By getting back into culture at its origin point, the academy, many hoped to see a new generation of equally Western and Christian artists like J. R. R. Tolkien, Rembrandt, and Handel. The country would then be amenable to Western Christian culture, our "worldview," with all its white, Jesusy beauty. The church would then have no pressure to drift from biblicism, and the conservative, capitalist power structures it has been molded to support. We—mostly white, and entirely Western-centric folks—would be safe. We would have influence.

As a journalist, I see overlapping agendas every time I look at campaign finance reports and boards of directors. For example, one of Worldview Academy's biggest supporters and longtime board members has been Tim Dunn, the Midland oil man behind Empower Texans, a lobbying group pulling the Texas legislature to the political right like a team of Clydesdales. Dunn is a sincere Christian. He's also promoting the continuation of fossil fuel dependence and underinvestment in public schools. If voters can be convinced that the two are synonymous—faith and the conservative political agenda—it creates a coalition with multiple entry points. Whether you care about low taxes, abortion, or saving souls, the Republican party has a plan for you. Training a bunch of teenagers to argue on behalf of that mixed agenda without telling them where one ends and the other begins seems like a worthwhile investment.

It would take me years to disentangle the agendas of conservatism and the genuine concern for the salvation of the world. As misguided as the latter can be within rigid theological traditions, I also think it can be held sincerely and humbly by people who fear damnation for themselves and others. I know a lot of people who sincerely believe the Bible can be trusted on matters of science and history, and souls depend on it. Those earnest apologists believe their faith can withstand a challenge. And that meant something to a teenage girl whose entire sense of self was bound up in religion. Worldview Academy gave me the tools I needed—not to battle atheists in college, but to withstand the slings and arrows of growing up. Having answers to my logical, intellectual questions was necessary for me, because I did not yet understand that integrated faith could exist apart from certainty. If my monolithic fundamentalist religion had been blown away by intellectual arguments at that time, I would have assumed that was all there was to faith, and been set adrift.

I was immature. I needed intellectual certainty to scaffold my immature faith.

Having that certainty, however unfounded, I grew up with a sense of purpose and safety. When I would doubt my faith, careening toward the fear of hell or annihilation, I would walk myself through the Socratic style questioning the Worldview Academy faculty taught us to use on unbelievers. I would ask myself, "Where are you going when you die?" and evangelize myself from there. I would evangelize my logical, skeptical mind. Unbeknownst to me, this intellectual process protected my infantile spirituality from scrutiny it was never intended to withstand. I engaged the certainty-based religion of my youth primarily with my mind, and a slowly growing spirituality continued to thrive, mitigating impulses toward depression, addiction, and risky behaviors. I was cultivating my mind, but God was cultivating my soul. Slowly, as I matured into adulthood, my mind and spirit became more and more integrated, and I traded monolithic religion for faith. I lost my religion, and it happened just like the worried grown-ups feared it would.

## Among the Casualties

In the end, I am a cautionary tale. Even with all the apologetics training and the C. S. Lewis, and the Christian high school and undergrad, I drifted. I went from Worldview Academy to the London School of Economics, and things started to fall apart.

Graduate school was the first time I'd been invited to look at current events and history through the lens of non-American, nonwhite people. It wasn't a logical debate about evolution or postmodernism that got to me. It was stepping outside my own perspective, seeing the world through the eyes of people who were not like me but who were not adhering to the script I'd been given for enemies of the faith.

There was Dr. Shani Orgad who wrote about message boards for breast cancer survivors. Dr. Raka Shome who challenged us to look for how people who had been objectified by colonial interest were writing and talking about themselves. They didn't want to debate. They wanted to listen. They wanted me to listen. My coursemates weren't cigar-smoking, turtleneck-wearing ideologues looking to start the revolution, either. Those of us who lived in the same student housing along the Thames would have "Bankside date nights," more devoted to silliness and chit-chat than debate. One member of the date night group was Kristen, a comedy nerd who, after I helped her move to Los Angeles, would eventually help me pack my honeymoon suitcase the night before my wedding. Another was Jessica, a sports fanatic who regularly visited her family in Ghana. And there was Nina, a competitive bodybuilder from Greece.

The monolith wasn't chipped away by debate, but by delight, by compassion, and by seeing truth in others. By summer my big, strong faith was a handful of sand in my pocket. I had Jesus and not much else, but I was more curious and excited to learn than ever. And I didn't feel lost or like my salvation was on the line. It felt like having my toes in sand that was warm, comforting, and real but not immutable. The sand had all the same protective elements of purpose and belonging, but I could use it to shape castles and mermaids instead of just sitting alone on my boulder, ready to explain it to curious onlookers.

The journey wasn't over yet. I would return to the United States with my pockets full of sand, start working for the church, and quickly find that the pressure to "reboulder" my faith was strong. I'd grown up thinking that my faith should be like a rock. Like the rock Jesus described in Matthew 7 on which the wise man built his house.

That passage seemed to be warning me about my new sandy faith, which would cause my house to collapse. But I don't think Jesus was talking about certainty in that parable. I don't think he was talking about having a big, solid, faith that delivers absolute answers on every single subject. That little parable starts with "Everyone who hears these words of mine and does them is like a wise man who built his house on the rock" (Matt. 7:24, ESV). Which words of his? This is the conclusion of the Sermon on the Mount, Jesus's big countercultural call to live lives of humility, generosity, and integrity. It's full of challenge and mystery, and he leaves a lot unexplained.

For instance, as the "salt of the earth," what exactly are we supposed to be preserving or enhancing? I mean, I'm plenty salty, but somehow I don't think that's what we're talking about here (Matt. 5:13).

How does the Bank of Heaven, where I'm supposed to be storing up my treasure, work? Can we get into the exact value of these various treasures once I'm there? Are there some high value items I should be prioritizing? Is the occasional almsgiving enough, or do we need, like, martyrdom (Matt 6:20)?

I have a whole *list* of hypothetical scenarios to run regarding this "give him your cloak" bit (Matt 5:40).

The vagueness and metaphor is a gift to pastors and teachers, who can go for miles on the Sermon on the Mount, finding novel applications and historical tidbits to milk new meaning out of each mystical verse. That's fine, but taken as a whole, the Sermon on the Mount paints a picture of embodied spirituality. It's a whole mood, as the kids would say. It's not a list of propositional truths. If we have been living in this flow of not judging others, of loving our enemies, of cultivating private spiritual practice, of refusing to worry, then that's when we have built the house of which Jesus says "the rains fell, and the floods came, and the wind blew and beat on that house, but it did not fall" (Matt. 7:25). He's telling us how to live, how to be resilient and transcendent, how not to fall apart when things get tough. It's a spirituality we live among others, not a debate.

Living the Sermon on the Mount has allowed me to weather the storms of uncertainty when the boulder of fundamentalism would have dragged me to the bottom of the floodwaters. And the ironic thing: Nothing has been more winsome, less combative, more well respected among my non-Christian classmates and colleagues. Nothing has been a better witness.

When Kristen, one of my grad school friends, was raising money for a charity event, she offered to write a limerick for anyone who donated. I donated, and this is the limerick she wrote:

> I am friends with one Bekah McNeel.
> Drove to LA with her at the wheel.
> It was back in grad school,
> I learned Jesus is cool,
> 'Cause she lives her life with such zeal.

I just don't think the guy on the UT campus had the same takeaway.

## The Quest

In our home my husband and I have opted for a wholehearted embrace of inquiry, science, and perspective-taking. We also embrace the spirituality of the Sermon on the Mount. We do not worry that facts and reality will destroy our children's faith, though they may learn things that change the way they understand God. We want our kids to ask "why" and "why not" (and boy oh boy do they oblige) not only of us but of all authority, because we believe authority should not be making arbitrary rules or overplaying its hand. But the answers they get may not be found in logical syllogisms or proofs. The answers may be instinctive or intuitive. They may lie in going counter to the logic, if the logic is harming people. I want my kids to be more comfortable with the great discomfort of my life: Answers are not the same as certainties.

Sometimes an answer is an action. An act of kindness that defies the law.

Sometimes the answer is the soul's response to beauty. The way artists and composers compel us.

Sometimes the answer is in paradox. When our ways of knowing collide, we must do the best we can until there is more to know.

Questions are quests. They are adventures. Answers are stepping stones, wells to draw from. They are not the end of the quest, but rather help along the way.

I don't know if my kids will need logical religious scaffolding while they develop spiritually. They might have my obsessive mind that cannot sleep unless it has seen the locked doors. They might need me to assure them of things I'm not sure of until they are ready to know more. I don't think I would send them to an apologetics training camp, for all the cultural reasons mentioned above. But I will encourage them to read whatever books put their minds at ease. If that's C. S. Lewis's *Mere Christianity*, so be it. If it is a catechism or a systematic theology book, that's fine too. I want their minds integrated with their spirituality. But I don't want their minds to control their spirituality, nor do I want a good argument to be enough to manipulate them. I want their hearts, minds, and bodies to be fully integrated. I want them to judge truth not just by airtight arguments, but by the peace it brings, how it leads them to live, and how it urges them to love.

I recently witnessed the fruit of such parental priorities, in my house but not with my kids. For a few months, a high school senior named Bel helped us out with childcare after school. Her dad, Patton, had been my editor at a previous journalism gig, and we bonded not just over our shared profession, but also over our similar faith journeys—hurt by churches, skeptical of specific doctrines, can't quite fully walk away. He wrote the book *My Faith So Far: A Story of Conversion and Confusion.*

So Patton and his wife, Michaela, had always been open about their doubts with their three kids, and when seven-, eight-, nine-year-old Bel came home with questions about God, they often said, "I don't know."

Having eighteen-year-old Bel in our home, I could tell that even her childhood questions had not been mindless chatter. Bel is more comfortable asking deep and probing questions than I might be when asking you where you got your shoes. She was completely nonjudgmental in our often chaotic home, with my pandemic-stressed kids acting out, and me and my millennial husband constantly failing to live up to Gen Z ideals. We chatted about faith, and she identified herself as Christian, but in an open, malleable way. In her college application essay, titled "Growing Up Gray," she wrote about how the unsettled faith of her household—manifested in a sort of perpetual church hop—had frustrated her, but also formed her.

"I've always been really independent, but it made me more independent," Bel said.

So when she'd been in college for a few months, I interviewed her, with Patton, over Zoom. We talked about how, as someone who had been deconstructing before it was a hot topic, Patton often just felt like he was failing to give his kids anything meaningful by way of faith, especially the lack of consistent church participation. "It's something I've always experienced as a struggle and frustration and a failure on my part," he told me. Bel too recalled frustrations with her parents' nonanswers and what she felt was an overly critical perspective on churches. But she also noted that they gave her plenty of resources for finding her own answers: Their dinner table hosted guests with different viewpoints, and the discussion regularly went into tough topics. They spent time in nature as a family and talked about meeting God there—Bel considers her evergreen tree tattoo a spiritual symbol. And they kept going to church. Patton would go visit all kinds of churches around San Antonio, mostly as a journalist who is interested in religion and social justice, and Bel would join him.

Then, Bel said something that surprised both Patton and me. When describing the difference between her and her peers who grew up with a more traditional religion, she said, "My relationship with the Lord was formed really individually from a really young age."

We both knew Bel had been forming her own faith from a young age; that wasn't surprising. But most exvangelicals don't feel comfortable using the term "the Lord." Tons of baggage there. In fact, when my husband finds a good parking spot, or gets the last box of granola bars at the grocery store or some other trivial score, he often says, sarcastically in an exaggerated Texas accent, "It was the Lord." But Bel isn't an exvangelical. Unburdened by cynicism, she comes to the idea of a caring and faithful God in a constructive way. Construction is a process, and that's what she has done. While so many of us are "de-" or "re-" constructing something given to us preprocessed, she was building a faith alongside the rest of her identity.

When Bel says "the Lord" she's referring to someone she has sought in the open spaces. Her faith is flexible but real. She experiences God profoundly, and it was the questions that led her there, not the answers.

*Part 3*

# FORKS IN THE ROAD

The next four chapters are the "how" of the book. As in "how does our shift in faith affect the other decisions we make as parents?" World-views are funny things. A tiny shift can ripple through our household, unsettling things that were settled, raising questions we thought were answered. We take a look at a few of the secondary issues that inevitably come up after we leave the one-way icy road to the top of the mountain, some we expected and some we didn't.

Chapter 10

# Hungover and Hunting for Church

If you'd been made to serve a master
You'd be frightened by the open hand, frightened by
the hand
Could I be made to serve a master?
Well, I'm never gonna understand, never understand.

—Vampire Weekend, "Everlasting Arms"

While in graduate school, I woke one morning, still in my clothes from the night before, with a headache like someone had been chopping through my skull with an ax, and a stomach like a witch's cauldron, all bubble, bubble, toil and trouble. I was hungover.

The night before had been what my classmate called a "Jesus Party." She baked bread for the thirty invitees, and we were all told to bring bottles of wine. We did, as did the additional thirty or so people who showed up. The bread ran out quickly, and the wine kept going.

Wine. That was the smell emanating from somewhere nearby as I groped the dark recesses of my oversized leather handbag, searching for my cell phone to check the time. What I found instead was a semi-dry, semi-crusted layer of vomit. At an unknown point between getting myself and all my friends thrown off a night bus somewhere in central London and tumbling into bed, I had thrown up in my bag.

I checked the time, forced myself out of bed, dressed, extracted my umbrella and wallet from my ruined handbag, and leaned against the cool metal of the elevator as I made my way out to the front porch, where a group of smokers huddled under the awning watching the fine mist of a typical British morning.

"You OK?" one of the smokers asked.

"I'm just hungover," I replied.

"Go back to bed, love. It's Sunday. You can sleep it off."

"I'm going to church."

"What?!? That sounds miserable. Why?"

"I just . . . need Jesus."

I then opened my umbrella, sending little bits of dried vomit flying in all directions, and walked the mile and a half to church, the only place where I knew how to find Jesus. The institutional church had so convinced me that it was the sole dispensary of God's grace and truth that after a night of drunkenness and mild blasphemy I dragged my ragged, blanched, nauseated self to church so I could slump in the back row and be—what? Forgiven? Restored? Less hungover?

I know there are well-intentioned folks involved, but from a historical standpoint the power structure of the church as we know it just invites corruption. It's an extreme hierarchy with license to demand all manner of things from people with very little clarity on what they are allowed to ask for in return.

The question at hand for readers of this book is whether we should take our kids to church, assuming that our relationship with at least one local institution has soured. But do we even know what church is? Do we really know our options?

The extensive history of religious communities is beyond the scope of this book, but have no fear, there are shelves upon shelves of religious history in every library and bookstore. You can go on a religious history tour of the Middle East or China or India. You can study it in school or seminary. You can watch a two-hour YouTube video with subtle spa music in the background while it describes the martyrdoms of Jesus's apostles.[1]

I've done a few of the things above, and here's my one sentence conclusion: Humans waste no time in the transition from mystery to dogma, from revolution to institution, from cooperating to competing. When something proves useful for consolidating power, they go all in. In the case of Christianity, the first four hundred years after Jesus the Christ were spent arguing about what he predicted would be the fundamental question for his followers: "Who do you say that I am?" (Matt. 16:15, ESV).

This poetic moment between Jesus and Peter in the Gospel of Matthew was followed by several centuries of conjecture and theory as to the meaning of Peter's gold-star answer, "You are the Christ, the son of the living God." The winning doctrines in these debates were called "orthodox" and the losers were dubbed "heresy." The orthodoxy we know today came to us by the less poetically named doctrine of "hypostatic union" articulated in the Athanasian Creed somewhere in the fifth or sixth century.

That didn't, of course, end the debate. Because we still don't really agree about what Jesus meant when he said, "On this rock I will build my church" (Matt. 16:19). Is Peter "the rock," making this the grounds for papal succession, as some in the Roman Catholic church believed? Or is the church built on Peter's statement of belief, incorporating those who affirm that statement as "living stones" (1 Pet. 2:5)? Is "church" based on shared authority, shared belief, or shared life?

And finally, what is included in this "church" of Jesus? Is it the universal church made up of all believers? Is it the institutional church manifested in local congregations? Is it those who, pre-Jesus, looked forward to the Christ's coming as well as those who identified Jesus as the Christ? Was Israel special? Are we Israel? Can infants be part of the church? Do you have to actually join? Who is in charge here?

Ah, Jesus. Always generating more questions than certainty.

What I know is this: Despite the bickering that has marked its *entire existence*, the Christ gave his followers a lot of mandates the world needs. They were told to love their neighbors, to care for the poor, to suffer for righteousness's sake. Peter and Jesus have another poetic Q&A at the end of the Gospel of John, wherein Jesus tells Peter to "feed my sheep" (John 21). He's telling him to take care of the people whom Jesus had gathered together into this radical, loving, way of life—his church.

Some of the US church's most vocal critics—Rachel Held Evans and Lyz Lenz come to mind—once tried to start a church specifically to be better at loving people. They so wanted to see the church do a new thing, they so wanted reform, that they were willing to do the nearly impossible work of starting a new entity entirely while seeking to avoid replicating an already successful and problematic model. That is such commitment and sacrificial love, and it is such pain and disappointment.

I've never tried to start a new church. I was born too tired for that. But my own church-burnt friends and I are still desperately trying to show God's acceptance to one another and our children, trying to live out God's love to the world, trying to find a way for people who claim to represent Jesus the Christ to embody God's justice, gentleness, and attention to human bodies, as he did. We're scraping along even as it's becoming clearer and clearer that church affiliation and embodiment of God aren't always synonymous.

## Who's in the Pews, Pew?

Participation in religious organizations—usually connected to local churches, temples, synagogues, or mosques—is a fascinating piece of social data.

The Pew Religious Landscape Survey asks participants to rate the importance they place on religious identity, as well as how frequently they study sacred texts, pray, meditate, and attend some kind of religious gathering. Religion journalists comb through reports from Pew, The Public Religion Research Institute, Gallup, and Lifeway Research looking for meaning in the subtle shifts in religious participation.

For example, in the past few years, the statistical decline in mainstream Protestant church attendance (even pre-pandemic) and the rise of nonreligious identification has fueled questions of whether Christianity is somehow under threat, even as evangelicals, Catholics, and all kinds of Protestants occupy high offices throughout the land. Editorials are written, sermons are preached, fundraising letters are drafted based on these speculations.

In some ways the obsession is merited. Participation in religious communities, including regular attendance to religious services, seems to correlate with more firm belief, at least belief in the existence of God. It certainly indicates how much influence formal religious organizations have on the country. But beyond that, there are a few subgroups not easily picked up by surveys, and these nonetheless shape religion as we know it. Just as the *Anna Karenina* principle tells us—on page one of Leo Tolstoy's classic novel—"Happy families are all alike; every unhappy family is unhappy in its own way." Happy worshipers align with their religious communities enough to claim the identity, beliefs, and ethics of the community. Unhappy worshipers have their own mix of angst about the whole thing.

The recent rise in the "none" religious affiliation may simply be a sign that it is now socially acceptable to admit the internal reality many have been living for far longer. In other words, the "nones" used to be in church on Sunday morning. I suspect some people still do this. A lot of people would have divorced the church a long time ago, but they're staying together for the kids. I've been surprised by the number of parents I meet who go to services despite not really believing the mystical, spiritual, or strictest moral teachings. They feel they've outgrown the need for religion, but they want their kids to grow up with regular exposure to it. They don't like the way a lot of religious people behave, and they don't feel beholden to the rules of their religious upbringing, but there's one thing or another about connection to religious community that they don't want their kids to miss.

Sometimes this is me. Sometimes I go to church because I want my kids to know that we're not the only people in the world who talk about Jesus, and I want them to have access to the language of an historic faith.

Some want their kids raised around "good people," which is endlessly ironic to me, because the people you find in church are a big reason why so many people are in another nuanced subcategory: the people who dislike the institution of the church but maintain at least the basic spirituality of their religion. These people may not yet be statistically significant, and their doubts and uncertainties stemming from a break with religious authority make it difficult to locate them on a survey. But they are there, searching for an embodiment of God. Some are finding God embodied in community organizations and support groups, service and advocacy. I know more than one person who describes Al Anon, Alcoholics Anonymous, or Celebrate Recovery as their connection to God's people. Some find transcendent worship in nature, and communion in their hiking group. Others are just drifting from church to church, hoping for the best.

Some are discussing Anne Lamott and Richard Rohr at the park on Sunday morning with one or two other families in the same predicament, wondering whether this counts as church, even though all the kids have done is climb on the play structure. As you can tell from the specificity of that last sentence, this is also me sometimes. Sometimes I need a break. Sometimes I wonder if the break is a breakup.

In some ways, organized gatherings of religious people are such easy things to let go of.

It's easy to stop hauling everyone's asses away from sleep, toys, or phone calls, sitting through a lecture you only listen to between half and three-quarters of the time, and making awkward chitchat with people whose names you know you're supposed to remember. It's easy to step away from constant, uncompensated requests for your "time, treasure, and talents." It's easy to remove yourself from the scrutiny, social hierarchies, and the politics inevitably found whenever two or more are gathered. It's easy to dissociate from racist, classist, misogynist, or bigoted groups claiming to follow the Way of the same *Middle Eastern mystic* as you. It's easy to come up for air after suffering under manipulative, narcissistic leadership.

But in other ways, letting go feels impossible.

It's difficult to lose that weekly touchpoint with your faith, or what's left of it. It's difficult to turn your back on an institution from which you derived a sense of purpose or identity. Whether you're leaving a local institution, or the idea of institutional religion, it's tough. It's difficult to go without regular encounters with the people who shared your purpose and identity, some of whom had known you for years, maybe even your whole life. It's difficult to explain what you believe now, and how it's different from what it was then. It's difficult to take control of your own spirituality, and to discern where God is moving through, between, and among people.

Now, by this point in the book, we know what's next. What makes the complication even stickier? Kids. Will you take your children to a regular weekly religious gathering or not? Will you encourage them to take communion or participate in vacation Bible school or youth group? What about baptism? (We know how tied up in knots I was about that.)

Social scientists tell us affiliation with a religious community has positive effects on young people and their mental health— it's one of the Search Institute's developmental assets. But that obviously doesn't mean that every religious community will have a positive mental health effect—and all God's exvangelicals

161

said, "Amen." For those of us struggling with the church and its teachings we must ask ourselves, constantly: Where is my child to see God embodied in people? In this children's ministry? This volunteer event? This fellowship group? Or is there something here that will lead them away from God? Are they being taught shame and legalism? Are they being taught that God hates certain people?

I believe our kids need embodied spirituality—in service, generosity, healing, repair, acceptance, and connection. They need to see it embodied so they can practice embodying it for others. As much as I want my kids to see and experience community based in God's love and to learn to live that way in the world, I truly question whether most institutional churches are the best place for that—because if there are so many people for whom it has not been, can it be for any of us?

## The Family of God

Even though she'd just sat through my lecture on "the gospel lived in the female body," it wasn't sex or sexuality that led Christina to find me, sitting beside a pool in a Florida conference center. It was the eternal destiny of her father, who had died a Buddhist.

I groan internally at how I probably answered Christina's questions that day by the pool. Her earnest face longing for a theological reconciliation between the destiny of the father she adored and the teachings of a church that had become central to her world. I didn't give her that reconciliation. Even if I'd wanted to, I couldn't risk getting caught dispensing poolside heresy. Whatever dissatisfaction she was harboring, I remember being impressed that she hung in there with the ministry.

She was a new Christian, completely smitten with this community she'd found through the University of Arizona chapter of Reformed University Fellowship, the college ministry of the

Presbyterian Church in America. She was one of those students college ministers dream will come through their doors. She was a leader, an enthusiast, and better yet, she had the kind of unchurched background that makes ministers feel like they are having an impact. Christina was the kind of kid we would have put in a newsletter, proof that RUF was fulfilling its goal not just to support Christian kids, but to build God's kingdom by getting kids connected to local churches.

Not only did she love RUF, but Christina dove headfirst into supporting a local Presbyterian church in Tucson. She hadn't been raised in church, but at a critical stage in her growing up, going from college into early adulthood, the church was her home.

Christina and I stayed loosely in touch on social media, the way our generation does, watching from afar for little signs to mark each other's journeys, reaching out through the virtual darkness to leave a little "like," a little affirmation. I liked when she married a petite woman with long dark hair and artful tattoos. Christina wore French braids and a bow tie for their Instagram-perfect cliffside wedding, drenched in hazy sunset hues. She liked when I posted something LGBTQIA-affirming on Facebook.

Those little "likes," those social media nods, mean a lot to people evolving in their faith. Because the stuff we post gets plenty of the other kind of feedback too. Our social media networks weren't built to absorb the shock. They were built for blowback. We build our social networks on agreement, and disagreement threatens the infrastructure. Not unlike local churches, in that regard.

Christina told me coming out as queer on Facebook, shortly after college, had ultimately ended her relationship with her church, long before those gorgeous wedding photos on Instagram were ever taken. Her willingness to subscribe to the various doctrines of the church had been strained by its condemning her father to hell, something I sadly took part in with whatever answer I'd given her back in college. But she continued to work in the church nursery, and her relationships with leadership and prominent families continued. Community was what had drawn her to church in the first place, not doctrine. She'd gone all in because she loved the people, admired their faith, and wanted to learn from them how to raise a loving family.

For as long as Christina's sexuality was kept private, whatever people suspected, they continued to treat her like a member of the community. After coming out on social media, she told me, "nobody really talked to me again." She has one or two friends from that time who remained supportive. She reconnected to another through the foster care community in Tucson when she and her wife were in the process of fostering and adopting their sons. By the time Christina came out publicly, she'd built up a new community outside the church, and while the "shunning" was painful, she had somewhere else to turn, which not everyone has. She feels lucky in that regard.

Because she was older and had come to the church with many of her own thoughts fully formed, she didn't waste too much time trying desperately to make the church accept her. "Maybe my questioning my beliefs was subconsciously setting myself up for dropping this big bomb on people," she mused as we spoke on the phone. "Maybe I was distancing myself." Now, as a mother of two boys and a girl, she wants to make sure they have the rhythms and community she found through the church. But she also wants them to have the acceptance she didn't have.

Many faiths have gone into her boys' spiritual inheritance. Christina's father was Buddhist, her stepmom is Catholic, as were her grandmothers, her stepdad is Jewish, and her mom is not religious. She and her wife feel free to make their spirituality as inclusive as their family, with a community to match. So instead of looking for a building full of people connected by a single belief system, she's building their "church" through their school and the autism support network she's been building for one of her kids—she's starting with people who are devoted to her family and their flourishing, and building from there. Maybe one day it will include an inclusive, liberal-minded church, maybe not.

Christina, I have no doubt, will find the community she's looking for. She will find the God who is love embodied in a place where she and her family are accepted and supported.

## "Aperfect" Church

Most recently, we found God embodied by the people in a little Anglican church in San Antonio, but we will never be enrolled or avowed members of it or any church. We will give, serve, and participate freely, and when we go we will do so freely.

As I write this, we are wrestling with some doctrinal stances of the church, particularly around the LGBTQIA community, as we realize there's not as much openness as we had thought there might be. I'm no longer in a place where I can give money and support to places that don't affirm those members of God's family. At the same time, there are some people in that church who need to feel the hands and feet of God, and I cannot simply walk away.

This is why we keep our consciences free when it comes to church membership.

While I see the ways the New Testament describes Christianity as a communal faith, and the encouragement to "bear with one another" in Paul's letters to churches implies commitment, I don't think that membership vows or rolls are necessarily part of that. The New Testament Christians also didn't have our predicament—with centuries of schism, dogma, and abuse of power to consider when choosing from the thousands of local congregations in our cities. The authority structures of the institutions were not then what they are now, and it certainly hadn't been co-opted by political and financial power the way the church has in the United States. Many organizations that start out as churches can over time, because of the way we structure modern churches, become more like clubs or businesses.

I don't believe God is embodied in every 501(c)(3) religious entity just because a certain name is spoken or a certain dogma is maintained. Nor do I believe those things are necessary—the name, the dogma, or the nonprofit status—for God to show up in people. Inside or outside the institutional church, God will never be embodied perfectly, but I choose to believe the Spirit of God is filling in the gaps. Our faith, and our children's faith, can flourish in imperfect places—or "aperfect" places, those that aren't trying to be the perfect church, or even a church at all.

We can share faith and fellowship with our friends and family, service organizations, teams, and support groups. If that's really where God is showing up, and our kids see it and share in it in explicitly spiritual ways, what are they missing? I know the seminary answer for what they are missing: the means of grace. Particularly the sacraments and teaching of the word. But if you're at the point where you seriously doubt the institutional church's exclusive authority to dispense God's grace, then obviously the church's doctrine of the means of grace probably means very little to you. If the institutional churches available to you aren't embodying God, if they are hateful and abusive places, I'd argue they can serve all the wine and crackers they want, but it's not grace. They can exposit all the Greek they want, but it's not grace.

If that's you—fully alienated from the institutional church—you'd probably experience God's grace more in fellowship, encouragement, nonchurchy prayer, maybe even some biblical or theological discussion, maybe musing together on the nature of God and love. This all sounds like it requires marijuana. It doesn't—but I'm not saying that wouldn't make it more fun.

I do want to put one qualifier on this: Not every group of people I like can be a faith community. I'm a spiritual being. You're a spiritual being. Our kids are spiritual beings. For a while during my deepest alienation from the local church, my most intimate friendships were with people I loved, and we shared great thoughts together, but they were not comfortable discussing matters of faith. I needed to be around people who could discuss faith, even if they weren't my best friends. Plus, I like communion as a means of grace even though the "teaching of the word" usually puts me in a bad mood. Thus I regularly find myself in church, but uncomfortable. There are no perfect churches, and I don't know any churches that have embraced aperfection—a total rejection of certainty and rightness as the goal—so I usually hang out in imperfect churches, looking for the other squirmers.

Sometimes hanging in there with an imperfect church is worth the extra work it creates. If we continue to go to a church where the children are taught, probably in Sunday School, things that, while not harmful, are not as nuanced as we'd like, it's OK to set the record straight at home. We can then explain that even when we disagree—it's probably going to be about creation timelines and Jonah—we can all still show God's love to one another and the world. It's probably OK if they want to go to youth group because their friends are there, but you might want to debrief after the purity talks. Make sure they know no one is a used band aid or a petal-less rose in God's eyes. Or just have them skip that one.

Of course, I understand the internal impulse to say "No! My children will go nowhere near any of that! They will never come within one hundred yards of anyone who believes these things!" We want to protect our kids from being shamed by people who believe certain things we abhor. But for me, ironically, that is actually more related to my bad habits of certainty than to my desire to live freely in the spirit. One of the unfortunate things about being raised in absolutism is that we can often turn our rejection into absolute rejection. I go through seasons of this regularly. They are lonely.

God's people can be about the business of loving in all those quirky, imperfect places, but we need to be clear about the difference between imperfect and destructive. The difference between one legalistic purity talk and a culture of sin-hunting and judg-ment. The difference between uninterrogated seven-day creation-ism and militant framing of science as "anti-God." The difference between conflict and abuse. Too often, I think, the truth of "no perfect church" is used by leaders and loyalists to justify abuse and destructiveness. The act of leaving a destructive community is an act of faith, and it is also useful to our children's understanding of what it means to embody God. Don't waste it. When you have to part ways with a church or a group of people because their teach-ing or actions are working against the purposes of God—meaning you find out your church is fundamentally racist, or something similar—that discussion is worth having with your kids in a devel-opmentally appropriate way. It's OK to explain to your kids, "We are looking for a place where Black people are seen and heard, because God sees and hears Black people" or, "We want to make sure that we are only giving money and time to organizations that welcome immigrants the way God's people have always been told to do." Or, for heaven's sake, "We need to be in a community that values our family the way God does."

It's actually pretty good accountability: Would I want to explain to my kids why we are leaving this community? Would I want to explain to them why we are staying? Would my reasons for leaving or staying line up with the values I'm trying to impart?

Searching is not a bad faith tradition to pass on to our kids. It's the tradition of the pilgrims and the mystics and in some ways even the prophets and reformers—people who know God well enough to look around and go, "This ain't it." Or at least, "There's gotta be more than this." People who took Jesus at his word when he said, in his mysterious way, "Seek and you will find."

Chapter 11

# Spanks for Your Soul

Oh I feel it coming back again
Like a rollin' thunder chasing the wind
Forces pullin' from the center of the earth again
I can feel it.

—Live, "Lightning Crashes"

If you really want to send me into a parenting tailspin, tell me
I'm disciplining my kids all wrong.

Tell me I should be more harsh, or they'll lack secure boundaries and end up in prison.

Tell me I should not be so harsh, or they'll be laden with shame and end up in prison.

I am an easy mark for this kind of torture because I grew up hearing that how a parent disciplines their child is the most important factor in how the child "turns out." (At what age someone has officially "turned out" I don't know. Every decade seems to present new opportunities for the wheels to come off.)

Whether or not anyone explicitly said this I don't know, but the overarching message was very strong: Discipline was how you turned a natural born sinner into a God-fearing contributor to society. It was better to err on the side of severity. Spanking was the most reliable. My mom likes to say that she rarely had to

169

spank me because I would repent if she just looked at me sternly. That's probably true; I'm a total people pleaser who was probably always going to end up in a middle-class job with lots of rules, voting Democratic because I like regulations. My sister, who endured tons of spankings, however, turned out to be a tattoo artist who makes pot gummies and votes Democratic because Republicans are assholes. In other words, spank or don't spank, you could still be raising a Democrat.

My parents did not spank me often as a child, but they made up for it in one, colossal grand finale when I was fifteen. Yes, years, not months. It was the week before spring break during my freshman year of high school. I was experiencing some success in the social market and felt ready to cash it in: I was throwing a party.

My social success, however, was not being equally enjoyed by all. It caught my mom in that miserable shuttle-driver phase of parenthood, and I was *not* interested in the express shuttle. I wanted a black car charter service. I wanted to be chauffeured to parties, to meals after the games, and to friends' houses. My "requests" were probably similar in tone to what airline customer service reps hear all day, every day. I was a varsity athlete, well on my way to dating an upperclassman, and regularly hanging out with whatever passed for "the cool kids" at my tiny Christian high school. I was insufferable, no doubt. Of course, internally I agonized over my desire to appear autonomous, my insatiable fear of missing out, and my lack of a driver's license constantly reminding my older, cooler friends what a baby I was. Also, my priorities were shifting. Developmentally, the opinions of my friends were starting to outweigh the opinions of my parents. I was regularly obnoxious toward my mom when she didn't want to drive me to wherever my friends would be. I wanted to run with the pack, not keep peace in the den.

At some point, apparently, my mom had taken all she could. On the Friday before spring break, one week before my party,

I had the phone in hand, dial tone rushing me along, when my mom asked me what I was doing. I told her I was calling a friend to plan something for the party, and she told me to hang up and go talk to my dad. "Why?" I asked. My trouble radar was not yet going off, probably because my brain was in what my therapist calls "reward." The excitement of the party had me blind to my surroundings. "Just please go talk to him," she said, not making eye contact, "Before you make any more plans."

That was enough to punch through the glass and pull the alarm. Something unpleasant was coming. Really unpleasant. I was no longer in "reward" but in what my therapist calls "threat." My brain now solely focused on figuring out what terrible thing was about to happen. As a teenager in threat mode, I responded . . . poorly.

"Oh my God, mother, *what is it?*" I snapped, dial tone still humming in my hand. The fact that I used the Lord's name in vain was a sign of just how far gone I was and did not help my case.

My mom didn't answer, she just sent me to my dad. I hate that I snapped at her like that, I really do, over two decades later. I'm a weary mom myself now, and I know how exhausting these conversations can be. I don't blame her for not wanting to get into it with me. At the time, though, it felt like she was refusing to prepare me. Like she was sending me in blind. To my parents it was obvious—I had it coming. To me, what happened next came out of nowhere. When the brain is in reward—which mine had been most of the time that spring—we don't hear ourselves. I had been brain deaf to the bratty pattern and the tension in its wake.

That was about to change.

My dad was waiting for me, Bible in hand, when I entered their room. For what seemed like an hour, but which was probably only about ten minutes, he read me a bunch of Scripture about children honoring their parents and told me how awful I'd been lately. He was totally right; I could see that once I was no longer in reward. I'd been tyrannical and disrespectful and rude, and I was devastated.

By the time he got to the consequence, I was already miserable. I was sick to my stomach, longing to apologize to my mother, feeling my status as "the perfect daughter" slipping away. I was the kid who only needed a stern look to repent, and here I was getting the "full Moses" (similar to a full Nelson in wrestling, but using the law of God instead of arms). I was crying, thinking that the lecture was the punishment for my imperious behavior. Oh no. It was only the preamble. The wind-up. The actual consequence: I would be grounded for all of spring break. I was to cancel the party.

Obviously, what composure was left fell apart. The reasons I crumbled were complicated and incredibly on brand for my particular pathologies, before and since.

I cried because of the party.

I cried because I was caught off guard.

I cried because I hated the way he was talking to me.

I cried because I was afraid I wasn't a good daughter anymore.

I tried to make the case for proportionality. For a kid who never got in trouble, who never made less than an A, I argued that it was overkill to take away my entire spring break and the party on which I was staking all my social capital. In a moment of compassion, my dad offered me an alternative. I could keep the party and spring break if I took two "licks" instead. (Licks, for those of you who were not raised by football players, are spankings.) Tears dried. It was a deal.

He went to the back of the house where our dog had commandeered some construction materials from a recent home renovation. When he came back, we looked at each other across the wide, thin piece of wood siding with chipping paint and Great Dane tooth marks. My eyes were swollen, but no longer crying. His eyes were grieved, like he was looking for a way out of this. He tried to get me to reconsider. But no way, I was all in. I'd overdosed on humiliation that night, my brain was addled with adrenaline and my throat was raw from crying, but I was winning back my party. In fact, it was still seven days away, so I might even be able to sit down by then.

The lava of panic and shame had cooled to dark igneous anger.

I didn't cry anymore that night. Not even when I got the licks, which hurt like hell and echoed through the house. Not when my dad threw the board to the ground and hugged me tightly, clearly in that moment hating what he felt were his obligations as a parent.

Now look, that story is intense, and, yes, it's very tempting to camp out on all the things I wish my parents had done differently. But now I'm a parent, and I understand a few things.

I understand how frustrating it is when your kids behave like Veruca Salt from *Willy Wonka and the Chocolate Factory*. I also know that most parents have absorbed some version of Veruca's Oompa Loompa song from the Gene Wilder movie adaptation:

> Who do you blame when your kid is a brat?
> . . .
> Blaming the kids is a lie and a shame
> You know exactly who's to blame
> The mother and the father.

Layered on top of frustration and fear was family tradition. Corporal punishment played a huge role in my family's mythology. Whuppins with paddles and wooden spoons were all regular features of family lore.

Layered on top of family tradition was the culture of the 1980s, 1990s, and 2000s. In a world that felt inundated with drugs, rebellion, punk rock, and STDs, keeping kids in line felt gravely consequential. There was no room for experimenting with all this mental health psychobabble.

Layered on top of cultural anxiety was religion. "He who spares his rod hates his son," was in the Bible (Prov. 13:24, NKJV).

God had told us how to avoid the aforementioned pitfalls: Use the rod. In my house, "disrespect" was the gravest of all offenses, because it challenged the authority of our parents, who represented God. Challenging God's authority was the first step toward apostasy. My dad's tortured face when administering the licks was that of a man making a sacrifice, doing something he believed he had to do because my soul was on the line.

## Sultans of Swat

For my parents, James Dobson and his ilk were the salesmen of spanking, this must-have for moral formation, this ShamWoW! of child rearing. Wash the disobedience away. Dry a lie. Polish those manners. Obviously they didn't invent spanking. They just repackaged it and sold it to a new generation of anxious parents, who were being told that AIDS and crack were going to steal their babies if they tried any of this psychobabble the atheist "child development experts" were peddling.

In some ways, spanking is traditional and thus feels reliable. Corporal punishment transcends cultures and religions and generations. However, the same could be said at one time of putting leeches on swelling, asbestos in walls, and lead in pipes. Parents have always spanked, kids have always bullied, men have always said sexually inappropriate things to women. You can't justify human behavior solely on its persistence.

But Dobson's new spankings were less rustic and crude than the whuppins doled out in the 1950s and 1960s, the ones our parents had endured. Spankings could be administered in love, in part because pain was seen in nature. Pain was the natural consequence of transgression, Dobson said. Parents were, I suppose, forces of nature. "Corporal punishment, when used lovingly and properly, is beneficial to a child because it is in harmony with nature itself," Dobson wrote in a 2014 article on his website.[1]

I know a lot of parents who would part with Dobson on just about everything but still believe that a controlled, lovingly dispensed swat on the bum is a clear and healthy way to set a boundary, especially with pre-rational children. I've also seen scholarship saying corporal punishment of any kind, no matter how judiciously applied, is not helpful. I've moderated panels of experts who urge parents, schools, and local governments to address generational cycles of domestic abuse, and most experts on those panels come out hard against any form of spanking.

Societally we focus a lot on spanking, I think, because it seems to draw such a line between barbarism and civility, or, seen from the other perspective, between parents who are serious about discipline and those who are wishy-washy. But spanking isn't the issue behind the issue. Spank or don't spank, you can still raise healthy kids. Spank or don't spank, you can still raise emotionally crippled kids. The issue behind the issue is authority—the right to exercise power. What kind of power do those in authority have? How do they exercise it? What are the consequences?

One of the regular features of Dobsonesque parenting is the idea of parents and children as opposing forces. It frames parenting as a series of battles that a parent must win to maintain authority from would-be usurpers. This way of seeing the world and our children did not come out of nowhere.

## Whupping Them into Shape

The abuses wrought by authoritarianism were disturbingly underscored in the summer of 2021 when news broke that mass graves had been discovered near former Indian Residential Schools in Saskatchewan and British Columbia, Canada, each holding between two hundred and six hundred bodies of First Nations adults and children. Many likely died of the diseases common in the schools, the reports said, not from direct beatings, but the disregard for human life at the nexus of racism, violence, and obedience was broadcast to the world. The excavation of the graves was part of the ongoing effort to expose the harm done to First Nations as colonists attempted to establish and exercise authority, not only during the initial conquests of land and resources, but during the continued effort to bring indigenous people into submission.

When the Canadian government commissioned a Truth and Reconciliation Commission in 2015 to address the harm done by the residential schools, one of the calls to action was the repeal of Section 43 of Canada's Criminal Code, the government's authority to inflict corporal punishment. A collection of theologians, educators, and scholars came together to create a philosophical framework for repeal, a series of essays published together under the title *Decolonizing Discipline: Children, Corporal Punishment, Christian Theologies, and Reconciliation*. The Indian Residential Schools were rooted first and foremost in colonialist racism, which the various scholars acknowledge from the get-go. However, they point out the ways theological beliefs about discipline shaped the particular ways racism played out for those children.

Within the hierarchies of church and family, professor Valerie Michaelson writes that obedience is the primary tool of spiritual development for children. "Without learning to submit to parents or others in authority, the argument goes, children will not learn to submit to God."[2] Submission to authority is the means of salvation, especially for women and children. Now embed this belief in a culture wherein physical and psychological violence are regularly used to bring enemies into submission.

While modern eyes look back on the residential schools, which also operated in the United States, as particularly barbaric, we have not fully abandoned their ethos. The racially disproportionate use of suspension and expulsion in schools, and solitary confinement in prisons—and prisons in general—prove that we still operate at that nexus, even when the violence is psychological.

But even separate from racism or colonial contexts, the emphasis on submission at any cost stays with us. I think we lose the ability to discern when we want submission because we're tired of the crap (and kids, let's be real, can dole out some crap), and when we want submission because we're trying to save their souls. With the authority chain going straight from us to God, you don't really have to discern. The benefit to them isn't the particular behavior or privilege in question. Submission itself, the act of losing the battle, is supposedly the spiritual benefit.

Authoritarianism isn't a tool in our toolbox, it's a culture and belief system. We don't know how to see conflict—even conflict with our own kids—as anything other than a battle, a challenge, something we must conquer by any means necessary. *For their own good.* We may not beat our kids, but do we yell, berate, shame, and punish? On my worst days, I take away toys, I shout, I arbitrarily revoke privileges. Why do I do it? What am I so afraid of that I am willing to inflict harm on my children in order to avoid it? From what, exactly am I trying to save them?

You don't have to believe in literal hell to fret over the long-term consequences of your kids' behavior.

## Developmentally Appropriate Sins

Before we even get to the "how" of dealing with kids' behavior, I think first we need to pour a little water on the flames of alarm.

The teaching that bad behavior is the sign of a rebellious soul is so deep in my bones that even as I pledge to never spank or shame my kids, even as I seriously doubt concepts like eternal damnation, I still panic when they get in trouble at school. I still fear not only earthly consequences, like jail, but also a corruption of their spirits. The flames of alarm may only be a stubborn ember in my motherly heart, but throw some kindling on them—a parent-teacher conference, a public meltdown, a fed-up babysitter—and the flames of alarm become a forest fire of anxiety and moral panic.

I signed up for a Mental Health First Aid course in a moment of such panic, after reading about the wave of youth mental health crises sweeping the globe as a result of the COVID-19 pandemic. The Mental Health First Aid course, which I eventually wrote about for *The 74 Million* and *The Texas Tribune*, was helpful in the face of the immediate crisis, but it was also helpful in another way. The course spelled out the difference between mental health challenges and ordinary childhood development. It never once mentioned "unacceptable behaviors" or "spiritual dangers." It removed the morally loaded interpretations, and suddenly raising kids seemed so much less fiery.

Pulling away from family happens on a biological timer. It's not rebellion.

Talking back or brooding is part of a hormonal surge that allows teens to make decisions independent of their parents, to own their opinions, beliefs, and *faith*. It's not rebellion.

Risky behaviors happen as the prefrontal cortex, where good decisions are made, lags behind curiosity, confidence, and passion. It's not rebellion.

Put in this context, raising kids seems more predictable, less dire. Adolescents push back on our authority because they have to *learn* to live without us. Independence doesn't just happen without practice. Boundaries around these developmentally appropriate behaviors are good and helpful, mental health professionals say. One of the great benefits of boundary-testing (kids' forte from day one) is the reassurance that boundaries exist.

Apparently maintaining a boundary can be done without punishment, or so I'm told. I'm horrible at this, but I cannot tell you how badly I want to be good at it. I default to consequences and quick control so often. As a Christian and an American, I've only ever seen a punitive approach to deterrence—make the consequences so scary they won't risk it. This is the failed strategy on immigration, the war on drugs, and numerous other "law-and-order" policies the American government has adopted. It's the essence of purity culture, which makes impurity sound like a death wish. It's the heart of corporal punishment, and the heart of the numerous toys I've taken away as various "consequences."

And it doesn't work. We have never been able to scare people into abiding by the law. That's why the jails are full, the immigration courts are backed up, and my kids are still throwing things.

Now, I can hear the "what about" brewing: What about running out into traffic? Should we just let our children run into traffic while we reason with them or listen to their feelings about traffic? No. Obviously, you run out there and scoop them up, and figure out the best way to keep them from doing that again. You use your power to protect them. But that's the point: Our children's pushback over wearing socks or going to bed or breaking curfew is *not the same as running into traffic*. It's not the same as running into literal traffic *or* running into traffic as a metaphor for spiritual peril. Being taught that our children's eternal destiny depends on our ability to discipline them has left a generation of parents unable to tell the difference.

Youth-oriented Mental Health First Aid helped me create some categories. It also raised another important point lost in the spank-them-to-heaven discourse: If the behavior isn't part of typical development—if they suddenly withdraw from both friends and family, cry or brood nonstop with little provocation, harm themselves or others, use drugs habitually—then it is a sign something is wrong. The child is in distress.

We were raised believing that sin is the bad things you do because you are sinful. You act bad because you have badness in your heart. You brood because you are ungrateful. You steal because you feel entitled. You bark orders at your mom because you believe you are the center of the universe. Actually, mental health professionals tell us, most of the time trouble outside signals hurt inside, not corruption. So the shame and pain of harsh punishment can actually backfire. Punishing someone who is acting out of pain or alienation doesn't fix the problem.

We know this. Even if it fixes the behavior, the underlying issue will create other problems. Addiction, disordered eating, and self-harm can all happen while minding your manners.

If we aren't willing to talk to our kids about how they feel, what they are worried about, where they feel unseen, unheard, and misunderstood, and what they wish was different about their life, then we are not going to be able to effectively address their hurtful words and destructive behaviors. We have to be willing to take their feedback on our behavior before they'll listen to our feedback on theirs.[3]

## Training Up a Child

As I discussed in chapter 6, on hell, restorative justice aligns with *shalom*. It addresses the best of what we want for our kids, regardless of where we are on sin and judgment. Good brain science is helpful as we try to help our children manage themselves and contribute to the world, but so is a restorative worldview.

In *Decolonizing Discipline,* the authors have restoration in mind. They don't leave us with a mere treatise on why corporal punishment is bad. They don't suggest that the First Nations who were subjected to colonization in the residential schools now be subjected to Western counseling and psychology. They suggest an alternative for repair in First Nations communities based on First Nations culture.

Outside the deep, place-based spirituality of First Nations people, some of this learning isn't possible. A white parent in a fully Euro-modern society isn't going to be able to crack open *Decolonizing Discipline*, read psychologist Martin Brokenleg's essay, "The Circle of Courage: Raising Respectful, Responsible Children through Indigenous Child Rearing Practices" and start doing it. Nor should she, really, because that sort of easy adoption could end with a white Instagram influencer publishing a book about how she's raising her kids with a carefully curated set of (highly photogenic) indigenous practices. Learning child rearing practices from other cultures should not be about the pursuit of perfection or optimizing our own children's lifestyles. Brokenleg's focus is doing what is best for indigenous children based on their culture, and that is enough.

At the same time, if we acknowledge the child-rearing culture we have inherited is bent on raising more colonizers, conquerors, and perfectionists, and that it's hurting our kids, then we might be well advised to observe the wisdom of other cultures, especially if the wisdom they draw, as Brokenleg explains, is derived from the earth we share.

He opens his essay explaining how his people, the Lakota, learned about the child's role in the community from buffalo herds—the animals they depended on for survival. When threatened, he writes, the herd forms three concentric rings of defense based on both vulnerability and preserving the future of the herd. The outer ring of adult males are the strongest and most expendable, the middle ring are the female adults who, while strong, are essential to building up the herd after loss, and the inner ring is the young—the future of the herd. Their place in the herd is not only defined by their vulnerability, but their importance. Importance, however, does not mean that they are expected to serve on the outer ring before they are ready.[4] The process of becoming ready is marked by four things, Brokenleg writes: belonging, mastery, independence, and generosity. Together they form what he calls "The Circle of Courage."

My best and highest commendation to you is to just go read this essay. If you do that, you can skip the next few paragraphs. I cannot do it justice, but if you want more of a preview, I'm going to attempt to summarize some of what he says—and I do so with Brokenleg's blessing. But I promise you, this summary is not a substitute for the real thing. The essay is that good.

*Belonging*, he writes, involves a kinship to the entire community and the earth. The child must see themselves as not just part of a nuclear family, but as part of a people and part of the natural world. They have a role to play that includes both nurturing and being nurtured.

*Mastery* is about both external and internal skills, honed through both natural and adult-provided practice. No one is expected to perform above their developmental age, either in school or life skills or in emotional regulation. At the same time, the joy they get through progress, when it is pointed out to them, spurs them forward. Teaching younger children enhances connection and shows the older child how far they have come in their mastery. We adults can remark on the progress, present next steps, and restrain ourselves from the temptation to intervene when mastery is not happening fast enough for our perfectionistic timelines.

Because the Lakota believe that resilience comes from internal power, Brokenleg writes, the goal of *independence* is getting a child to the point where adults are no longer needed for decision-making, behavioral oversight, or emotional regulation. In this pursuit, he says, "discipline and punishment are so antithetical they cannot exist at the same time."[5]

Discipline is about teaching, putting more and more inside the child so that they will have more to draw on. Punishment is about controlling the outside, and it will always depend on who is enforcing the rules from the outside. Discipline requires lots of listening from the adult side, Brokenleg explains. Listening implies that the child's emotions, perceptions, and thoughts on the matter are crucial to the response. When the emotions are processed and the child is ready to engage their rational brain, he writes, "Explanations are carefully used so that children understand their own dignity and responsibilities."[6]

All of this culminates in *generosity*—the giving and receiving of kindness, sustenance, and nurture. It is about making sure that everyone has what they need, and about trusting that you will have what you need.

As I was reading the essay, underlining like a fiend and yelling, "You have to read this!" to my husband in the next room, I have to admit that my heart sank when I got to generosity. It reminded me that so much more needs to change if we really want to change the way we raise our kids.

Brokenleg's essay isn't like the parenting books that can be mined for information, helpful hints, and tools. It's a holistic vision inherently absent from our perfectionist culture. It is absent because colonial powers wanted it to be absent and because restoration has never been completed. We had the chance to learn from the First Nations, to adapt as newcomers, and we chose to eradicate and replace instead.

As I read Brokenleg's essay, my heart yearned for this kind of holistic heart-knowing for my kids, and yet I realized that cultural change isn't just about how we resolve conflict. You cannot create this kind of integrated, holistic experience only when dealing with thrown toys, tantrums, broken curfews, or shoplifting.

When I was having my babies, everyone was reading books about how to raise their kids like the French or the Scandinavians do. This is not problematic in the same way as appropriating indigenous child-rearing. The same power imbalance does not exist between Europeans and white Americans. But for Americans, trying to emulate European baby-raising bumps into one similar problem: They will have a very difficult time raising American kids to eat like French kids because French food culture is different from American food culture. Unless you eat like a French person, your kids are probably not going to either, and one step outside your kitchen will put the whole enterprise to the test. You cannot raise Scandinavian kids in a society with no social safety net, because having a social safety net allows Scandinavians to raise their kids the way they do. If college is paid for, the college rat race, which dictates so much of American childhood, looks different.

FORKS IN THE ROAD

If we want to adopt child-rearing practices from other cultures, we have to adopt the worldview of other cultures. We have to stop insisting that our way is best and consider all the ways that our relationship to land, culture, economy, and body go hand in hand with how we discipline our kids.

## The Decolonization of Mary Catherine

Mary Catherine knew she didn't want to discipline her son the way she had been disciplined as a child—discipline so harsh that eventually Child Protective Services got involved. But no matter how much she tried, she still found herself threatening to spank her son. It was the only way she had ever seen adults handle the inevitable frustrations of raising children.

To reverse the habits she had been given by a lifetime of hierarchical gender roles in her family and her charismatic church, Mary Catherine knew she was going to have to relearn more than just discipline strategies. "I had to unpack the ways in which religion played a role in some toxic beliefs i.e. misogyny/patriarchy, homophobia, colonization and that influenced the way I parented. Keep the good but ditch the bad," she said. First, she had to leave the pastor's son who had gotten her pregnant and then eloped with her at twenty-one. Next, she needed new ideas. New outlooks. New opportunities. She enrolled at a local university and began working toward a degree in the sociology of religion. There she started to learn about her own indigenous roots. "That's changed the way I view the Christianity I was raised with," Mary Catherine said. "I felt like I had to dig into a humans-first culture in order to feel a sense of pride and self esteem."[7]

As a Latina woman, she has inherited a dual past: She has a genetic and spiritual inheritance from indigenous peoples, but family ties to the complicated European colonial history shared by many in Latin America and the Southwestern United States. Indigenous philosophy was giving her pride, changing the way she saw the world, but she still had to do the day-to-day as a young, single mom. And it was lonely. Like many of us, her mind was growing and changing, but the old fears and habits still shook her confidence, particularly when it came to parenting.

Mary Catherine had a hard time relating to "traditional route" moms, she said, largely because she had been raised to believe that their lives were somehow superior to the path she was now forging. "In a lot of ways it was self-sabotaging. I was isolating myself," Mary Catherine said. "I felt judged already." Again, as a single mom trying to recover from a lifetime of being dominated, Mary Catherine found that her indigenous roots came to her rescue. After being raised to be a "good wife" and to submit to authority, even when it was abusive, this self-described "lost soul" found hope in the matriarchal systems of the indigenous people. It gave her dignity as a mother and comfort as a member of the "village."

Indigenous children are parented by the whole community, and Mary Catherine needed exactly that. Her son still needed to be parented; he still needed boundaries and instruction and role models. Her female friends took on new importance as "elders" for her son. She filled her village with people who affirmed her, who did not raise an eyebrow at her decisions not to spank or shame.

Meanwhile, her son was enrolled in Catholic school, the best option she could afford for preschool. He was coming home with some of the words and phrases that hinted at the old patriarchal hierarchy with its strict discipline and punitive God. "He was becoming more indoctrinated as I was becoming more radical," she reflected. Mary Catherine doubled down on explicitly anti-colonial conversations at home. They talked about gender, race, and the dangers of imbalances of power. "I try to parent high-autonomy and high-respect," Mary Catherine explains. She drops to her son's eye level when speaking to him; she doesn't demand he hug her or anyone else.

Then one day, in one of those end-of-the-rope parenting moments, Mary Catherine physically picked up her son and placed him in his room. He was indignant, far more hurt by it than Mary Catherine had expected. It wasn't fair, her son explained, that she was able to dominate him physically and as an authority. She made the rules and enforced them—he felt helpless, like he had no say in what was happening to him.

"It really shocked me, because I had never had conversations like that with my parents," Mary Catherine said. She was humbled, and immediately sought to repair the obvious breach of trust. But she was also encouraged. He had spoken up for himself, articulated the very values she was trying to impart. He was holding her to her decolonization agenda. "Mutual respect is working."

It's working in our home too. Slowly but surely, I'm saying things like, "I can see you're upset, and I want to help. Please stop screaming so we can hear each other." Sometimes they stop screaming. Sometimes they don't. However, they *can* tell me things like, "I know I sound mad, but underneath I'm really sad."

Well, that's helpful to know.

They tell me, "When you talk to me with that voice I cannot think of all the words I want to tell you."

Aha. This is a familiar feeling for me as well.

We're getting there. Like Mary Catherine, I've had to do some work. For me, that has meant going to what my kids call "the temper doctor."

## The Temper Doctor

I had been in talk therapy on and off for years after my big church meltdown in 2012. I should have done more when Asa was born in 2016, as I was clearly knocked sideways by postpartum anxiety. But it wasn't until 2020, the year the world collectively lost it, that I decided to take a more aggressive approach to deal with the anxiety, shame and anger spewing like toxic ash from a volcano I kept insisting was a mere mountain.

The anxiety had been a sporadic, benign feature until after I had kids. The shame was a more constant companion, but nothing a little meditation and worship music couldn't soothe. Until ever so recently, anxiety and shame had been under my control. The anger was another story. That had been there for a long, long time, and it was terrifying. It hadn't started when I left my ministry career. It didn't start on the night of the epic spanking. It's not anyone's fault. My anger goes deep and far back, and I refused to admit it even existed until I was about twenty-five. I still have to work really hard to acknowledge it in the moment. My husband teases me, because whenever he asks if I'm angry, I answer, unironically, "No! I'm (synonym for angry)."

Whenever I went to battle with parental authority—because that's what we'd been told our relationship was, a battle—the lava of panic and shame in my heart flowed and cooled to anger again, like it did on the night of the spanking, adding another layer of igneous rock on the seabed. It stayed below the surface of the ocean for most of my childhood, erupting and cooling until eventually it was clearly visible, unavoidable, a looming island of my personality.

So of course, when my own kids challenged my authority, when they refused to buckle a seatbelt, turn off an iPad, or stop licking windows, Mount Anger erupted. I yelled. I hissed. I growled. I threatened to revoke all the privileges and throw away all the toys.

Out came the shame, another reliable feature of my psychological landscape, at having lost my temper again. The tearful apologies, the pacing and mumbling.

Out came the anxiety. What was this volatility doing to my kids? What sort of emotional scars was I creating? What sort of lava would flow through their hearts?

It was love for my kids that finally got me into Radically Open Dialectical Behavioral Therapy (RO-DBT). My therapist does not tell me to stop being angry, anxious, or ashamed. She doesn't let me ruminate on the volcano, how it got there, and how to make it go away. It might never go away. My shame and anxiety, especially, might never go away. I have to learn to connect to my husband and kids *even when I'm angry*. The volcano of anger. The ashy rain of shame. The churning magma chamber of anxiety. Those may not be fixable, at least not right away. But my relationships are. When I cause harm, I can repair it.

Lewis and I have been honest and transparent with our kids as much as possible without making their world feel scary and insecure. So we apologize. We admit when we're wrong. We acknowledge when a change of course makes sense. We seek to make amends.

When I was apologizing to Moira one day, after a full cycle of anger-shame-anxiety, I decided that she needed to see that I was serious about my apology, that I really was doing something to keep it from happening again. So I told her I was going to see a special doctor to help with my anger and stress. She called it a temper doctor. And if you need one, you should find one too.

## Chapter 12

# The Sex Talks

Oh and we get it wrong sometimes
And then we get it right
Oh yeah we try and we try, till we get it right.

—Amy Cook, "Get It Right"

L ike most evangelikids of my age, I have, seared into my memory, a graphic illustration of what premarital sex would do to me.

I watched my seventh grade Sunday school teachers trying to separate two paper hearts that had been glued together. The pink heart was torn to shreds. The blue heart was left streaked with pink scraps. Sex was meant to unify two souls, and it would accomplish that, whether or not we intended it to. This is the most factually sound part of the illustration. Bonding is a biological function of oxytocin, one of the hormones released during sex. If we had sex, we were then told, we would be destroyed emotionally. Now we're getting into conjecture. We've made a leap from hormones to horror. But then comes the kicker, the main point: do you want to give your future spouse this tattered heart? Or this heart covered in the pink scraps of some other woman?

189

The pain of a broken bond was *secondary* to the shame of giving your future spouse a messed-up paper heart.

Some of my friends in other youth groups were shown roses denuded of their petals, each petal representing a sex partner, and in this problematic metaphor, the "specialness" of sex. Others were shown M&Ms passed from hand to hand. The M&M is a mess by the end, and the kids are asked, "Do you want to eat this?" Leaving one to assume that sex partners, as a commodity, are best straight from the package. Some were asked if they wanted a piece of gum that had already been chewed. You get the idea: Sex with a virgin is the only special sex—an idea shared by both youth groups and the sex trade, which charges a premium to clients who want to take a girl's virginity.

Even progressive, secular, sex-positive narratives venerate virginity. In the girl-power movie *Moxie* the main character's boyfriend insists on making sure her first time is special. It's super sweet, the boy choosing to hold back instead of push harder. I get it. But after that first time, I guess, the back seat of the car is fine?

It's tempting to make a joke about the ruse being up once a teenage girl has sex with a teenage boy for the first time. After that, sex may as well be a couple of thrusts in the back seat with the buckle digging into your back. But who am I to say that all teenage boys are hopelessly awkward, except for the ones that are overconfident? Gen Z seems to have its act together in a lot of ways. Maybe they are awesome at sex. Also, who am I to even speculate? *I was never a teenage girl having sex with teenage boys.* It could have all been terrific. Maybe men have always peaked sexually at sixteen but no one wants to tell them.

Whether or not the second-time-and-beyond sex was good, the messages around us in both church and culture are clear: It's not special.

Waiting to have sex until marriage is not a new ethic. It's shared across many faiths and cultures. A certain amount of misogyny and shame goes along with it as well. There's no virginity testing for men.

Abstinence teaching and virginity worship is often harsh, but "purity culture" is the uniquely American evangelical adaptation of this global obsession. It was an all-or-nothing gambit to make kids not have sex once the cultural norms of the early twentieth century shifted in favor of the sexual revolution. It was a scare tactic and a shame tactic; it was a mixture of hearts-and-minds campaigning and carpet bombing.

Linda Kay Klein recounts the role federal and state money has played in abstinence-only teaching since the 1980s, and the industry of purity rings, journals, curricula, and more that flooded the United States as a result.[1] The merchandising of virginity worked well with some trend-sensitive teens who may have been less interested in other aspects of the culture wars. Purity paraphernalia went hand in hand with contemporary Christian music and wacky games at youth groups to create a youth culture where cool and good were not opposites. While defiant teen culture had been giving parents the sweats since *Rebel Without a Cause*, purity culture tied belonging to being good.

Which created problems for kids like Kayla.

**Like a Virgin, Shamed for the Very First Time**

By the time Kayla had encountered her first graphic youth group illustration about sexual purity—this one was a Band-Aid that lost its stickiness as it was passed around—she already felt like an outsider. She had been sexually abused the year before and figured, "I'm just a Band-Aid that's no longer going to stick."

The idea of autonomy over one's body is not part of most church purity curricula, and Kayla spent most of her adolescence confused about who, exactly, her body was for. The True Love Waits ring she wore out of peer pressure told her that her body belonged to her future husband, and that it was already tarnished. It wasn't something anyone would want. Her family system told her she was to be obliging, giving others what they wanted, even when it opened the door to sexual abuse. For someone who was told that "no one will want you," it was confusing when someone *did* want her.

Not being one of those pristine, holy girls with something to lose, Kayla found herself drawn into increasingly risky situations, saying "yes" because she didn't know what else to say, given that she didn't really have anything to protect anymore.

The sad reality is that sexual abusers often, though not exclusively, target people who have been told they don't deserve respect, who will be easy to intimidate into submission or discredit if they do come forward. Young people who have been isolated—common in cultures that use shame to maintain control—make particularly safe targets. Kayla's first abuser would not be her last.

Her healing journey didn't happen in the church. It happened at the Rape Crisis Center, where, at eighteen, she finally found words to describe the things done to her, without adding more hair, dirt, and filth to the Band-Aid. She is now married and is raising a son alongside her now teenage daughter. She found a progressive spiritual community, a local chapter of The Liturgists. Healing sexual trauma—whether it results from violence or from shame—is her calling.

Kayla founded For Her, a nonprofit dedicated to serving women whose social and financial situations put them at risk of sexual exploitation in San Antonio, Texas. She goes into strip clubs with gifts and words of encouragement for the mothers, daughters, and students working to support themselves inside. The goal isn't to cozy up and get them to quit their wicked ways, though helping women pursue empowering options is part of the nonprofit's work. The point is to remind them that their work doesn't mean that they lose all right to say who touches them, when, and how. They have not become worthless stems, grimy candies, or chewed gum. They have as much dignity as any virgin or housewife.

Kayla is passing the same sexual ethic to her own children, based in dignity and autonomy. They decide who, when, how, and where to give affection or intimacy. Whatever they decide, they do not lose the right to set their own boundaries in the future. Just because they have sex once, it doesn't mean they have to next time. Just because they didn't want to kiss one paramour, it doesn't mean they can't kiss the next one. If they cross a boundary, they are not forever ruined. Boundary setting is part of learning.

If they decide to reserve sex for marriage, Kayla said, that's great, and she would obviously support them, but that's not the end goal. "What's more important is my kids understanding healthy relationships. To have dignity, boundaries, mutuality," she said.[2] Learning who can be trusted, who should have access, and how to set boundaries are life skills that go way beyond sex. Sex is only one part of our intimate life, and Kayla and I noted when we spoke that the church did very little to help us understand healthy emotional and spiritual relationships either. "Boundaries were so lacking in my life, even though I had all this religious structure," Kayla said. Along with the risky sex, the emotional side of even her nonsexual relationships tended toward codependence. She didn't know how to separate what belonged to her and what belonged to others, but she wants her kids to have that skill set.

Even in a consensual relationship, having sex freely without coercion or obligation isn't always guaranteed. Not every thought or resentment needs to be shared, but neither should every fear or fantasy be kept secret either. The better we are at boundaries, the better our relationships will be across the board—with family members, romantic partners, friends, and coworkers. It's important to know what to share and with whom to share it, and to be able to make that decision without shame.

As the mother of two kids who have almost zero inhibitions, this feels like an impossible needle to thread. But it's necessary.

## The Difference between Shame and Privacy

We always thought we would tell our kids about sex early. We wanted to demystify it, set clear boundaries, give them facts before someone else gave them fiction, and equip them in all the ways Kayla described when we met for sushi. But then my daughter's preschool teacher called to let me know that Moira had told the entire class of three-, four-, and five-year-olds that Santa Claus was not real. I didn't want to get a similar call from her kindergarten teacher when she told the class about sex. So we've waited.

We answer questions honestly here and there, and we probably won't ever have a big sit-down talk with either of our kids. Not because those are wrong, but because I know my kids, and the ceremony around a formal discussion would set up my particular children to treat sex like Santa Claus—some fantastical mix of taboo and reward separate from daily life. Definitely something to share with the class. Definitely something to worry about.

Lewis and I feel we've done a pretty good job of keeping shame out of the conversations. Now we have to figure out how to extol the power of privacy. Nothing is more culturally malleable than modesty and privacy. One culture's wrist is another culture's cleavage. What's appropriate on the beach is not appropriate in a deli. If we try to make our kids abide by some sort of rules by invoking absolute or timeless morality, we're making a house of cards that any self-respecting teenager is going to flick. We might as well embrace the ever-shifting, context-dependent, yes-today-no-tomorrow thing that is the social contract.

Blogger Christina Miller Larsen invokes Jean-Jacques Rousseau's concept of the social contract to explain to her children why they must wear clothes outside.[3] It's not the historical definition of the social contract, but it's a brilliant adaptation. Rousseau was referring to the freedoms we surrender to government in exchange for protection, but as Larsen uses it, it's more like neighborly agreements. It's how we make each other feel socially safe and secure. We wear clothes because it's something all the people decided to do, and we have not developed social structures to account for nakedness in public. We only touch our penises when we are alone, because our neighbors have not regularly been around people touching their penises in public.

When you're young, the line between public and private is forgiving. A toddler disrobing at the splash pad, as mine often did, is no biggie. By the time you're an adult though, the line between public and private is often enforced by law. An adult disrobing at the splash pad is a problem. Our country isn't good at nuance, on the whole, but we've done a decent job with public nudity. In most schools, kindergarteners who show each other their butts once or twice don't get sent home; high school students will. We have an inherent learning curve built into the social contract, and it's OK to use it.

Social contracts don't replace morality. They exist to help us make decisions when the issues aren't moral ones, but concern living together harmoniously. The social contract needs to be amended at times, sure. It can be wrong and even oppressive. But where it works, it explains a lot of what is private and what is shared.

We have household social contracts as well. Some families walk around in their underwear. Some fart at the dinner table. Some leave the door open when they pee. Yet they don't do any of these things in public.

Many social contracts will be more permissive than our individual comfort levels or even family social contracts, and that's fine, but I think we need to be careful with our reasons. For instance, in our culture, bikinis are OK. Our family rule right now is that the kids wear long sleeve rash guards for sun protection. When a grandma buys Moira two-piece bathing suits, those become "grandma's house" bathing suits, to be worn once or twice in the backyard pool before they are outgrown, and grandma can do the unpleasant duty of slathering on the SPF 75. At some point, as

Moira develops in both physical and social ways and is able to apply her own sunblock, we will need to decide if our opposition to bikinis can be maintained without shame or judginess. If it can't, we have to relent. Check back with me in about five years.

On the other hand, I suspect our current culture will one day seem reckless on the issue of oversharing. Anyone who has listened to NPR for longer than a day has probably heard a researcher or psychologist fretting over what the oversharing on social media is doing to our brains, what market and government data collection is doing to our security, and what algorithms are doing to our perception of reality. We put a lot out into the world, and the world is using that information. Amid the fretting lies real danger—security concerns, social division, extremist recruitment, social media addiction—though it's often difficult to tell what's harmful and what's just change.

I share things on my blog that would make my grandparents blush, yet my peers don't balk at discussing our vaginal and mental health struggles. Ads for sex-proof menstrual cups litter my Facebook feed, and there are people talking about fecal odor in my Instagram stories. I have no doubt my kids, if the internet continues to spin its tangled webs, will share the kinds of things that make me blush. But they also might be aghast that I allowed Twitter to track my location. Or used Facebook, period. The boundaries of appropriate behavior and privacy seem to shift with each generation as technology brings us deeper and deeper into one another's lives, and it's really hard not to make absolutes out of norms.

One norm, however, seems to have endured: You can't masturbate in front of people.

## When God Kills Kittens

Kayla and I had a laugh at this point in our interview. We were in a crowded Japanese restaurant for lunch, right as COVID-19 vaccinations were starting to roll out and people were venturing back into the world. In the background of the recording I can hear children shrieking and groups of men laughing.

When we got to the topic of masturbation, our voices dropped instinctively.

And then we laughed at ourselves.

No one would have overheard us in the noisy restaurant, and if they could, we'd already discussed rape, molestation, and sex work. But masturbation—*the thing everyone does*, probably including the kids at the table next to us—that's what needed an extra layer of discretion?

Purity culture made a sport of seeing how much self-deprivation one could endure. Couples were constantly vowing to save their first kiss for their wedding day, or to never say I love you to anyone until they were proposing marriage. It was all very theatrical, led mostly by boys who turned purity culture into a very particular kind of dick-measuring contest. The kind with no dicks involved. To add some levity to their spartan sexual suppression, my friends in college hung a little homemade poster on the inside of their dorm room door, so that they would see it on their way out each day. It was the popular 2002 meme, "Every time you masturbate, God kills a kitten." The meme was ironic; the reminder not.

That's right, masturbation is off the table in purity culture. At issue are two arguments, strained to their breaking point. Argument 1: It's impossible to masturbate without lusting after another person, which, in Matthew 5:28, Jesus said was just as serious as adultery. Argument 2: Sex is sinful if it's selfish, and the only person masturbation pleases is oneself. To which I, who have quietly masturbated for most of my life with zero guilt, reply as follows. Rebuttal to Argument 1: That is not what that verse is talking about; it's an indictment of hollow piety and self-righteousness. Rebuttal to Argument 2: That's an odd interpretation given how many wives are not as pleased as their husbands with the sex they are having, because purity culture warped their minds about sexual pleasure. Plus, those wives never masturbated freely to figure out what they liked, and now they are afraid to admit that their sex life is anything but perfect because the whole point of all that purity was to make their husbands feel like demigods in bed.

But I digress.

It's funny to me that I never felt guilty about masturbation. I felt shame and guilt over *everything else*, why not that? With God as the all-knowing hall monitor, "secret sins" weren't even really a thing. I felt guilt over mean thoughts and lies that remain undiscovered to this day! No, somewhere deep inside there was something defiant that said, "If I'm going to survive the sex desert, I'm taking this little canteen with me."

Both Kayla and I are perfectly comfortable with our children naturally exploring their own body parts in this way, but talking about it in public illustrated the challenge of creating boundaries and privacy without shame. Masturbation, sex organs, and sexual behaviors are not shameful things. But they are private. Private and good.

### You've Got a Good Body

Growing up, neither Kayla nor I ever heard the body described as "good." She recalled hearing it talked about as something ephemeral that would be left behind when we went to heaven. I remember it being treated as a liability, full of lust and dangerous appetites. My own bosomy figure was a particular hazard for myself and the boys around me. Bodies could be a lesser good or an eternal bad. But a body couldn't worship God the way a mind could. A body could not bring glory and shalom, except in our willingness to deny its appetites.

As a young person growing up in purity culture, Linda Kay Klein learned that physical pleasure was selfish at best and sinful at worst. Today, she is committed to giving her daughters a different perspective on pleasure. For example, she told me that after giving her infant her nightly baby massage, she often gives a little massage to her own shoulders, demonstrating to her baby that feeling good is something we all deserve and can enjoy. That doesn't sound radical, unless you grew up in a culture like ours where pleasure was suspect and suffering—even beyond simply denying the body's appetites—was revered. "We've been taught that our bodies and our desires are inherently rooted in the earthly, sinful world, and that pleasure or anything that feels good is to be deeply mistrusted," Klein told me.[4] Even things like peace and contentment were under suspicion because they meant you were probably doing something selfish or wrong.

Suffering, by contrast, is somehow seen as the body's path to God. In *Pure*, Klein expounded more on this idea that suffering, especially for women, was next to godliness. Martyrdom, selfless denial, and even the kind of suffering you can't really control can bring you closer to God, who, in the form of Jesus, put his body through crucifixion.[5] A suffering woman is safe and holy. A satisfied woman is dangerous and suspicious.[6]

Purity culture goes hand in hand with what I call "worm theology"—the obsessive exploration of ways to denigrate humanity, hold our desires in deeper contempt, and wallow more pitifully in our sinfulness. Worm theology leads me to believe that if even my spiritual desires are probably corrupt, my body's desires are laughably debased. We talk a lot about "guilty pleasure" but never holy delights. If we come across some poem or meditation with a promising name it ends up being about prayer and avoiding sin, for instance "Desires" in *The Valley of Vision*, or Hildegard von Bingen's *Book of the Rewards of Life*. Spoiler, virtue is the reward, not a massage.

But in the Bible we see David dance before the Lord. We see the lovers in the Song of Solomon delight in each other's bodies—though there are plenty of commentators ready to allegorize that to death. We see Thomas request to touch the wounds of the risen Christ. Our bodies, in their actions, their delights, and their scars, are part of creation, and creation has a special relationship with God. The stuff of creation groans for freedom, cries out in praise, and testifies to the oneness. The stuff of creation, the nerve endings and hormones and urges are all things that our sacred texts teach that God called "good." When we call them "dangerous," "unruly," or, heaven forbid, "bad," we're breaking the communication between body and soul, and we're also probably breaking down the lines of communication with our kids.

### It's a Penis, Not a Wee-Wee

Anatomically and functionally, Kayla uses real words, not euphemisms. Euphemism literally means "good speech," which is unnecessary if you believe the words themselves are good. She wants them to understand sex, how it works, and its inherent risks. As she explains how bodies in general work, it opens the door for her kids to explore how their unique bodies work. What feels good? What is comforting or exciting or upsetting?

In addition to giving kids the words to describe the goodness of their bodies, using accurate words also helps young people explain when something goes wrong. When someone violates their agency or casts doubt upon their boundaries.

Euphemisms, Kayla explained, create misunderstandings.

I thought back to middle school when *everything* seemed to be a euphemism for a penis. Sometimes I play a game wherein I just type random words into Urban Dictionary and see what kind of horribly awkward situations I've been creating by saying things like "tap" and "teabag" and "banister." Try it. You'll never speak again. We compared stories of grandmothers who went by Yaya or TiTi, the same words some families use for genitalia. This can complicate a victim's outcry.

"Outcry" is the word professionals use in trauma-informed care to refer to the moment a person signals they need help. It's an incredibly vulnerable process, and misunderstandings make it more difficult. Most people, especially kids, don't sit their parents down and say, "We need to talk about the neighbor's constant innuendo." Or, "My older cousin is showing sexual predatory behavior." They express it in whatever way they know, and so the more exact language they have, the better. Clear language also helps kids set their boundaries when sexually exploring or developing. Like, who really knows what second base is? Using clear, medical grade language leaves little room for going further than you'd wanted to go, because you realized too late that the boundary was given in a terrible metaphor.

Clear language is good, Kayla explained, and clear opportunities to use it are also good. She tries to create regular space in her house for her kids to ask questions, outcry, or share their thoughts.

## Speaking of Sex

Klein has talked to a lot of people about sex, having spent sixteen years interviewing individuals raised in purity culture and helping them recover from the trauma many of them endured there. She speaks regularly, offers coaching, and runs a non-profit—Break Free Together—that connects individuals recovering from purity culture to one another.

She's also a mom to two daughters. When I asked her how she approaches the topic of sexuality with her own children, she said it's not about having "the talk" with them; it's about having one thousand little talks. If parents can listen nonjudgmentally and respond with curiosity and openness in little, inconsequential conversations, it's more likely that kids will be the ones to bring up big questions and concerns about sex when they arise.

If kids are used to us criticizing and shaming them for bad grades or odd fashion, if we freak out at developmentally appropriate pushback, of course they aren't going to want to ask whether French kissing is sex. Of course they won't ask for advice about a girlfriend who wants to make their relationship more "special" by having sex.

In addition to being kind and open, she encourages parents to be unflappable—not to show on the outside how distressed they might be at the thought of their child as a sexual being. So the sitcom tropes of the awkward mom "birds and bees" talk or the freaked out dad yelling something about "no boys till you're thirty!" aren't the directions you want to go. The goal in these conversations is to set yourself up as a trusted source of guidance, the place they go first, Klein said, because there are a lot of bad information sources just a Google search or catty comment away.

Thinking of sex as an ongoing discussion takes the pressure off the parents, too, Klein pointed out. "Our job isn't to say everything right all the time," she said. "It's simply to show them that they can talk openly with us without fear of judgement."

In my experience, any conversation beyond the logistics of getting from home to school to lessons and back again requires intentionality. We have to make room somewhere amid the shuttling. There has to be a lull in the frenzy, and we have to create it. As a compulsive striver, I'm not great at this. I'm also not great at being the kind of person my kids want to talk to. I ask too many questions, get flustered too easily, and overexplain most things. I have so many intrusive thoughts and anxiety about their development that I have a hard time calming down enough to just talk. I'm a little smothery, because I'm a lot obsessive.

So I got help.

I was in therapy for three hours every week for almost a year, just so I could learn to create the kind of environment where my kids feel like they can talk to me about their deepest personal truths without feeling like they're on an emotional carnival ride. I want to start having these intimate conversations now, before we're in drugs and sex territory. While we're talking about Pokémon and playground crushes.

I've never met anyone who says talking to their kids about sex is comfortable, but practice definitely helps.

## Chapter 13

# The Big Fear

You gotta go for what you know
To make everybody see, in order to fight the powers
that be.

—Public Enemy, "Fight the Power"

When we went on vacation during the summer of 2021 we carted a lot of books around with us. Nestled in a cabin, I finally read *Educated*, Tara Westover's 2018 memoir of being saved by education after growing up in a family of conservative Mormon survivalists in Idaho. That's about as light as reading gets for me. I'm super fun at parties. My kids, who are far more on trend, had us read aloud to them *Luca*, the junior novelization of Pixar's latest animated movie. Luca is an overprotected sea monster from a provincial goatfish shepherding family who, like all sea monsters, turns into a human when he's outside the water. He goes to a little town on the Italian coast, makes friends, and realizes that what he really wants to do is to go to school.

Reading about these two knowledge-hungry, persistent young . . . beings, I looked at my own kids in consternation. "Why aren't you two more desperate to get to school every day?" I wondered. Of course, I know the answer. We're not withholding it from them. Quite the opposite. There is no interest too obscure for me to indulge. Entomology? Pokémon Eeveelutions? DJing? Speleology? I want them to devour it all like a smorgasbord of wonder. I promise you, my overly enthusiastic support of casual interests will come up in therapy.

School, books, and learning, for me were and still are freedom and power, how I know myself as an individual when the religion still buried in my bones tries to make me into a sin-hunting, idol-smashing, rule-following robot. I get why people are afraid of education; I feel its unruly effects every day.

At the same time, education can also be a tool to encourage conformity—like religious or patriotic education—or to usher someone onto the icy slope of competitive perfectionism. Many white evangelicals are of two minds on education—they dislike the kind that makes you question authority and like the kind that gives you an economic advantage.

My parents encouraged my academic pursuits and my genuine curiosity—for Christmas in fifth grade they gave me, as I had requested, the *American Dictionary of the English Language*, 1828 facsimile edition, and an MIT sweatshirt. (Like I said, great at parties.) No matter how conservative my family got, they were never so conservative that we were allowed to even *consider* not going to college. College was part of our family culture and middle-class lifestyle, even if the people around us were fretting over the dangerous ideas we would find there. My parents had to make choices when their multigenerational family culture of high achievement in education bumped up against their relatively new religious culture. So they split the difference and sent us to Christian schools through high school, encouraged but did not mandate Christian college, and supported graduate school of any kind. Together we struggled to reconcile two messages: Education is essential, and education is dangerous. Remembering that tension, Luca's and Westover's experiences were not foreign to me. I resonate with many of the sentiments expressed by

Deborah Feldman in her quest for knowledge.[1] I can get really worked up talking about the work of Pakistani education activist Malala Yousafzai.

I was never forbidden to study, especially not on account of my gender. But I understand the root of the fear and control these brave hearts went up against.

The backdrop to the stories of people like Westover, Feldman, Malala, and even Luca the sea monster is this big fear: If the kids are educated, they will leave. Maybe physically, maybe spiritually, maybe politically. They will slip our grasp. They will no longer be under our authority. While we may shudder at these extreme stories—we may even feel angry at the forces that kept these hungry minds in darkness—every parent experiences some version of the big fear.

In chapter 10 we discussed the ongoing war between fundamentalism and reason, and how the almost absurd anti-intellectualism of fundamentalism was a breaking point for some. But for many of us, raising our kids to be open to learning, science, and reason is not a one-and-done decision. Long before Berkeley and MIT are on the table, our kids' quest for knowledge puts us in a few tough spots. Not all knowledge flows through a classroom. We don't want our kids exposed to language, images, and experiences that will fill their heads with violence, sexualization, or bigotry. We don't want them to join cults or extremist political movements.

Classrooms themselves can be fraught. While we are in a state of uncertainty, it may increase our unease to know others out there are quite certain, and quite willing to project that certainty onto our kids. To varying degrees we worry about what they are picking up at school—not just the f-word and the stomach flu, but other people's certainty about religion, God, gender, culture, race, authority, influence, and prosperity. We worry that before they know who they are, someone else will tell them. The struggle over what kids learn, who teaches it to them, and how far they should go in questioning authority seems to be intrinsic to parenthood, and our release of certainty and perfectionism only makes it murkier.

However, as I mentioned in my own story, a competing big fear also plays a role: the big fear of losing financial ground for their children. Many parents are balancing moral and economic fear, making trade-offs between protection and achievement. Like most fear-based decisions, a common boogeyman has emerged. Chapter 10 dealt with the boogeyman at the university level, because that's where many of us parted ways with certainty. However, there's another boogeyman who shows up sooner in our children's lives, when we must make the earliest decisions on how we will relate to their education. In this case the boogeyman is public schools.

I started working as an education journalist in 2013. I've dug deeply into public education's struggles at the personal, local, state, and national level, and I've seen one big fear or another moving beneath the surface countless times. I can't tell you what books, schools, lessons, and clubs to choose for your kids, or to what degree you should just let them choose. What I'd like to do, instead, is to offer an informed look at the ideas and values that shape our K–12 school systems, so that you, whether you resonate more with the MIT-bound fifth grader or with Luca the sea monster, can make decisions based on something other than a big fear.

### Authority's Big Fear of Being Challenged

At the very least, exposing your child to more knowledge is going to make your life harder.

When my daughter Moira figured out how to connect her iPad to the Wi-Fi, her whole demeanor changed. She would pull it out at the coffee shop or the airport, search for networks, follow the prompts, ask for a password if needed, and be on her way to playing her favorite math game or watching Pokémon drawing videos on YouTube. She no longer had to wait for us to finish the phone call, chaperone her little brother in the bathroom, or get everyone's boarding passes sorted. Knowing how to navigate this modern tool gave Moira the power to entertain herself during the interminable waiting of errands, travel, and leisurely adult coffees. But I was torn. I liked being able to use, "Sorry, no Wi-Fi" as a deflection when I didn't want to have to monitor her YouTube consumption or argue about it. Once she knew for herself, she had power in the relationship, and that made my job more difficult.

There's no doubt that maxims like "knowledge is power" stick with us for a reason. Ignorance, like poverty, can keep you under the thumb of authority in numerous ways. In the Middle Ages, the lack of understanding allowed authority to wield fear and superstition as tools of control. In our modern justice system, the esoteric language and various chutes and ladders of the law make it so that legal representation is all but mandatory for a favorable outcome. In civil cases where there is no right to an attorney, justice tends to tip toward whoever can afford to hire one.

People in authority—whether they run governments, banks, or gyms with labyrinthine membership contracts—want to keep people ignorant for numerous reasons. They mostly profit from ignorance. Banks make money when customers sign without reading the fine print. People who don't know their rights don't sue you. It's easier when subordinates do what you say, traveling along the most profitable path for you.

But even authority with good intentions is tempted to keep people ignorant. As a journalist, I run into this at least as often as I run into nefarious secret-keeping. I run into superintendents who want to make a research-backed decision without having to convince thousands of worried parents that it's the best one. I run into churches that have to fire a beloved minister quietly and don't want to fuel the gossip mill by explaining why. I run into nonprofits that won't be able to keep doing the good work they are doing if word gets out that they are going beyond the scope of a grant. We have to have a conversation about whether transparency or outcomes are the ethical imperative. We rarely agree.

When it comes to Moira and the Wi-Fi, the authority I have over her screen time is beneficent. I limit because I care. But her empowerment—the knowledge of how Wi-Fi works—means I have to make my case, have a discussion. If I shortcut to, "Because I said so," then she has the power to sneak behind my back. So I have to get her into agreement. We have to talk about screen time, maturity ratings, bad words, and damaging images. We have to learn etiquette and set boundaries. Rather than my narrative of "There's no Wi-Fi" or "Authority should be obeyed without question," we have to agree on a new narrative integrating my responsibility to keep her safe and her ability to make choices.

Education gives the power of knowledge and invites our children to shape the narrative of our past, present, and future. It empowers them to interpret and ultimately change the world. But not everybody wants a new narrative. Not everybody wants the world to change.

### Religion's Big Fear of Secularism

Those invested in keeping things the same—the same people in power, the same behaviors acceptable, the same revenue streams flowing—have various strategies for keeping the bomb of knowledge from blowing up in their face.

The most extreme authoritarian regimes—like the plantations of the antebellum United States—fear even literacy, because the ability to read for oneself leads to questioning the claims of those in authority. Enslaved people were often severely punished for learning to read. Most regimes don't go quite that far, at least not as a matter of broad practice. More often religious communities, like Feldman's Hasidic Jewish community and Westover's survivalist family, fear teaching from outside the community. They carefully curate secular instruction so as not to create a competing authority to the religious authority.

Others, like Malala's community, limit who has access to what kind of learning.[2] In patriarchal systems throughout the world, women's education is secondary to attending to men and their needs, secondary to the duties of the home. When men put a stop to the learning, at whatever level, for whatever reason, that stop is absolute. Resisting those rules is why Malala was shot.

As I mentioned, my education-loving parents weren't totally immune to the evangelical version of the big fear, which contended that the modern, Marxist academy and secular state wanted to turn Christian kids into atheists. They sent us to conservative Christian high schools and colleges where we learned all the same subjects as public school students, filtered through the lenses of biblicism—the belief that the Bible is the ultimate authority over any textbook. That filter, I would argue, also caught a lot of basic pedagogy, but that's another story for another day. I'm literate, and that's what matters.

Christian schools, Bible schools, Jewish yeshivas, and Muslim madrasas exist along a spectrum of conservatism and antagonism to the secular academy. That said, Jewish and Muslim communities in the United States know that the teaching of their religion and history will only happen through private, community-based effort. They may want to establish authority over their children, sure, but teaching their worldview is also an act of resistance to the dominant cultural power. They recognize that Christianity is baked into American public schools. The only people who don't seem to realize that, ironically enough, are Christians.

## Evangelicalism's Big Fear of Pluralism

A Brooklyn-based colleague was surprised to hear that my kids would not be off school for Yom Kippur. "What do the Jewish kids do?" she asked. In San Antonio, I answered, they either miss school or go to one of the Hebrew academies. She was aghast.

But at least she had precedent to be aghast. My Muslim friends do not even expect to hear an occasional "*Eid mubarak!*" in an American public school.

In addition to having our sacred holidays celebrated in secular state schools, most public education is amenable to white, broadly Christian values as well, though you'd never know it to listen to the group representing Christianity in debates over sex education, access to gendered or nongendered bathrooms, and school-led prayers. Those battles are almost entirely about values some Christians feel are at risk—they aren't fighting for things that they've never had, like those who fought for racially integrated schools, special education services, or girls' sports. People of color, people with mental and physical differences, and women have had to fight to make the public school system work for them at the most basic level. Christians are fighting to keep the wall-to-wall dominance their values have always had. They're fighting against pluralism, a system where everyone's values are respected.

"What about *my* values?" many Christians, especially evangelicals, have said.

Yes, yes. That is a problem. Because evangelicals don't just not value pluralism. They highly value its mutually exclusive opposite. Evangelicals earned that name because they urge "evangelism"; they are compelled to tell people about Jesus in hopes that the person will convert to Christianity. Inherent to evangelizing isn't just a concern with how *I* am living, what *I* believe; but also how *you* are living, what *you* believe. However altruistic their desire to save souls, evangelism is an investment in expanding religious homogeneity. So, Christianity has a clearly favored status in American culture, and yet those Christians who fear religious pluralism often hunt for boogeymen under every desk.

Here's one example that recently blew my mind:

I have written a lot about the rise of social and emotional learning in public schools. Social and emotional learning encompasses everything from loving-kindness meditation to feelings charts to making amends. It teaches internal regulation, cooperation, and emotional intelligence, and it has broad support among educators and the business sector. However, social and emotional learning has found itself in a peculiar set of crosshairs, because these skills and competencies have always been the domain of morality, character, and religion.

In October 2019, I was reporting at an international social and emotional learning conference, and an American Indian educator expressed concerns that the curriculum was, like many things in public school curriculum, overly aligned to the values of Christianity. He questioned whether the things being taught were really based on brain science and not laden with religious presuppositions. Two months later, I covered a panel discussion, and one panelist highlighted the anxiety of those who feel social and emotional learning is the secular academy taking one more step to render religion irrelevant.[3] "It's as though we're trying to start another religion," University of Arkansas researcher Jay Green said during the panel.

In an effort to harness the good of spirituality and ethics, social and emotional learning bumped into the nation's religious anxiety in both directions. Christianity is still embedded in the dominant narrative of the United States. It continues to exercise power. It has influence. But it is not the state religion and therefore cannot be rightfully enforced. It has no authority. So there's anxiety in both camps—those who resent Christianity's influence and those who desire its authority.

Social and emotional learning soon got caught up in another iteration of the big fear. While it may smell of Judeo-Christian values, almost all social and emotional learning curricula explicitly teaches students to consider others' viewpoints, which is a threat not only to Christianity, but to the other identities that often overlap it in the United States: whiteness and nationalism.

In the summer of 2021, Utah State Board of Education member Natalie Cline made an explicit link between social and emotional learning and another hot-button issue that has been roiling white conservatives: critical race theory.[4]

## White Christian America's Big Fear of Discomfort

Elected, often partisan, governing bodies like legislatures, school boards, and state boards of education make it clear that learning history should lead to patriotism and pride in what their state or nation has done in the world. Because we've also invested heavily in the idea of the United States as a Christian nation, being a Christian gets lumped in with patriotism and pride. That pride is difficult to maintain while teaching that Americans live on stolen lands and have systematically denied rights to Black people, and that missionaries often used violently coercive techniques throughout the Americas. It's even more difficult if we talk about how history has led to modern disparities in wealth and power.

Christians who oppose historical accuracy, social justice, and ethnic studies are operating more out of deference to whiteness and nationalism than to their Christianity, of course. But the lines between Christianity, whiteness, and Americanness are blurry for many. America as a Christian nation is a powerful narrative, especially for white folks trying to feel better about some of the very not-Christlike things the United States government has done in their behalf. We omit white supremacy's systemic impact, relegate it to the historical, extrajudicial actions of groups like the Ku Klux Klan, and tell kids that they are living in the glorious age of equality. Implied: If you aren't prosperous in this glorious age, it's your own fault.

Kids are inconveniently good at siphoning this message from between the lines. Over the past few years, wealthy, white schools have found themselves in the news after students reported racial slurs and racist bullying.[5] The parents in the story, of course, are mortified. Where did they get this kind of talk, these reprehensible ideas? They connected the dots, folks. The kids put a name and a face to the way their parents spent money, to the composition of their neighborhoods and their AP classes. They, in that plucky teenage way, put an uncouth label on the socially acceptable racism they live with every day.

Teaching about systemic injustice and ethnic studies presents a major challenge to the "winner's" version of history, with its huge omissions and glossy claims of progress. Teaching about systemic injustice and ethnic studies threatens to raise a generation of people who might feel compelled to change a few things. The things they might change could have a negative effect on the authority, influence, and prosperity of those currently in power. So those in power spring into action. These teachings, they insist, aren't just debatable history. They are the work of one of American Christianity's favorite boogeymen: Marxism.[6] Marxism hates America, it hates Christianity. It doesn't matter whether Marxist analysis is accurate because it is the enemy.

In 2021, conservative legislatures in states like Texas, Florida, and Tennessee tried to ban as much "anti-American" teaching from public schools as they could.[7] When the particular clause "an individual should feel discomfort, guilt, anguish, or any other form of psychological distress on account of the individual's race or sex"[8] showed up in Texas's education code as something to be forbidden, I felt a sea-change in how we talk about education. Not only was the state doubling down on a sort of white supremacist agenda, but it was missing a fundamental tenet of education: Becoming educated is uncomfortable. It is uncomfortable because it challenges our ignorance, demands that we grow.[9] If we believe that the authority in our life is based on a certain set of facts and realities, then challenging those realities challenges the authority. If we find our identity in relation to that authority, our very identity can be challenged. That's unsettling. An individual might even feel discomfort, guilt, anguish, or any other form of psychological distress on account of the ways their race and sex show up in history.

When we consider what we're exposing our children to and how we're educating them, I wonder how much we're trying to protect them from discomfort. How much we're trying to protect ourselves from discomfort. I wonder whether we are sending them to school to be educated, or to have the walls of their comfortable ignorance reinforced.

No matter what happens with the teaching of history, ethnic studies, and social emotional learning in public schools, uncomfortable families will always be able to turn to the private sector. After the 1954 *Brown v. Board of Education* decision when the national government began desegregating America's schools, Christian "segregation academies" started popping up across the South. When public schools mandated virtual instruction and later mask-wearing during the coronavirus pandemic that started in 2020, many private Christian schools did not follow suit. The pandemic was thoroughly politicized, with communities of color being most severely hit by the virus and its economic consequences. Many white evangelicals followed Donald Trump's lead in minimizing the severity of the outbreak, and refusal to observe restrictive mandates was framed as religious and political resistance.

Many Christian schools became havens to escape public health regulations, just as some Christian schools have been havens to avoid civil rights regulation. Whether the connection is overt or a couple of steps removed, white supremacy thrives where there are efforts to escape the regulating arm of the government.

## Parents' Big Fear of Failure

Not all private schools scrapped mask mandates or opened their doors against the advice of public health officials. Some were far more careful. Some went above and beyond, giving families a safety protocol in keeping with the well-resourced learning environment they are used to providing. But whether or not they have any racist, nationalist, or even politically conserva-tive leanings, private schools more broadly have contributed to our perfectionist culture in insidious ways.

Inherent to the private school idea is that parents, not the state, are responsible for the education of their children, for de-ciding what kinds of knowledge they have access to. Many still function as guardians of influence—religious schools in partic-ular. But to get parents to pay tuition in the tens of thousands of dollars, they also must promise a certain degree of prosperity as well. Elite private schools claim to be entry points into the pros-perity pipeline, even as their tuition, culture, and the luxury cars in the pickup line would seem to indicate that the school is not the entry point, but rather a midway point on the pipeline.

Private schools aren't the only schools in that pipeline though! Public schools in expensive neighborhoods can serve the same purpose, insulating a school with resources so that kids have access to whatever academic, extracurricular, or social resources they need to get into the best colleges, get the best internships, and ultimately land the lucrative careers of their (or their parents') dreams. With racial segregation being illegal, public schools across the United States are set up to be economically segregated because their attendance zones cover (and are sometimes carefully engineered around) economically homogenous homes.[10] At a population level, even if not at an individual level, this still amounts to racial segregation. Sixty percent of Black students attend schools whose student bodies are high poverty and nonwhite.[11] States are required by federal law to rate their schools, and study after study indicates that a school's rating tracks with its socioeconomic status.[12] Colleges want to see high SAT scores, which also track with income.[13]

"Good schools"—these well-resourced, predominantly white, highly rated schools—in turn, influence real estate purchases. That's why websites like Zillow and Redfin let you search for a house by school boundary and look up the ratings of schools near the house. Even as state rating systems and rating organizations like Great Schools try to account for economic disparities in their ranking systems, the norm persists: Expensive neighborhoods have highly rated public schools.

"Good schools," whether public or private, are only the tip of the iceberg in the blood sport that is modern parenting. I was talking to a Pilates instructor at our local YMCA about her kids' sports schedules—practices before the sun came up, driving around the state for swim meets, hundreds of dollars spent on athletic gear, including a swimsuit alone with a price tag over $200.

"I'll never be able to do all that," I told her, "I'm not that mom."

"Yeah you are," she said. "Believe me, you'll do it."

I've been taking Pilates from this woman for years. She knows me, knows my positions on social justice, my journalistic work, my disdain for elitism. Still, she knows the pressure. What she's doing isn't exceptional. She's not "that mom" either. The other moms in the YMCA Pilates class agreed with her. It's incredibly hard to tell your kids no when everyone around them is wearing a $200 swimsuit, showing up for practice at 5 a.m.

That's not even academics. The scholastic rat race is even more intense. I briefly worked as a tutor to make extra money during the Great Recession. I spent my evenings helping unmotivated students, who would naturally be making high Cs at best, earn the As they would need to get into top tier regional liberal arts schools. I often wondered how they would fare when they got there. Then one night a student's mom asked me if I would consider online tutoring her older child who was struggling at one of these competitive regional liberal arts universities. This college student not only struggled in first-year classes, but also didn't know how to ask their professor for help.

Study after study shows how "helicopter" parents who hover over their kids and "lawn-mower" parents who mow down obstacles ahead of their kids do more harm than good to their children's sense of agency, self-worth, and resilience.[14]

By this time, I hope you're asking: What does all this have to do with shifting faith? With uncertainty? We may not fear hell for our children, but we still fear failure. This rat race, this pursuit of prosperity is a complementary status quo to the absolute, certain religion. It waits to catch us when our faith falters, offering us a sanitized, pragmatic religion of achievement to replace what we lost. I've tried to build the case for you, however, that it is the same perfectionist, supremacist trap, just by a different name. It has rituals, dogmas, and ethics that have grown up parallel to those of fundamentalist religions, offering an easy way to lose the spiritual component of religion but keep the striving.

### Replacing Big Fear

I can't tell you how many times white or middle class parents tell me they just want a school where people share their "values." This is usually a coded word for white or middle class lifestyles—the kids wear nice clothes, listen to music that isn't rap, and compete hard in school and sports. They do drugs and drink, but only in a teenagery fun way, not in a scary gangsta way. They have sex but not babies.

But if your values, along with your faith, are shifting and changing, you have a unique opportunity to change what your kids get out of their education. I can't promise your kids will not be "led astray" at a public school and that they won't hear words and phrases they shouldn't. If they go to a school with a true socioeconomic and racial mix of kids, I can't tell you they'll have all the AP classes and enrichment clubs you wish they'd had. They might not come out ahead in the end. Rethinking education isn't about winning the game by breaking the rules. It's about redefining the game entirely.

Having seen the societal and personal consequences of doing things the way we've been doing them, we have so much to gain by bravely considering our children's education as an opportunity to embrace uncertainty and reject perfectionism. We might lose control over their beliefs. They might give into unsanctioned influences. They might deviate from the path that so many others are walking. But the path they walk may be more free, more redemptive, more equitable. Instead of the challenges we fear, we might find the warmth of struggling together. Our disagreements don't have to push us apart. I always feel warmer toward my kids at the end of a long-ass day of boundary setting (mine) and pushing (theirs). Our commitment to love amid struggle is a powerful source of resilience.

Instead of the secularism we fear, we might find the joy of inquiry. Whatever you believe about God and the universe, exploration and asking questions are embedded in human nature. Spirituality can weave in and out of science, arts, and mathematics because spirituality feeds inquiry and curiosity. It asks big questions in an effort to connect to the transcendent. Instead of the pluralism we fear, we might find the beauty of diversity. Instead of looking for ways our worldviews and beliefs are better or more correct than others, we can look for the ways the good and the truth shows up in all of us. This isn't relativism or postmodernism. It's an acknowledgment that the good and the truth is bigger and in more than just our little group.

Instead of the discomfort we fear, we might find the peace of reconciliation. If we believe the future is brighter than the past and that America can one day be greater than it has ever been, we will endure some discomfort to get there. We all know how to sacrifice to get what we want. We just have to actually want a better society for our marginalized brothers and sisters.

Instead of the failure we fear, we might find the pleasure of the work. As a nervous fundamentalist, I used to ask myself, "What if Jesus comes back before I reach my goal?" For years it made me anxious, and then one day I saw the question differently. If there's a real possibility that you won't reach your goal—whether because of Jesus coming back or death or a climate apocalypse or a kid who just is not interested in your goals for their life—shouldn't the things we do along the way be as filled with delight, purpose, and pleasure as possible?

In the end, that's what this chapter has been—a challenge to think about our kids' education not as a means to an end, but as a process full of meaning and value. Our uncertainty allows us to ask more of it, to learn along with our kids.

# *Paedobaptism-ish*

Soon we'll all know that we don't know nothing
It's a new world to behold
A golden hour to stand for something
To find the power in your Mighty Soul.

—Langhorne Slim, "Mighty Soul"

So, you ask, did you baptize the baby?

We did.

In February 2015 we stood in front of a little Anglican church and vowed to treat baby Moira as a child of God. The priest anointed her with oil and dribbled water on her head. Eleven-month-old Moira, ever the extrovert, hammed endlessly for the crowd. She waved and crinkled her tiny nose. She clapped when the other babies were either dedicated or baptized. (The church practices both paedobaptism and credobaptism, for those keeping track. Dedication is when parents commit publicly to raising their baby as a Christian, but they don't baptize them yet).

As part of the baptism ritual, the congregation is asked if they will support, pray for, and work with us to raise the child. They answer, "we will." After the event, Moira was passed from family member to family member, friend to friend, down the two pews filled solely with people there to see her. Then the larger church family began to buzz around her, placing hands on her head and blessing her, congratulating us, and laughing at her antics.

I felt warmer toward the church than I had in years. Instead of policies and politics, that day there was only love. Only belonging. We were standing in the center of what Columbia University researcher Lisa Miller calls "the field of love," and while I remain uncertain about the efficacy of the water and the oil on my daughter's head, Miller claims that the field of love is a powerful force of good in a child's life:

> Into the child's daily field of relationship, her innate spirituality and support for this natural spirituality, we find a promising world for a child. Into the child's daily field of relationship, her innate spirituality and support for this natural spirituality from parents and others can now be infused. Spiritual presence, guidance, and values can come from extended family, close friends, psychologists, youth workers and clergy, coaches, and educators. Each of these important adults has a personal choice to decide to be a spiritual presence and model of love, and as they choose to do so, the child's routine social world becomes what I call the *field of love*: a place to learn spirituality in daily life.[1]

Spirituality—not a specific religion, but a connection to the transcendent—has lifelong benefits, including resilience against depression and addiction, Miller writes. The Search Institute lists connection to a community of faith as a developmental asset, something to help children thrive and overcome many of the challenges that scare parents most: suicidal thoughts, risky behaviors, and aimlessness.[2]

Spirituality is innate to children, Miller writes, and parents, even parents who are doubting, play a primary role in cultivating it. Even if we have moved far away from religion or grown

uneasy with spiritual language, she encourages parents to fa-
cilitate their children's exploration. It's daunting for parents,
especially those who are struggling, to feel like their child is going on a journey that is as uncertain and murky for them as for
the parents. As adults we've done school, we've done puberty,
we've brushed our teeth thousands of times. All the challenges
of survival we have, by virtue of being grown up, overcome. But
when it comes to emotional and spiritual development, many
of us are no "further along" than children. As perfectionists, we
often eschew what we cannot master, so when we return to our
discarded spirituality or emotional development, we make a dis-
concerting discovery: We are right where our kids are. Waking
up in a whole new world.

That's where Miller's research is so reassuring. We might feel
lost, but our children are not. They are fully seeing and discovering and will at times lead us. I think Jesus knew this too. When
he said that those who enter the kingdom of heaven must be as
little children, I think this is what he meant. That we must not
be masters of our universe, but explorers and learners awash in
wonder. The road into the kingdom of God—shalom, peace on
earth—is not an icy mountain road. It is a field of love.

As soon as Moira could talk, I began to ask her, "Who loves
you?"

"Mommy!"

"Daddy!"

"God!"

"Granny!"

She would go on to name her whole extended family, care-
givers, and whichever friends she had most recently seen. This
game continued as her memory improved and could soon go on
for several minutes.

One day, after a particularly joyful trip to the grocery store
filled with chatty cashiers and helpful baggers, I asked Moira,
"Who loves you?"

"Oh Mommy," she said, chuckling at my naivete, "Everybody in this city loves me!"

Moira's sprawling field of love stood in sharp contrast to my own view of the world, which had grown more hostile and combative in the years since I'd left my ministry job. Overwhelmed with cynicism, it would be years before I assessed my own field of love and found it largely defensive and transactional, lacking in the real conversations and vulnerability needed to sustain connection.

As a journalist it is easy to end up in this situation. We swim in a world of bad news and "deep" conversations solely for the purpose of work. It's easy, and yet dangerous, because the more I saw the world as hostile, the more I felt like I had to be perfect to get anything good. I believed if I stopped performing, no one would help me. Worse, if I let the wrong person get too close, they would take advantage of me. People became liabilities, threats to my time and peace of mind.

God seemed hostile too, or at least distant, shrouded in the fog of past hurts and twisted theologies. I was trying to hold up my end of all the bargains. Atonement's promise that "when God looks at you, God sees Jesus" should have comforted me, I told myself. So why couldn't I get past the hurt that God would never be able to stand the sight of me as me? I was grateful . . . but sad. God and I were not close. We had reached détente, but not allyship. That was the most I felt I could expect, despite ample evidence of abundance in my life: healthy kids, loving marriage, professional success, helpful extended family, great grocery stores.

Through prayer and therapy, I ultimately found my way back. Following Moira was part of it: We grew together in our ability to name and express emotions. We explored God and social justice together. Her baptism and love of church gave me a reason to stay connected.

One day, during a meditative prayer, I asked myself: Why am I still doing this? With all the crap that came along with religion,

how am I still praying? Immediately, pictures of my own baptism came to my mind. I could hear things my parents had said
about God's love. I remember the talk my dad had with me before
my first communion. I could feel the passion of my early teenage
recommitment to following Jesus. I remembered hearing God's
voice clearly as I moved to a new city, became desperately lonely,
found a church, and took communion. My parents had given
me access to words and rituals that would connect me to God in
ways they could not have predicted, ways beyond their control or
the control of the pastors and priests who would follow. I came
back to the church not out of fear, but because it was where God
had been meeting me for thirty years, sometimes through the
words and teaching and songs. Sometimes in spite of them.

I also expanded my spirituality. I left behind the church's
obsession with certainty and fought tooth and nail to rid toxic
certainty and perfectionism from my work, relationships, and
parenting. Sometimes the best I could do was apathy. Sometimes
it was defiance. There were moments of genuine openness.

In the middle of this journey, we had another child. On November 5, 2017, our son Asa was baptized, this time under a tent
in a special All Saints' Day service with two Anglican churches
combined. Less of a ham than his sister, Asa endured the anoint-
ing and christening with a stoic face, only slightly more animated when the priest walked him down the center aisle, showing the congregation its newest family member.

Meanwhile, thirty-three miles away in Sutherland Springs,
minutes before the water touched my son's head, a gunman
burst into another church. He killed twenty-five people, including grandparents, little children, and a pregnant woman.

Looking back at my blog post from the following day, I can
now see that I was struggling to make sense of several things:
(1) the maddening juxtaposition of the two church services, ours
so happy and theirs unspeakably tragic; (2) the role of Christians
in the gun culture that made it so easy for an unstable person to

get hold of an assault rifle; and (3) my own decisions to bring children into a violent world and expose them to a community complicit in that violence. I wrote: "I can imagine God in my chaos . . . but what about THAT chaos? What about the chaos of violence and tragedy? Does his [sic] grace go there? Does our baptism mean anything in that context?"[3] My conclusion that day, and now, is yes.

In the post, I reflect on the child being baptized: Asa. His name means "healer." To raise him into that promise, he does need a connection to that wellspring of spiritual health. He also needs freedom from the rigid certainty and control of what American religion has become. His baptism, and his sister's, their father's and my own, are not about particular churches or particular creeds. Our baptism is about acceptance and identification as children of God. Not in a way that makes us more malleable and dependable voters and tithers, but in a way that makes us deeply secure, confident, and generous.

I still identify as a Christian—it is the spiritual tradition by which I know God. Every day I feel like something new is coming into question, some old doctrine feels like ill-fitting pants, squeezing a body that wants to breathe. With each exploration, I find myself further from the white evangelical parenting industrial complex, with fewer satisfying books and Sunday School curricula to give my kids. Even though I identify as Christian, the identity is not something I'm trying to ingrain in my kids. We don't sing songs like "I am a C- / I am a C-H-/ I am a C-H-R-I-S-T-I-A-N." In fact, Moira was seven years old before she heard the word Christian, despite a budding lifetime of prayer, Bible stories, church family, and chats about God. We were driving past the Greek Orthodox church in our neighborhood, and she asked what the building was.

"It's a church," I answered.

"What kind?" she asked, doubtless noticing the mosaics and statues that were more ornate and colorful than those of the

Catholic church down the street or the Presbyterian church we drove by on the way to my husband's office.

"Christian, like ours," I said. Our church meets in an elementary school, so I understood why the connection wasn't immediate.

"What? Croissant?" she said.

Lewis and I looked at each other. Had we never uttered the word "Christian" to her?

We explained that Christians were people who follow the way of Jesus. She mumbled the word a few times, and we have not really revisited it since.

As Richard Rohr points out, Jesus's goal wasn't to set up a new religion, in the sense of a new cultural in-group or orthodoxy. He came to radically expand our understanding of how God moves and inhabits the universe. The whole universe.[4] When we baptized our children, we were not inducting them into a particular religion, a particular in-group of right thinkers and orthodox believers. We were not giving them a group to belong to, we were giving them belonging.

Belonging is constantly expanding. It favors connectedness over certainty. It's not conditional on being "right." Belonging is the precondition, the wellspring, the source, and it is constantly accommodating all those who are part of it. Christianity as a bound set of beliefs is not what we are after. It is union with Christ, participation in his death and resurrection, which looks as much like us and our neighbors in our current context as it does like Jesus the God-man of the Bible.

We have to do our best to translate this evolving faith to our kids. We have to come up with new answers to old questions. But in the process something beautiful has happened. Before I had kids, I was angry. I was sardonic and bitter. But when I look into the hopeful, curious eyes of my children, who want so much to live in harmony with the world, I can't put that on them. Those wounds are mine, not theirs.

This book was born from parenting through my own struggles with faith, and maybe I always will struggle. But turning the bitter rejection of the old into the hopeful embrace of uncertainty in the new has also revived my faith. I have seen scriptural transformation—the experience of eternal truths in our context. I have hoped for restoration rather than vengeance. I have opened my heart to racial righteousness, solidarity, and public activity. I have allowed my mind to entertain questions, inquiry, and curiosity in places that once felt dangerous. I have a relationship with a church on my terms and am helping my kids grow into autonomy on their terms. I have chosen to give them a better world instead of a winning formula.

It has been a life-giving, shalom-seeking, engaged, inclusive, curious, communal, instructive, but overall uncertain journey, and I'm OK if I'm on it forever.

# Discussion Questions

## Introduction: Baptism and Burritos

1. I go into detail about my struggles with infant baptism. Was there a doctrine or teaching in your religious tradition that never quite sat well with you? Or perhaps a first brick to come loose in the wall of your faith?

2. Who are some of the authors, speakers, teachers, podcasters, or theologians who have offered alternative perspectives from the ones you were used to? Did you feel like you were making things up as you went, or did someone come along to help you?

3. My kids recently asked me to explain a genderless God. What's the toughest question your kids have asked you about faith?

## Chapter One: How to Lose the Faith and Keep It Off

1. A therapist recently commented to me that she sees a lot of people who were shut out of community for asking hard questions about their honest doubts. What is your experience with doubt? Was it welcomed by you, your family, and community? Was it discouraged?

2. What is your experience with disgust? How did it manifest for you? Were you critical, cynical, or snarky? Maybe depressed

and disillusioned? How did you put distance between yourself and what disgusted you? Did you go so far as to cut out friends or family?

3. What is your experience with hurt? Take some time to think about what was most painful at the core of the hurt—maybe it was the defensiveness of the leadership, as Jonathan Holmes talks about. Or maybe it was Lilly Hope Lucario's "having the knife twisted" when you were not believed. Once you have thought about that, listen to your spirit to see if you should talk to someone about it, either a friend or a counselor or a licensed therapist.

## Chapter Two: White-Knuckle Parenting

1. I fought the perfectionist label for a long time, because I'm not very detail-oriented and don't present as the buttoned up, crisp lines kind of gal. Obviously I didn't understand perfectionism. Before reading this chapter, would you have described yourself as a perfectionist? What about now? Even if that doesn't feel like the core of who you are, do you see its effects?

2. For many, this is not the first time they've seen Kenneth Jones and Tema Okun's link between perfectionism and white supremacist culture. When you first saw that connection—whether it was something you experienced personally, a previous encounter with their workbook, or in reading this book—was it an "Aha!" or was it a "Wait, what?!?" Where have you seen perfectionism and white supremacy working hand in hand?

3. Where does your life need to be decolonized? Is that even the right term for you? If you are struggling with specific beliefs or pain you feel around parenting and faith, have you traced those struggles to the wider agenda of capitalism or white supremacy in the world?

## Chapter Three: Sleep Training for Jesus

1. The schools of parenting advice tend to lean either more disciplinarian or more attachment focused. Which school of thought were you raised with? Which do you tend to favor in your own parenting? Is that intentional or do you find yourself defaulting to one or the other?
2. This chapter talks a lot about the role of mothers in creating a perfectionist society. What about dads? How do fathers further perfectionism and how does it hurt them?
3. Why do you think "family values" became such a rallying cry for the religious right? What is it about families that raises the alarms so effectively?

## Chapter Four: Sword Drills

1. I struggled with the how of having my kids memorize Scripture, mostly because I wasn't super clear about the why. Do you have—or have you seen someone else with—a healthy why and how for Scripture memory? What about reading Bible stories before bed? Praying before meals? Celebrating Christmas and Easter?
2. Think back to hearing the fantastical stories of the Bible as a child. What was your reaction?
3. Which Scripture has been used to shame you, and have you been able to reclaim it as a source of freedom?

## Chapter Five: Theater for the Damned

1. Alright let's hear it: What are the best and worst answers you've ever heard for "Why would a loving God send someone to hell?"
2. Jean-Paul Sartre, who famously penned the line, "Hell is other people," explained that he really meant hell is bring trapped in

other people's judgment of you, and never being able to know yourself apart from that. As someone with profound social anxiety and shame issues, this speaks to me. What conception of hell speaks to you?

3. The people in the play *The Christians* fought Pastor Paul's "no hell" doctrine for a number of different reasons. If you were raised with the doctrine of a literal hell, which argument do you most relate to: (a) that people will have no reason to be good, or (b) that we will have to share eternity with the most evil people ever to have lived?

## Chapter Six: Black Jesus and Confederate Pastors

1. Think back on how you learned about race and racism. What was and was not spoken of in your home? Were there people of different races in your life, and if so, how were you taught to relate to them? What were you taught explicitly and implicitly? As you look back, what sort of learning and unlearning do you need to do?

2. At this book's writing, in 2021, it feels like racial reckoning is knocking on a lot of doors. And the people answering those doors are not always ready to hear that their institution has played a role in injustice. As someone who has done more than my fair share of systems justification—explaining away things I could see with my own eyes because the answer *simply could not be* "the system is creating this outcome"—I see familiar discomfort in the responses on social media, mainstream media, and in conversations. Which spear are you most hesitant to lean on? Which systems do you tend to want to justify, especially as it pertains to racism? Your family system? Your school system? Religion? Capitalism? Why?

3. What are five resources you have gone to for racial reeducation?

## Chapter Seven: Holy Unions

1. Who was the perfect family in your faith community? Was there a family that was specifically marginalized or excluded? Obviously, if you're discussing this in a group, be careful with this one. But find a way to describe what it was that was celebrated and exiled in your faith community of origin.

2. It's getting more common for churches to say they are "accepting but not affirming" of LGBTQIA people—meaning they can attend, but the church will not marry, baptize, or publicly bless their family. What do you think families like Sicily's hear when they are told they cannot be publicly acknowledged by the church in marriage, baptism, or other sacred rites? Do you think they feel "accepted but not affirmed"?

3. In this chapter I argue that perfectionism eventually renders us all impure, or at least scared of becoming impure. Think of a time when someone spiritually (or physically, if appropriate) touched you in a moment when you felt untouchable. What does that memory tell you about God?

## Chapter Eight: Unholy Unions

1. If you're reading this book and you supported Trump, I am fascinated and would love to learn more about you. My suspicion is that most of the people drawn to this book did not support him. So if you're among those who did not support Trump: What were the Trump years like for you? Are you among the many for whom evangelical support for Trump spurred deconstruction? Accelerated it? Didn't touch it? Did it stress your relationships with family and faith community? Were you surprised by evangelical support or did it make sense for you?

2. Think of a "leader." Where does the image come from? In your faith community of origin, was leadership explicitly talked

about, or did you pick things up from watching who was "called" to lead? How much do the lines blur between faith leaders and public or business leaders for you?

3. Social Darwinism is the belief that status, like survival, is self-justifying. The ability to be "on top" of society means that you should be there. Though few would say they adhere to social Darwinism, where do you see that in religion, business, and politics? What is it called?

## Chapter Nine: War Games

1. For me, the logical, rational arguments for faith were important because I had only been taught to trust my mind. In what ways is it important to meet our children where they are? How can we equip them to handle doubt and debate in a healthy way?

2. Rejecting toxic certainty is a big theme of this book. But at the same time, most progressive people of faith believe in science and facts. Is certainty ever appropriate? How do we know when and where?

3. When Bel used the term "the Lord," her father and I both started a bit. Are there words that unsettle you but that might be different if you didn't have baggage attached to them?

## Chapter Ten: Hungover and Hunting for Church

1. Someone recently asked me why I have, at times, stayed at churches when I know it's a doomed relationship. If you've ever stayed in a church for longer than you maybe should have, why?

2. If you've given up on "church" or formal gatherings of faith, with what have you replaced them? Where do you find community?

3. When you think of a community of faith, what are the essential components? What are the pros and cons of having an

institutional church? Of having an informal fellowship with others? Of keeping faith private?

## Chapter Eleven: Spanks for Your Soul

1.  I really had a hard time deciding whether to include the story about my last spanking. It was formative, but I don't want anyone to judge my parents. Can you hear that hesitancy? Do you share it when you tell stories about your past?

2.  At the same time, sharing my thoughts on discipline was scary; even sharing other people's thoughts was a little nerve-racking. Mostly because my kids are still growing up and I didn't want to invite people to judge them as a way of judging whether my thoughts were valid. Are you ever tempted to pressure your kids to act a certain way so that people will think you're a good parent?

3.  Both of the preceding questions were about the connection between judgment and discipline. Why do you think the topic of discipline is so hot? What does that tell us about how we view parents and children?

## Chapter Twelve: The Sex Talks

1.  Think about how you would, if you could perfectly script the conversation(s), talk to your kids about sex. What points would you include? What would you avoid? How old would you introduce different components of human sexuality?

2.  Now, with that perfect script in mind, think of all the ways it might be derailed. Think of questions you dread. Circumstances that might confuse the discussion. Talking to kids about sex rarely goes as planned—what truths encourage you in spite of this?

3.  What was missing from your own sex-ed (formal or informal)? What were the consequences?

## Chapter Thirteen: The Big Fear

1.  Take some time to read up on the schools in your area and discuss how the effects of segregation, white flight, and school funding have created unequal opportunities.
2.  How do the parents in your community justify participating in this unequal system?
3.  Whenever I write about this, and it's often, someone will inevitably say they don't want to sacrifice their kids for the sake of their ideals. What is your response to that? Do you agree? Do you disagree but feel that is a real concern? Do you feel that is a smokescreen for a different concern? (Pro Tip: If you don't have kids yet, be very careful about how you enter this conversation, because the realities of sending one's kids to school every day are heavy!)

## Conclusion: Paedobaptism-ish

1.  It's possible (probable?) you do not care whether we baptized our children. But if not entirely apathetic, were you disappointed with the choice we made? It's fine if you were! If so, why? Were you at all encouraged? How so?
2.  Looking at your own life, try to talk through the difference between spirituality and religion. Where do you see them merging and diverging? Where do you feel the tension between them in your early, middle, and late deconstruction?
3.  What are the burning questions you still have? What are the issues most pressing on your mind? Who can you talk to about them? Who is in the "field of love" for your family as you grapple with these tough questions?

# Acknowledgments

Everyone interviewed in the book gave me an invaluable piece of wisdom, humanity, and beauty, and I feel infinite gratitude for their trust. Extra thanks to Denise Ojeda for connecting me to her special people.

This book wouldn't exist if Patton Dodd hadn't heard my idea and said, "You know, I have this friend . . ." and if that friend had not been Don Pape. Both of those people caught the vision and lent their expertise to making it happen. I am thankful for the good people of Eerdmans, who didn't just allow me to publish a book, but invested in me as an author, and made the whole process lovely.

I feel really lucky that I get to thank one of my best friends, Liz Frels, for being my test audience and first editor on the manuscript. It was a vulnerable process, and I was glad I knew that even if the first draft was terrible, she wouldn't tell anyone, and she'd still be my friend.

I owe thanks to my parents for being happy to see me thrive, even if that has meant talking about them in public sometimes.

To Jack Simons, who taught me how to write.

To the freelance editors at various journalism outlets who gave me ridiculously generous deadlines so I could have income while working on the book.

ACKNOWLEDGMENTS

To my kids, who made this process just challenging enough to remind me why I'm doing it and provided great anecdotes.

To Lewis, who listened to a lot of impostor syndrome and catastrophizing with a calm heart and endless reassurance. He is the parent and partner we all wish we were. I'm so glad he likes me.

# Notes

### Introduction

1. Nefertiti Austin, *Motherhood So White: A Memoir of Race, Gender, and Parenting in America* (Naperville, IL: Sourcebooks, 2019), 159.

2. Austin, *Motherhood So White*, 159.

3. Peter Enns, *The Sin of Certainty* (San Francisco: HarperOne, 2016), 157.

4. Pete Holmes, *Comedy Sex God* (New York: HarperCollins, 2019), 150.

5. See Randy S. Woodley and Bo C. Sanders, *Decolonizing Evangelicalism* (Eugene, OR: Wipf & Stock, 2020). This is a great resource for those wanting to learn more about this. I received a lot of training from the Racial Equity Institute as well, which I highly recommend.

6. Rachel Held Evans, *Inspired: Slaying Giants, Walking on Water, and Loving the Bible Again* (Nashville: Thomas Nelson, 2018), xx.

### Chapter 1

1. Michael Hakmin Lee, "From Faith and Advocacy to Unbelief and Defection: Exploring the Concomitants and Consequences of Deconversion among Evangelical Ministers and Ministries," PhD diss., Trinity Evangelical Divinity School, 2015. In addition to loss of confidence in biblical authority, Lee also found that dissent from Christian teaching and values, disappointment with God and the

Christian experience, and personal disposition were the four most salient factors in deconversion.

2. Rachel Held Evans, *Inspired: Slaying Giants, Walking on Water, and Loving the Bible Again* (Nashville: Thomas Nelson, 2018), xvii.

3. Richard Dawkins, *The God Delusion* (London: Bantam, 2006).

4. Daniel Silliman, "An Evangelical Is Anyone Who Likes Billy Graham: Defining Evangelicalism with Carl Henry and Networks of Trust," *Church History* 90, no. 3 (2021): 621–43.

5. Frank Schaeffer, foreword to *Empty the Pews*, by Chrissy Stroop and Lauren O'Neal (Indianapolis: Epiphany, 2019), xi.

6. *Lord Save Us from Your Followers*, directed by Dan Merchant (New York: Virgil Films, 2010).

7. Pew Research Center, "In U.S., Decline of Christianity Continues at Rapid Pace," published October 17, 2019, https://www.pewforum.org/2019/10/17/in-u-s-decline-of-christianity-continues-at-rapid-pace/.

8. Christopher Rhodes, "Why 1492 Was Even More Important Than You Learned in History Class," *Political Religions*, published October 14, 2019, http://politicalreligions.com/why-1492-was-even-more-important-than-you-learned-in-history-class/.

9. Bertrand Russell, "Why I'm Not a Christian" (speech, London, March 6, 1927), YouTube, https://www.youtube.com/watch?v=NdDYvvevLZk.

10. Jonathan Holmes, *The Company We Keep: In Search of Biblical Friendship* (Minneapolis: Cruciform Press, 2014).

11. Jonathan Holmes, phone interview by the author, January 18, 2021.

12. Lilly Hope Lucario, "The Psychological, Emotional Twisting of the Knife in the Wounds, Caused by Non Belief/Doubting Victims of Abuse," Healing from Complex Trauma & PTSD/CPTSD, August 19, 2014, https://healingfromcomplextraumaandptsd.wordpress.com/2014/08/19/the-psychological-emotional-twisting-of-wounds-caused-by-non-beliefdoubting-victims-of-abuse/.

13. Holmes interview, 2021.

**Chapter 2**

1. Kenneth Jones and Tema Okun, *Dismantling Racism: A Workbook for Social Change Groups* (ChangeWork, 2001).

2. Nefertiti Austin, *Motherhood So White: A Memoir of Race, Gender, and Parenting in America* (Naperville, IL: Sourcebooks, 2019), 117.

3. The Racial Equity Institute, which conducts antiracism workshops for organizations, includes this concept in its training. The power of white supremacy is the ability to get everyone—white and nonwhite people—to buy into the false promises of capitalism and white supremacy. In order for us to reach solidarity in the struggle to end white supremacy, they argue, we must all see where it's shaped us and where it's killing us.

4. Isabel Wilkerson, *Caste: The Origins of Our Discontents* (New York: Random House, 2020). This book explains how race works as a caste system, an inherent hierarchy we are born into, one that shapes the expectations and resistance we meet as racialized members of society. Caste doesn't hand us a set of tangible, particular life circumstances (income, education, etc.), but rather dictates which opportunities we will have to achieve those life circumstances. The number of chances you get, the penalties you incur under the law, the access to networks and capital—all are influenced by what people expect of you because of your caste. In my analogy, it determines our entry point to the slippery road.

5. Austin, *Motherhood So White*, 44.

6. Ekemini Uwan, "Decolonized Discipleship," *Sistamatic Theology* (blog), February 8, 2018, https://www.sistamatictheology.com/blog/2018/2/6/decolonized-discipleship.

7. Austin, *Motherhood So White*, 29.

8. Andrew Solomon, *Far from the Tree: Parents, Children, and the Search for Identity* (New York: Scribner, 2012), 700.

9. St. John of the Cross, "Dark Night of the Soul," in *Dark Night of the Soul*, trans. E. Allison Peers (Mineola, NY: Dover, 2003), 1–2.

10. Cindy Wang Brandt, *Parenting Forward: How to Raise Kids with Justice, Mercy, and Kindness* (Grand Rapids: Eerdmans, 2019).

11. Josh Link and Adrian Gibbs, interview with Cindy Wang Brandt, *Dirty Rotten Church Kids*, podcast audio, November 11, 2020, https://podcasts.apple.com/us/podcast/security-and-clarity-w-cindy -wang-brandt/id1487820978?i=1000498263787.

## Chapter 3

1. Ann Hulbert, *Raising America: Experts, Parents, and a Century of Advice about Children* (New York: Knopf, 2003), 9.

2. Hulbert, *Raising America*, 7.

3. Elizabeth Gilbert McRae, *Mothers of Massive Resistance: White Women and the Politics of White Supremacy* (New York: Oxford University Press, 2018), 1.

4. McRae, *Mothers*, 14.

5. See also Matthew Delmont, *Why Busing Failed: Race, Media, and the National Resistance to School Desegregation* (Oakland, CA: University of California Press, 2016).

6. This specifically refers to a 2018 meeting on the Upper West Side of Manhattan when New York schools were considering changing enrollment policies at the city's competitive exam schools. I've seen versions of this at school board meetings in my hometown as well—I just didn't film and upload them to Twitter.

7. A culture war is any public disagreement between segments of society that disagree about how life should be lived. In the United States, that fight became incredibly bitter and ubiquitous in the 1970s, 1980s, and 1990s as the American right and the American left developed monolithic worldviews with opposing stances on more and more and more aspects of American life.

8. Denene Millner, "Millionaire Ann Romney and the Fake Mommy Wars: What We Moms REALLY Want," *MyBrownBaby*, blog, April 16, 2012, http://mybrownbaby.com/2012/04/millionaire-ann -romney-and-the-fake-mommy-wars-what-we-moms-really-want/

9. Jemar Tisby, *The Color of Compromise* (Grand Rapids: Zondervan, 2019), 84–87, 121–22, 170.

10. Hulbert, *Raising America*, 354.

11. James Davison Hunter, *Culture Wars: The Struggle to Define America* (New York: Basic Books, 1991), 180.

12. Google "permissive vs. authoritarian vs. authoritative parenting" on a day when you have nothing else to do, and have all of your comfort items nearby.

13. David John Seel Jr., *Parenting without Perfection* (Colorado Springs: NavPress, 2000), 15.


## Chapter 4

1. Dictionary of Christianese, "sword drill, Bible baseball, Bible drill," August 26, 2013, https://www.dictionaryofchristianese.com/sword-drill-bible-baseball-bible-drill/.

2. Karen Armstrong, *The Lost Art of Scripture: Rescuing the Sacred Texts* (New York: Anchor Books, 2020), 14–15.

3. Armstrong, *The Lost Art of Scripture*, 340.

4. Armstrong, *The Lost Art of Scripture*, 347.

5. Deborah Feldman, *Unorthodox: The Scandalous Rejection of My Hasidic Roots* (New York: Simon & Schuster, 2012), 101.

6. Feldman, *Unorthodox*, 29.

7. Rachel Held Evans and Matthew Paul Turner, *What Is God Like?* (New York: Convergent, 2021).

8. Eugene H. Peterson, *The Message: The Bible in Contemporary Language* (Colorado Springs: NavPress, 2005).


## Chapter 5

1. Brené Brown, "Brené Brown," website, accessed July 16, 2021, https://brenebrown.com/. What follows is a sweeping summary of talks, books, and podcasts produced by Brown, all of which can and should be found on her website. You're welcome.

2. There are other definitions and constructions of shame. In Radically Open Dialectical Behavior Therapy, to which I owe a great deal

of happiness, shame is the feeling we get when we have violated community values. It is prosocial and restorative, as it leads us to make amends. What Brown and others mean when they talk about shame is an internalization of unworthiness that comes with rejection and belittlement. The taking of external signals and grafting them onto an internal conception of self.

3. Lisa Miller, *The Spiritual Child: The New Science of Parenting for Health and Lifelong Thriving* (London: Picador, 2015), 107.

4. See Edward Tronick, "The Still Face Experiment," 2007, YouTube video, 2:48, https://www.youtube.com/watch?v=apzXGEb Zhto. Babies have a strong negative reaction to a parent withholding a smile. The babies try everything to make the parent engage, and then begin to cry, so great is their need for social feedback, even as rudimentary as a facial expression, from the parent.

5. Mr. Rogers' Neighborhood, "Episode 0031," *Mr. Rogers' Neighborhood* video, 28:45, 1968, https://www.misterrogers.org/episode -playlist/batch-13-episodes-0031-0032-0033-0034-0035/.

6. Vinson Cunningham, "How the Idea of Hell Has Shaped the Way We Think," *New Yorker*, January 14, 2019, https://www.new yorker.com/magazine/2019/01/21/how-the-idea-of-hell-has-shaped -the-way-we-think.

7. PBS Kids, "Daniel Tiger's Neighborhood: Saying I'm Sorry Is the First Step (Song)," YouTube video, 1:28, March 10, 2016, https://www .youtube.com/watch?v=oICZVpmtL4c.

8. Richard Rohr, *The Universal Christ: How a Forgotten Reality Can Change Everything We See, Hope For, and Believe* (New York: Convergent, 2019), 142.

9. Texas State Legislature, *Relating to the social studies curriculum in public schools*, HB 3979, 8th Legislature, introduced in House June 15, 2021, https://legiscan.com/TX/text/HB3979/id/2339637/Texas-2021 -HB3979-Introduced.html.

10. Marta W. Aldrich, "Protesters Confront Tennessee Education Commissioner over Claims of Critical Race Theory in Curriculum," *Chalkbeat Tennessee*, July 1, 2021, https://tn.chalkbeat.org

/2021/6/30/22558296/critical-race-theory-crt-protesters-confront
-tennessee-education-penny-schwinn.

11. Lucas Hnath, *The Christians* (New York: The Overlook Press, 2016), 10.

12. Rob Bell, *Love Wins: A Book about Heaven, Hell, and the Fate of Every Person Who Ever Lived* (New York: Harper One, 2011), xi.

**Chapter 6**

1. Jaime L. Napier, Anesu N. Mandisodza, Susan M. Andersen, and John T. Jost, "System Justification in Responding to the Poor and Displaced in the Aftermath of Hurricane Katrina," *Analyses of Social Issues and Public Policy* 6, no. 1 (2006): 57–73.

2. Jemar Tisby, *The Color of Compromise* (Grand Rapids: Zondervan, 2019), 94.

3. Randy S. Woodley and Bo C. Sanders, *Decolonizing Evangelicalism* (Eugene, OR: Cascade, 2020), 21–22.

4. Woodley and Sanders, *Decolonizing Evangelicalism*, 23.

5. Woodley and Sanders, *Decolonizing Evangelicalism*, 33.

6. R. Buana Kibongi, "Priesthood," quoted in Kwesi Dickinson and Paul Ellingworth, *Biblical Revelation and African Beliefs* (Cambridge: Lutterworth, 1969), 50.

7. Diane B. Stinton, *Jesus of Africa: Voices of Contemporary African Christology* (Maryknoll, NY: Orbis Books, 2004), 54–108.

8. When I sent this quote to Denise to fact-check during the editing process, she asked if we could capitalize the roles and identities as proper nouns. That's how sacred she feels they are.

9. Jacquelyn Grant, *White Women's Christ and Black Women's Jesus: Feminist Christology and Womanist Response* (Atlanta: Scholars Press, 1989), 216–17.

10. Grant, *White Women's Christ*, 217. James Cone would later go on to credit Grant with this idea in his book *Said I Wasn't Gonna Tell Nobody: The Making of a Black Theologian* (Maryknoll, NY: Orbis, 2018).

11. Korie Little Edwards, "The Multiethnic Church Movement Hasn't Lived Up to Its Promise," *Christianity Today*, February 16, 2021, https://www.christianitytoday.com/ct/2021/march/race-diversity -multiethnic-church-movement-promise.html.

12. Esau McCaulley, *Reading While Black: African American Biblical Interpretation as an Exercise in Hope* (Downers Grove, IL: InterVarsity Press, 2020), 6.

13. Martin Brokenleg, "The Circle of Courage," in *Decolonizing Discipline: Children, Corporal Punishment, Christian Theologies, and Reconciliation* (Winnepeg, Manitoba: University of Manitoba Press, 2020), 136.

## Chapter 7

1. Augustine of Hippo, *On Christian Doctrine*, trans. D. W. Robertson Jr. (Indianapolis, IN: Bobb-Merrill, 1958), 1.36.40.

2. Amy Laura Hall, *Conceiving Parenthood: American Protestantism and the Spirit of Reproduction* (Grand Rapids: Eerdmans, 2008), 3.

3. The Catholic church has a rough track record with unwed mothers. The Magdalene Laundries scandal in Ireland came to light in the same era as the sex scandal, revealing the physical and psychological torment of "fallen women" who were taken into servitude while their babies were given away by the church for over two centuries.

4. Andrzej Grzybowski and Małgorzata Nita, "Leprosy in the Bible," *Clinics in Dermatology* 34, no. 1 (January 2016): 3–7.

## Chapter 8

1. Gregory Smith, "White Christians Still Favor Trump over Biden, but Support Has Slipped," *Pew Research Center*, October 13, 2020, https://www.pewresearch.org/fact-tank/2020/10/13/white -christians-continue-to-favor-trump-over-biden-but-support-has -slipped/.

2. Alejandra Molina and Religion News Service, "Latino Evan-

gelicals Narrowly Favor Trump," *Christianity Today*, October 6, 2020, https://www.christianitytoday.com/news/2020/october/latino -evangelical-christian-voters-survey-trump-biden.html.

3. Tim Keller, "Can Evangelicalism Survive Donald Trump and Roy Moore?," *New Yorker*, December 19, 2017, https://www.new yorker.com/news/news-desk/can-evangelicalism-survive-donald -trump-and-roy-moore.

4. I'm not a political theorist, there are other, probably better, ways to conceptualize power, but these have helped me as I examined my own political life.

5. Kathryn and Cameron Archer, Zoom interview, July 21, 2021.

6. Adam Serwer, *The Cruelty Is the Point: The Past, Present, and Future of Trump's America* (New York: Penguin Random House, 2021), 98.

7. Amanda Taub, "The Rise of American Authoritarianism," *Vox*, March 1, 2016, https://www.vox.com/2016/3/1/11127424/trump -authoritarianism.

8. Kathryn and Cameron Archer, Zoom interview, July 21, 2021.

9. Popularized by Ronald Reagan, "trickle-down economics" promotes the idea that the more money businesses have, the more they will spend on hiring and wages. It was used to justify tax cuts during the Reagan administration, and it continues to be part of the businesses-as-job-creators discourse. What we have, however, is not that at all, but rather additional profits ballooning salaries and stock portfolios at the top without any real benefits at the bottom. Meanwhile, automation replaces those minimum wage jobs at the bottom, increasing profits further.

10. Layton E. Williams, *Holy Disunity: How What Separates Us Can Save Us* (Louisville, KY: Westminster John Knox, 2019), 137.

11. Nikole Hannah-Jones, "America Wasn't a Democracy Until Black Americans Made It So," *New York Times*, August 14, 2019, https://www.nytimes.com/interactive/2019/08/14/magazine/black -history-american-democracy.html.

12. Williams, *Holy Disunity*, 47.

## Chapter 9

1. That's the year John Calvin's contemporary, Martin Luther, wrote the Ninety-five Theses.

2. In addition to this modernist challenge, Worldview Academy also takes on what it sees as the postmodernist challenges to Christianity's status as exclusive, objective truth. They used Scripture to take on multiculturalism, pluralism, and universalism, which inevitably ended in a lot of blog posts about being pro-life and one about being anti-Patagonia, the outdoor gear brand. Threats to Christianity, it would seem, are everywhere, including your local outdoor sports outfitter. The wholesale conservatism of the camp isn't a surprise, given the interest convergence of political and cultural conservatism and Christian fundamentalism.

3. J. Budziszewski, *How to Stay Christian in College*, Think Edition (Colorado Springs: NavPress, 2004), 17.

4. Aurora Griffin, *How I Stayed Catholic at Harvard: 40 Tips for Faithful College Students* (San Francisco: Ignatius Press, 2016), 16.

5. Francisco Sanches, *Quod Nihil Scitur*, quoted in Karen Armstrong, *The Lost Art of Scripture: Rescuing the Sacred Texts* (New York: Penguin Random House, 2019), 380.

6. Armstrong, *The Lost Art of Scripture*, 380.

7. Armstrong, *The Lost Art of Scripture*, 398.

8. Armstrong, *The Lost Art of Scripture*, 401.

9. Francis Schaeffer, *How Shall We Then Live? The Rise and Decline of Western Thought and Culture* (Wheaton, IL: Crossway, 1983).

## Chapter 10

1. Church History, "Church History: Complete Documentary 33 AD to the Present," September 7, 2012, YouTube video, 2:11:24, https://www.youtube.com/watch?v=xFIXMM1KWyc.

## Chapter 11

1. James Dobson, "Is Spanking Healthy Discipline?," *Dr. James Dobson Family Institute*, June 9, 2014, https://www.drjamesdobson .org/blogs/dr-james-dobson/spanking-healthy-discipline.

2. Valerie E. Michaelson, "Lies That Have Shaped Us," in *Decolonizing Discipline: Children, Corporal Punishment, Christian Theologies, and Reconciliation*, edited by Joan Durrant and Valerie Michaelson (Winnipeg, Manitoba: University of Manitoba Press, 2020), 54.

3. The psychology behind this kind of parenting is beyond the scope of this book, but if you want really helpful parenting books based on brain science, child development, and the presupposition that mental health and secure connection are better than harsh punishment at yielding long-term results, here's a list:

> Daniel J. Siegel and Tina Payne Bryson, *The Yes Brain: How to Cultivate Courage, Curiosity, and Resilience in Your Child* (New York: Bantam Books, 2018).
> Daniel J. Siegel and Tina Payne Bryson, *No-Drama Discipline: The Whole-Brain Way to Calm the Chaos and Nurture Your Child's Developing Mind* (New York: Bantam Books, 2014).
> Marc Brackett, *Permission to Feel: Unlocking the Power of Emotions to Help Our Kids, Ourselves, and Our Society Thrive* (London: Quercus, 2019).
> Brené Brown, *The Gifts of Imperfect Parenting*, audiobook (Louisville, CO: Sounds True, 2013).

*No-Drama Discipline*, in particular, helped me bridge the divide between my smoldering hellfire panic and the kind, responsible children I was hoping to raise. It emphasizes the training aspect of discipline.

Training implies practice. Practice implies imperfection. Imperfection is our happy place, friends. Not failure to live up to a real but unattainable perfection, but a rejection of the idea of perfection as a legitimate goal. Aperfection.

4. Martin Brokenleg, "The Circle of Courage: Raising Respectful,

Responsible Children through Indigenous Child Rearing Practices," in *Decolonizing Discipline: Children, Corporal Punishment, Christian Theologies, and Reconciliation* (Winnipeg, Manitoba: University of Manitoba Press, 2020), 125–26.

5. Brokenleg, "Circle of Courage," 133.

6. Brokenleg, "Circle of Courage," 134.

7. I spoke to Mary Catherine over Zoom in February 2021.

## Chapter 12

1. Linda Kay Klein, *Pure: Inside the Evangelical Movement That Shamed a Generation of Young Women and How I Broke Free* (New York: Atria, 2018), 22–23.

2. Kayla Carter-Moilanen, interview, March 31, 2021.

3. Christina Miller Larsen, "Teaching Modesty without Shame: The Social Contract," *Smarty Mommies*, blog, April 19, 2017, https://www.smartymommies.com/single-post/2017/04/19/teaching-modesty-without-shame-the-social-contract.

4. Klein, phone interview with the author, February 4, 2021.

5. Klein, *Pure*, 41–52.

6. I think this message has been twisted for men, mostly by hyper-masculine culture. To suffer is to notice your pain and need, which, as best I can tell, men are not encouraged to do. It's beyond suffering in silence. We seem to think they are holiest when they feel nothing at all.

## Chapter 13

1. Deborah Feldman, *Unorthodox: The Scandalous Rejection of My Hasidic Roots* (New York: Simon & Schuster, 2012).

2. Even in places where women are given some kind of education, like Feldman's community or my own Christian college, women were steered away from any academic pursuit in the service of a profession outside the home. They might need to take a job one day, but they should not choose profession over family.

3. Bekah McNeel, "How to Avoid the Ghost of the Common Core in Social-Emotional Learning's Rollout? Emphasize Local Control and Community Connection, Experts Say," *The 74 Million*, December 16, 2019, https://www.the74million.org/article/how-to-avoid-the -ghost-of-the-common-core-in-social-emotional-learnings-rollout -emphasize-local-control-and-community-connection-experts-say/.

4. Marjorie Cortez, "Utah Teachers Now Have Rule That Clarifies What They Cannot Teach about Diversity, Equity and Inclusion," *Deseret News*, August 5, 2021, https://www.deseret.com /utah/2021/8/5/22611408/utah-teachers-have-rule-about-teaching -diversity-equity-inclusion-critical-race-theory.

5. Emily Donaldson, "Video of Alamo Heights Student Using N-Word Prompts Examination of Racism in Small, Affluent School District," *San Antonio Report*, June 30, 2020, https://sanantonio report.org/video-of-alamo-heights-students-using-n-word-prompts -examination-of-racism-in-small-affluent-school-district/.

6. The trope that any criticism of the United States, any reference to systemic inequality or racism is "Marxist" is a red herring of reddest degree, usually lobbed as a political scare tactic and not a deep interrogation of the arguments, or, for that matter, a functional understanding of Marxism. Marxism is a way of interpreting history by looking not at what people were thinking about, but by looking at the resources and labor available to them, and how humans gained and lost power based on their access to resources and labor. Marxism concludes that capitalism is based in ideology, not reality, and that socialism will be the inevitable outcome of society's embrace of this reality, which will come in the form of a workers' revolution.

Most of the laws crafted to prevent the teaching of "critical race theory" actually wouldn't have prevented it. The laws were aimed at a basic teaching of enduring racism, but the academic-sounding title allowed politicians to hit the trigger of academic resentment in conservative communities.

7. Linda Jacobson and The 74 staff, "Chaos Theory: Amid Pandemic Recovery Efforts, School Leaders Fear Critical Race Furor Will

'Paralyze' Teachers," *The 74 Million*, June 28, 2021, https://www.the 74million.org/article/chaos-theory-amid-pandemic-recovery-efforts -educators-fear-critical-race-furor-will-paralyze-teachers/.

8. Texas State Legislature, *Relating to the social studies curriculum in public schools*, HB 3979, 8th Legislature, introduced in House June 15, 2021, https://legiscan.com/TX/text/HB3979/id/2339637/Texas-2021 -HB3979-Introduced.html.

9. Contributing to Linda Jacobson's article in the footnote above this one, I interviewed two educators, Ryan York and Asia Klekowicz, about how their school's social justice curriculum would be affected by Texas's new law. They were the ones who brought up the inherent discomfort of learning.

10. See the work of education funding nonprofit EdBuild for more on how this works. I don't have the space to go into great detail here, but this inherently unequal design was the subject of most of my own education reporting from 2017 through 2020.

11. Emma Garcia, "Schools Are Still Segregated and Black Children Are Paying a Price," *Economic Policy Institute*, February 12, 2020, https://www.epi.org/publication/schools-are-still-segregated-and -black-children-are-paying-a-price/.

12. Bekah McNeel, "Location, Segregation, and Accountability: The Quest for Better School Ratings," *BekahMcNeel.com*, blog, October 17, 2019, https://bekahmcneel.com/location-segregation-and -accountability-the-quest-for-better-school-ratings/.

13. Bekah McNeel, "Higher Education Remains Committed to the SAT, but Scores of San Antonio Students Tell Us More about Income Than Aptitude," *San Antonio Current*, October 24, 2018, https://www .sacurrent.com/the-daily/archives/2018/10/24/i-scored-a-1380-on-my -sat-higher-education-remains-committed-to-the-sat-but-scores-tell -us-more-about-income-than-aptitude.

14. Madeline Levine and Wendy Mogul are my go-to resources for this research. Their work will scare the blades right off your helicopter and your lawn mower.

## Conclusion

1. Lisa Miller, *The Spiritual Child: The New Science of Parenting for Health and Lifelong Thriving* (London: Picador, 2015), 137.

2. The Search Institute, "The Developmental Assets Framework," accessed September 1, 2021, https://www.search-institute.org/our-research/development-assets/developmental-assets-framework/.

3. Bekah McNeel, "Baptisms and Tragedies," *BekahMcNeel.com*, blog, November 6, 2017, https://bekahmcneel.com/baptisms-and-tragedies/.

4. Richard Rohr, *The Universal Christ: How a Forgotten Reality Can Change Everything We See, Hope For, and Believe* (New York: Convergent, 2019), 17.

# Selected Bibliography

Armstrong, Karen. *The Lost Art of Scripture: Rescuing the Sacred Texts*. New York: Anchor Books, 2020.

Austin, Nefertiti. *Motherhood So White: A Memoir of Race, Gender, and Parenting in America*. Naperville: Sourcebooks, 2019.

Bell, Rob. *Love Wins: A Book About Heaven, Hell, and the Fate of Every Person Who Ever Lived*. New York: Harper One, 2011. Kindle edition.

Brandt, Cindy Wang. *Parenting Forward: How to Raise Kids with Justice, Mercy, and Kindness*. Grand Rapids: Eerdmans, 2019.

Brokenleg, Martin. "The Circle of Courage." In *Decolonizing Discipline: Children, Corporal Punishment, Christian Theologies, and Reconciliation*, 125–36. Edited by Joan Durrant and Valerie Michaelson. Winnipeg, Manitoba: University of Manitoba Press, 2020.

Cone, James H. *Said I Wasn't Gonna Tell Nobody: The Making of a Black Theologian*. Maryknoll, NY: Orbis Books, 2018.

Cunningham, Vinson. "How the Idea of Hell Has Shaped the Way We Think." *New Yorker*, January 14, 2019. https://www.new yorker.com/magazine/2019/01/21/how-the-idea-of-hell-has -shaped-the-way-we-think.

Delmont, Matthew. *Why Busing Failed: Race, Media, and the National Resistance to School Desegregation*. Oakland: University of California Press, 2016.

Edwards, Korie Little. "The Multiethnic Church Movement Hasn't

Lived Up to Its Promise." *Christianity Today*, February 16, 2021. https://www.christianitytoday.com/ct/2021/march/race-diver sity-multiethnic-church-movement-promise.html.

Enns, Peter. *The Sin of Certainty*. San Francisco: HarperOne, 2016.

Evans, Rachel Held. *A Year of Biblical Womanhood*. Nashville: Nelson, 2012.

———. *Inspired: Slaying Giants, Walking on Water, and Loving the Bible Again*. Nashville: Nelson, 2018.

Evans, Rachel Held, and Matthew Paul Turner. *What Is God Like?* New York: Convergent, 2021.

Feldman, Deborah. *Unorthodox: The Scandalous Rejection of My Hasidic Roots*. New York: Simon & Schuster, 2012.

FitzGerald, Frances. *The Evangelicals: The Struggle to Shape America*. New York: Simon & Schuster, 2017.

Grant, Jacquelyn. *White Women's Christ and Black Women's Jesus: Feminist Christology and Womanist Response*. Atlanta: Scholars Press, 1989.

Hall, Amy Laura. *Conceiving Parenthood: American Protestantism and the Spirit of Reproduction*. Grand Rapids: Ecrdmans, 2008.

Hnath, Lucas. *The Christians*. New York: The Overlook Press, 2016.

Holmes, Pete. *Comedy Sex God*. New York: Harper Wave, 2019.

Hulbert, Ann. *Raising America: Experts, Parents, and a Century of Advice about Children*. New York: Knopf, 2003.

Hunter, James Davison. *Culture Wars: The Struggle to Define America*. New York: Basic Books, 1991.

John of the Cross. "Dark Night of the Soul." In *Dark Night of the Soul*, 1–2. Translated by E. Allison Peers. Mineola, NY: Dover Publications, 2003.

Jones, Kenneth, and Tema Okun. *Dismantling Racism: A Workbook for Social Change Groups*. ChangeWork, 2001.

Klein, Linda Kay. *Pure: Inside the Evangelical Movement That Shamed a Generation of Young Women and How I Broke Free*. New York: Atria, 2018.

Kruse, Kevin. *One Nation Under God: How Corporate America Invented Christian America*. New York: Basic Books, 2015.

McCaulley, Esau. *Reading While Black: African American Biblical Interpretation as an Exercise in Hope*. Downers Grove, IL: InterVarsity, 2020.

McRae, Elizabeth Gilbert. *Mothers of Massive Resistance: White Women and the Politics of White Supremacy*. New York: Oxford University Press, 2018.

Michaelson, Valerie E. "Lies That Have Shaped Us." In *Decolonizing Discipline: Children, Corporal Punishment, Christian Theologies, and Reconciliation*, 51–60. Edited by Joan Durrant and Valerie Michaelson. Winnipeg, Manitoba: University of Manitoba Press, 2020.

Miller, Claire Cain. "The Relentlessness of Modern Parenting." *New York Times*, December 25, 2018. https://www.nytimes.com /2018/12/25/upshot/the-relentlessness-of-modern-parenting .html.

Miller, Lisa. *The Spiritual Child: The New Science of Parenting for Health and Lifelong Thriving*. London: Picador, 2015.

Rohr, Richard. *The Universal Christ: How a Forgotten Reality Can Change Everything We See, Hope For, and Believe*. New York: Convergent Books, 2019.

Seel, David John, Jr. *Parenting Without Perfection*. Colorado Springs: NavPress, 2000.

Serwer, Adam. *The Cruelty Is the Point: The Past, Present, and Future of Trump's America*. New York: Penguin Random House, 2021.

Solomon, Andrew. *Far from the Tree: Parents, Children, and the Search for Identity*. New York: Scribner, 2012.

Stinton, Diane B. *Jesus of Africa: Voices of Contemporary African Christology*. Maryknoll, NY: Orbis Books, 2004.

Taub, Amanda. "The Rise of American Authoritarianism." *Vox*, March 1, 2016. https://www.vox.com/2016/3/1/11127424/trump -authoritarianism.

Tisby, Jemar. *The Color of Compromise*. Grand Rapids: Zondervan, 2019.

Westover, Tara. *Educated*. New York: Random House, 2018.

Wilkerson, Isabel. *Caste: The Origins of Our Discontents*. New York: Random House, 2020.

Williams, Layton E. *Holy Disunity: How What Separates Us Can Save Us*. Louisville, KY: Westminster John Knox Press, 2019.

Woodley, Randy S., and Bo C. Sanders. *Decolonizing Evangelicalism*. Eugene, OR: Cascade, 2020.